The
New
GLOBAL
BANKER

What Every
U.S. Bank
Must Know
to Compete
Internationally

Hazel J. Johnson

PROBUS PUBLISHING COMPANY
Chicago, Illinois
Cambridge, England

A Bankline Publication

ISBN 1-55738-358-8

Printed in the United States of America

BB

1 2 3 4 5 6 7 8 9 0

CB

To my son,
Derrick M. Johnson,
for his help and moral support over the years.
May his sons,
Michael M. Johnson and Alexander T. Johnson,
be as supportive and understanding
as he has been.

Table of Contents

v

Table of Contents

Preface

The U.S. commercial banking industry is currently undergoing important structural and competitive changes. Pressure is being felt from nonbank financial sectors and from foreign banks operating within the United States. Thirty years ago, the commercial bank share of assets among U.S. financial institutions was almost 60 percent. Today it is below 50 percent—and within this reduced market share *foreign banks* account for 36 percent of all commercial bank loans. In its first two weeks of operation in New York, China Trust (the largest private bank in Taiwan) attracted $6 million in deposits from 400 depositors. Union Bank (the San Francisco-based subsidiary of the Bank of Japan) recently bought 28 branches of Security Pacific. Other Japanese banks serve the more than 1,000 subsidiaries of Japanese industrial firms in California alone.

Because of bank failures and mergers, the banking industry has consolidated from 15,000 U.S. institutions to less than 12,000 in a matter of a few years. This trend promises to continue if U.S. banks are to remain competitive internationally. How else can the average U.S. bank of $260 million in assets compete with much larger institutions in Germany ($2.5 billion), the United Kingdom ($16 billion), or Japan ($37 billion)?

At the same time, the traditional deposit-taking and lending activities are being deemphasized, as bankers search for fee-generating market niches that will supply as much as one half of their operating income. This shift in focus is necessary because top-tier corporate clients have found it much easier to access money and capital markets directly and by-pass the banking system. Thirty years ago, bank loans were the primary source of short-term funds for these companies and commercial paper represented only 5 percent of total bank loans. Today, the commercial paper market has grown to 30 percent of bank loans. Nevertheless, regulatory constraints limit bank access to many potentially profitable fee-generating lines of business such as securities and insurance.

At a time when international trade is increasingly important to U.S. economic vitality, U.S. banks are retrenching from international activities under pressure from the lingering effects of troubled Third World debt, a feeble real estate market, and regulatory requirements to improve capital ratios. Yet the fact remains that banks in other industrialized countries are building a much more aggressive international presence. Finding the retrenchment of U.S. commercial banks perplexing, the head of the international division of the expansionist French bank Crédit Lyonnais remarked,

> "I don't understand the American banks; they are giving up markets and relationships that took years to build. This is a loss to the United States; it gives it less influence in the world."

Robert L. Clarke, former Comptroller of the Currency, voiced concern about U.S. bank retrenchment when he testified during a Congressional hearing on the competitiveness of U.S. banks. He said that there is a danger that the United States could "decline into a second-rate banking and financial power."

The New Global Banker sorts out the dynamics of the banking industry in the United States, Canada, the United Kingdom, Germany, France, Switzerland, Japan, and China. This book describes current banking practices and future market trends. Compelling regulatory issues are contrasted in the United States and abroad. In this context, market niches and synergies for U.S. commercial banks are identified and explored.

In spite of the obvious challenges, this is one of the most exciting periods in commercial banking history. Longstanding barriers are falling on many fronts. The line between commercial banking and securities activities in the United States is blurring as the result of stopgap regulatory measures and strategic alliances among banks, securities firms, and investment companies. U.S. banks are universally recognized as the industry's most technologically advanced and innovative. The European market presents opportunities to take part in the privatization of enterprises in such varied industries as banking, insurance, telecommunications, transportation, utilities, mining, and manufacturing. There are also long-term opportunities in trade finance, foreign currency transactions, corporate finance, and retail banking in Asia, and more specifically, Greater China—the dynamic region of South China, Hong Kong, and Taiwan.

These and other opportunities may be exploited not only by the large, multinational banks, but also by ambitious regional banks. Even in the context of constraining regulations, U.S. institutions can capitalize on their comparative strengths. Through strategic alliances, commercial banks are being transformed into internationally competitive providers of a wide range of financial services.

Hazel J. Johnson, Ph.D., C.P.A.

1 Financial Services: A Changing Industry

INTRODUCTION

Financial institutions facilitate economic growth in modern society by performing essential functions. In the past, each institution had a narrow band of services that it offered to its consumer and business clients. The payments system was controlled by commercial banks that cleared checks and drafts. Today money is transferred electronically among any number of financial firms in volumes that could never be efficiently handled in the physical form. Residential mortgage finance was available primarily from savings and loan associations that held the loans to maturity. This mortgage finance is now available from a wide array of sources and the mortgage loans themselves are traded as securities. Securities firms offered corporate and government securities as investment vehicles. Now these firms offer close substitutes for bank deposits and help industrial firms bypass the commercial banking system in their pursuit of short-term financing. The mainstay for insurance companies was the traditional whole life insurance policy. Today insurance companies offer products that compete with investments obtainable through securities firms. Mutual funds have emerged to permanently change the dynamics of the banking industry.

Over time, traditional roles have been blurred and it is not always easy to distinguish the product of a commercial bank from that of another financial institution. The competitive forces in the banking industry are not limited to domestic firms. There is increased pressure from foreign institutions. The financial services industry is in the process of significant change in a time of new alignments in domestic markets and increased international competition.

THE TRADITIONAL ROLES

Commercial banks are one of several financial institutions that serve the economy. Others include thrifts (savings and loan associations and mutual savings banks), credit unions, investment companies, pension funds, insurance companies, and finance companies. An examination of their traditional roles helps an observer of the industry to appreciate the dramatic transformation that has taken place.

In the classification of *depository institutions* are *commercial banks, savings and loan associations, mutual savings banks,* and *credit unions.* That is, they all issue deposits—money that can be withdrawn upon demand or according to terms of the deposit agreement. For many years, these deposits formed the basis for the country's payments mechanism. That was before money took the form of electronic impulses rather than physical currency and coin.

Savings and loan associations (S&Ls) were originally established to provide real estate finance by accepting small savers' deposits and investing in residential mortgages. *Mutual savings banks* were also originally geared to the small investor. These institutions made mortgage loans and accepted primarily savings deposits. Like S&Ls and mutual savings banks, *credit unions* provide a savings vehicle for the small investor. They originally invested these funds in small consumer loans for purposes other than residential housing. Members of credit unions shared some form of common bond, frequently employment or occupation.

Other *nondepository institutions* include *investment companies, pension funds, insurance companies*, and *finance companies*. Traditionally, the financial instruments that they offered for sale to the public could not be used as money. But advances in technology have minimized this apparent limitation. *Investment companies* (for example, Fidelity mutual funds) pool money in small denominations to make large purchases of corporate and government securities. To this extent, they are similar to commercial banks, but investment companies issue ownership shares, not deposits, to their investors. The rate of return from an investment company share depends on the rate of return of the securities in which the company invests, with no guarantee or insurance for the investor.

Pension funds offer their investors deferred income. Contributors to pension funds receive the promise of lump-sum or periodic payments at or during retirement from employment. Contributions into pension funds are made by both employers and employees. Funds are invested in loans to industry and in securities issued by industrial firms.

Insurance companies promise protection from a variety of specified risks in exchange for investor funds. This promised protection is documented in an insurance policy. The two major types of insurance companies are life insurers and property and casualty insurers. Life insurers protect investors from death and disability during the term of the policy. (Some life insurance policies also include a savings component.) Property and casualty insurers protect against all other risks—automobile insurance is an example. Like pension funds, insurance companies invest policyholder funds in loans to and securities of commercial enterprises.

Finance companies offer services for both consumers and businesses. In one sense, they are similar to commercial banks, because they make loans. But finance companies generally make riskier loans than banks—that is, there is often a higher probability of nonrepayment of loans that finance companies make. As a result, finance company loan rates have historically been higher than bank loan rates. Also, finance companies do not accept deposits, but issue securities similar to those of nonfinancial firms.

THE INDUSTRY TRANSFORMATION

In the past, these financial institutions tended to specialize. For example, commercial banks have been an important part of the economy's payments system and a major source of short-term finance for industry. Banks now offer consumer, real estate, and longer-term commercial services. Over time, many institutions diversified into other activities so that functions now frequently overlap, with the result that commercial banks are subject to increasingly intense competition.

Competition in financial services has blurred the difference between many formerly distinct institutions. For example, all depository institutions along with life insurance companies now provide mortgage finance. Also, all depository institutions, investment companies, and securities brokers and dealers offer accounts that are checking accounts for all intents and purposes. Investment companies offer rates of return to small investors that are often more attractive than rates available at depository institutions.

Changing Market Shares

The effect of the blurring of niches has been a decline in the importance of commercial banks and other depository institutions. Exhibit 1-1 shows this change. In 1964, depository institutions had 58 percent of the total financial assets held by financial institutions. That share is now below 50 percent. The primary beneficiaries of this shift have been investment companies (mutual funds) and pension funds. The competitive rates of return available through investment companies have clearly attracted investors, particularly small investors, away from depository institutions. At the same time, the significant growth in assets under management at both investment companies and pension funds has given corporations alternatives to bank loans. Thus, banks face threats to both their deposit base and loan portfolio.

Particularly hard-hit, the savings and loan industry has shrunk from almost 4,100 in 1960 to fewer than 2,000 currently. The income on long-term, fixed-rate mortgage loans was insufficient to cover the cost of maintaining their deposit base as money market interest rates

EXHIBIT 1-1

CHANGING MARKET SHARE OF FINANCIAL INSTITUTIONS

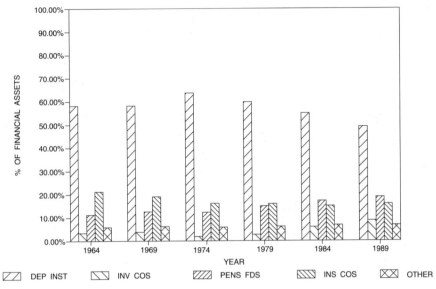

Legend:

DEP INST   Depository institutions (commercial banks, savings and loan associations, mutual savings banks, and credit unions)
INV COS   Investment companies
PENS FDS Pension funds
INS COS   Insurance companies
OTHER   Finance companies and securities brokers and dealers

Source

Author's calculations and graphic based on:
Board of Governors of the Federal Reserve System, *Flow of Funds Accounts: Financial Assets and Liabilities*, various issues.

rose dramatically during the 1970s. During the 1980s the riskier investments that S&Ls were permitted only served to worsen the situation. The S&L industry severly contracted and probably will never resume its former importance as a provider of mortgage finance.

For their part, banks have lost much of their low-cost deposits and top-tier corporate loan business. At the heart of this effect is a change in the interest rate environment, which has produced a trend toward direct financing of corporate America. Major corporate clients have found it more economical to borrow short-term funds in the commercial paper market directly from the investing public, rather than to borrow from a bank. Commercial paper allows large, credit-worthy firms to borrow for periods of up to 270 days. Exhibit 1-2 shows that the commercial paper rate has been only slightly higher than the Treasury Bill rate (the lowest short-term rate available) since 1975, while the prime rate (charged to such large bank borrowers) has been significantly higher.

As Exhibit 1-3 shows, the amount of commercial paper outstanding represented less than 5 percent of the amount of domestic bank loans in 1964. This percentage has increased steadily, so that now commercial paper represents almost 30 percent of the dollar value of outstanding bank loans, a trend that has significantly contributed to a decline in commercial bank market share.

Exhibit 1-4 also helps to illustrate the trend of more direct financing by U.S. businesses. While bank loans to nonfarm business have more than doubled from $277 billion to $669 billion since 1979, the share of total business financial liabilities represented by bank loans dropped from 17 to 14 percent. Clearly, many industrial firms have replaced the commercial bank loan with commercial paper and long-term debt instruments such as bonds.

But what has been lost in the business sector has been gained in the mortgage market. In 1979 bank mortgage loans amounted to $244 billion or 18.5 percent of all mortgages, as shown in Exhibit 1-5. Currently, commercial bank mortgage loans are closer to $860 billion or 22.1 percent of all mortgages outstanding. Within the general category, multifamily and commercial mortgages have grown even faster—from 23.5 percent to 35.5 percent during the same period.

In the consumer sector, as Exhibit 1-6 shows, the share has been somewhat more consistent. Commercial banks provided 52.8 percent of all consumer credit in 1979 and currently provide 47.4 percent.

Banks are important providers of finance in all three markets. Mortgage lending has been an important growth sector. Competitive forces have created some erosion in the bank market share for con-

EXHIBIT 1-2

INTEREST RATE VOLATILITY—T-BILLS, COMM PAPER, AND PRIME
(Averages 1964–1989)

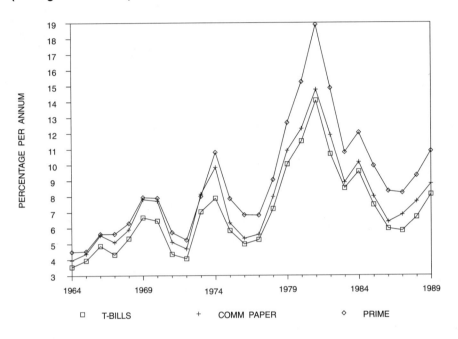

Source

Author's graphic based on data from:
United States Department of Commerce, Bureau of Economic Analysis, *Business Statistics 1961–1988* and *Survey of Current Business, April 1991.*

sumer credit. Unfortunately, business loans show much less promise for growth in future commercial lending.

Foreign Competition

The ability of financial institutions to compete is of central importance as global markets continue to develop. Domestic commercial banks compete at home not only with other domestic financial institutions, but also increasingly with foreign banks. Exhibit 1-7 shows

EXHIBIT 1-3

GROWTH IN THE COMMERCIAL PAPER MARKET

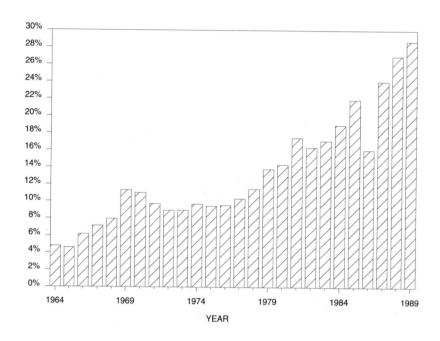

Represents commercial paper outstanding as a percentage of domestic bank loans.

Source

Author's calculations and graphic based on:

that foreign bank loans during the 1960s represented less than 2 percent of the amount of domestic bank loans. Now the share is closer to 10 percent.

In terms of total assets, the foreign presence is even more obvious. As shown in Exhibit 1-8, total assets of foreign banks exceeded 10 percent of all banking assets in the United States as early as 1980. By 1989, the percentage exceeded 22 percent.

EXHIBIT 1-4

COMMERCIAL BANK SHARE OF BUSINESS FINANCE

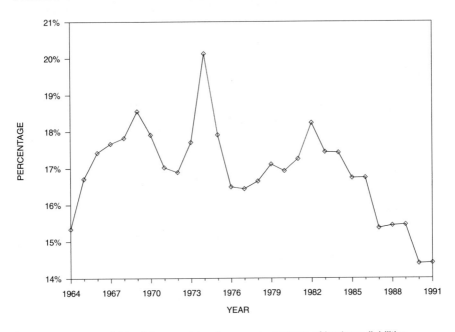

Represents commercial bank loans outstanding as a percentage of business liabilities.

Source

Author's graphic based on data from:
Board of Governors of the Federal Reserve System, *Flow of Funds Accounts: Financial Assets and Liabilities*, various issues.

THE NEW GLOBAL BANKING ENVIRONMENT

The banking environment has indeed become more international. There is more evidence of foreign bank presence in the United States even as U.S. banks retrench from their previous international activities.

U.S. Banks Overseas

Since the early 1980s, U.S. banks have deemphasized growth in their international asset portfolios. There are several reasons for this.

EXHIBIT 1-5

COMMERCIAL BANK MORTGAGE LOANS

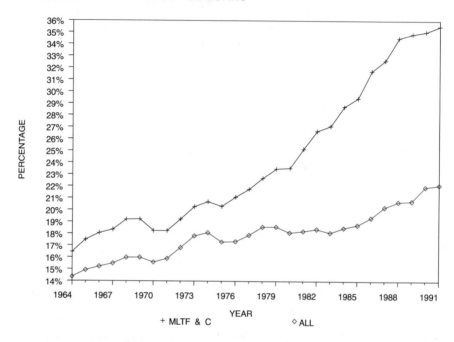

Represents commercial bank mortgage loans as a percentage of applicable mortgage loan category.

Legend:

MLTF & C   Multifamily and commercial
ALL   Home, farm, multifamily, and commercial

Source

Author's graphic based on data from:
Board of Governors of the Federal Reserve System, *Flow of Funds Accounts: Financial Assets and Liabilities*, various issues.

Third-world loan losses have prompted U.S. banks to withdraw from lending to developing countries. Also, U.S. banks have divested of foreign affiliates in order to purchase domestic banks and failed depository institutions (savings and loan associations and other com-

EXHIBIT 1-6

COMMERCIAL BANK SHARE OF CONSUMER CREDIT

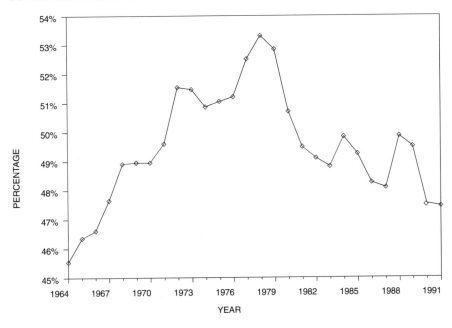

Represents commercial bank loans as a percentage of consumer credit.

Source

Author's graphic based on data from:
Board of Governors of the Federal Reserve System, *Flow of Funds Accounts: Financial Assets and Liabilities*, various issues.

mercial banks). Lastly, the new capital standards of the Basel Accord have made it necessary for money center banks to raise their capital ratios. Selling overseas affiliates serves this purpose because it reduces the amount of risk-weighted assets.

There are several notable examples of this trend:

- Chase Manhattan (New York) sold its affiliate in the Netherlands with assets of over $5 billion to Credit Lyonnais of France. In total, Chase Manhattan has reduced its foreign presence from fifty-five countries to thirty-three.

EXHIBIT 1-7

EXPANDING FOREIGN BANK LOANS

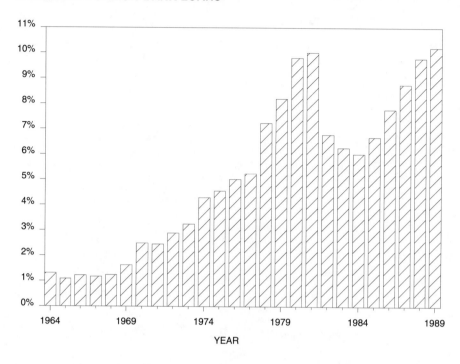

YEAR

Represents foreign bank loans as a percentage of domestic bank loans.

Source

Author's calculations and graphic based on:
Board of Governors of the Federal Reserve System, *Flow of Funds Accounts: Financial Assets and Liabilities*, various issues.

- Bank of America (California) sold its profitable Italian affiliate to Deutsche Bank of Germany.

- Wells Fargo and Company (California) divested of all its foreign offices before its merger with Security Pacific.

- Chemical Bank (New York) once had operations in thirty foreign countries (before its merger with Manufacturers Hanover

EXHIBIT 1-8

ASSETS OF FOREIGN BANKS IN THE UNITED STATES

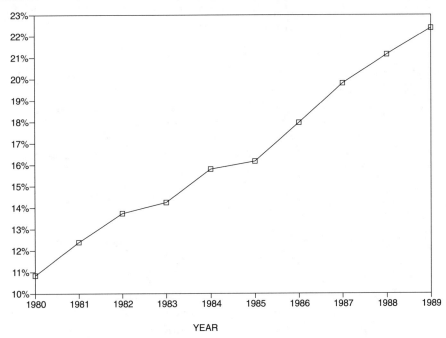

YEAR

Represents assets of foreign banks in the United States as a percentage of total bank assets.

Sources

Author's calculations and graphic based on:
1. Task Force on the International Competitiveness of U.S. Financial Institutions. *Report of the Subcommittee on Financial Institutions Supervision, Regulation, and Insurance*, U.S. Government Printing Office, October 1990. (foreign bank assets)

2. James R. Barth, R. Dan Brumbaugh, Jr., and Robert E. Litan, *Banking Industry in Turmoil: A Report on the Condition of the U.S. Banking Industry and the Bank Insurance Fund*, U.S. Government Printing Office, December 1990. (total bank assets)

of New York). The number is now nine. Many of the eliminated offices had been in Europe.

Citicorp is currently the most aggressive U.S. bank in terms of international operations. For example, the bank continues to increase its Asian personnel, targeting affluent Asians. The strategies and services of its Asian program include the following:

- In Asia, the name of Citibank is readily recognized as a high-quality provider of financial service. The bank capitalizes on this image.

- Each customer with a minimum $100,000 deposit has a personal banker.

- These clients are seen in a luxurious private office and served tea or coffee in fine China.

- Financial transactions can be conducted in eight different currencies.

- The same type of service is available to these clients when they travel to other countries.

This Asian program is considered highly profitable. For example, the 1992 revenues of the Singapore affiliate of Citibank were in the $1 billion range with net profits of $200 million.

In fact, as money center banks have generally retrenched from international operations, especially European operations, Asia appears to be an area of future growth potential where annual earnings increases range from 20 to 100 percent. Bank of America had reduced its Asian operations in the latter half of the 1980s. Upon merging with Security Pacific, however, it inherited Security Pacific Asian Bank Ltd., a strong, established network with connections with medium-sized, ethnic Chinese companies. Chemical Banking (the result of the combination of Chemical Bank and Manufacturers Hanover) anticipates that the combined networks of the two predecessor banks will make the merged firm very competitive in the Asian rim. However, none of these is as aggressive as Citibank in its pursuit of the Asian market. Citibank looks to penetrate new markets there and to expand its consumer products throughout the region.

Foreign Bank Presence

Even as U.S. banks only selectively expand their international horizons, foreign banks in the United States are providing services for consumers and businesses, with Japanese banks dominating this activity. While the U.S. banks that followed their corporate clients abroad in the 1960s and 1970s have withdrawn in many cases, the banks in other countries that followed their clients to the United States have not retreated in this manner. Also, the large size of the U.S. market has also been an attraction for foreign banks. The importance of the dollar in trade with the U.S. has also played a role in the expansion of foreign banks in the United States.

An interesting example of the cultural advantage that foreign banks sometimes enjoy in the United States can be seen in the area of Chinese banks. A few years ago, the Flushing area of Queens, New York, had few Asian residents. Currently, more than 140,000 Chinese and Korean immigrants reside there. Oriental banks are, likewise, an important element of the economy. The oldest Chinese-American bank in Flushing is Asia Bank. Others include Amerasia Bank and Hong Kong-Shanghai Banking Corporation.

One of the newest entrants is China Trust, the largest private bank in Taiwan. In its first two weeks of operation, China Trust took in $6 million from 400 depositors. Of course, American banks compete aggressively for Oriental deposits. For example, American banks' ATMs in Flushing offer transactions in three languages and the employees in Citibank's Asian Banking Center speak Korean, Mandarin, and Cantonese. Nevertheless, the Oriental banks have certain competitive advantages:

- Deposit interest rates are higher than at American banks.

- Weekend banking hours are maintained.

- In some cases, free parking (a rare commodity) is provided.

- The reputations and past records of customers from the home country are considered in credit evaluations.

- Gifts are often distributed during Chinese New Year.

The success of Oriental banks in Flushing is not an accident. Competitive pricing, a high level of service, and cultural links all contribute.

The influence of foreign banks goes far beyond Flushing. Exhibit 1-9 is a list of the 25 largest foreign banks in the United States and their U.S. assets. Fifteen of the 25 are Japanese banks. Three are Italian and two each are based in the United Kingdom and France. Hong Kong, Canada, and Switzerland are the home countries for the remaining three. Together, these banks control $440 billion in assets or 13.3 percent of the total assets of all FDIC-insured banks.

This is clearly a significant share of U.S. bank assets. In terms of location, however, these banks are concentrated in larger cities. Exhibit 1-10 shows their geographical breakdown. Almost half are located in New York, with other large concentrations in Los Angeles, Chicago, Houston, and San Francisco. Representative offices and branches are the most common organizational form, followed by agencies.[1]

In terms of the markets that these banks serve, most are involved in corporate banking. This is also true of Japanese banks that serve more than 1,000 subsidiaries of Japanese industrial firms in California. In addition, these banks also cater to the large Japanese population in that state. They have also gained significant market share by offering banking services with thin profit margins. Bank acquisitions have helped increase their market share. For example, Union Bank (the San Francisco-based subsidiary of Bank of Tokyo) recently acquired 28 branches of Security Pacific that were sold in connection with that bank's merger with Bank of America. As a result of these business and cultural advantages, Japanese banks hold almost 25 percent of total bank deposits in California.

These banks do not act in isolation, however. For example, Mitsubishi Bank owns the Bank of California. With the help of Mitsubishi Bank (and Mitsubishi Trust and Tokio Marine and Fire Insurance companies), Mitsubishi companies have purchased a metal company, a power plant, and a mining concern in the state of California. Elsewhere in the United States, Mitsubishi financial companies have been involved in the acquisition or construction of a nonferrous smelting facility, a forklift operation, a chemical company, a glass

EXHIBIT 1-9

FOREIGN BANKS OPERATING IN THE UNITED STATES

Bank	Total Assets[1]
1. Bank of Tokyo (Japan)	$ 45.2
2. Dai-Ichi Kangyo (Japan)	34.0
3. Mitsubishi Bank (Japan)	31.5
4. Fuji Bank Limited (Japan)	29.7
5. Industrial Bank (Japan)	28.1
6. Sanwa Bank (Japan)	28.0
7. Hong Kong and Shanghai Bank (Hong Kong)	24.8
8. Sumitomo Bank (Japan)	24.5
9. National Westminster Bank (United Kingdom)	22.3
10. Bank of Montreal (Canada)	17.8
11. Tokai Bank (Japan)	17.7
12. Mitsui Trust and Banking Corp. (Japan)	12.1
13. Daiwa Bank (Japan)	11.5
14. Swiss Bank Corp. (Switzerland)	11.4
15. Mitsui Bank (Japan)	11.2
16. Long-Term Credit Bank of Japan (Japan)	10.5
17. Mitsubishi Trust and Banking Corp. (Japan)	10.2
18. Sumitomo Trust and Banking Corp. (Japan)	9.8
19. Banque National de Paris (France)	9.4
20. Banca Nazional del Lavoro (Italy)	9.1
21. Banco di Roma (Italy)	8.7
22. Barclays Group (United Kingdom)	8.6
23. Taiyo Kobe Bank (Japan)	8.4
24. Credit Lyonnais (France)	8.2
25. Banco di Napoli (Italy)	7.7
	$440.4

Memorandum:

Total assets of FDIC-insured banks—1989 $3,299

[1] Billions of dollars

Source

Subcommittee on Financial Institutions Supervision, Regulation, and Insurance, *Task Force Report on the International Competitiveness of U.S. Financial Institutions*, 1991, p. 53.

EXHIBIT 1-10

LOCATION OF FOREIGN BANKS

City	Number of Locations				
	Representative Offices	Agencies	Branches	Subsidiaries	Edge Act Banks and Investment Companies	Total
New York	161	35	233	33	17	479
Los Angeles	24	60	30	13	—	127
Chicago	29	—	53	5	2	89
Houston	55	14	—	—	6	75
San Francisco	19	28	7	7	2	63
Miami	7	35	—	3	9	54
Atlanta	12	15	—	—	—	27
Washington, D.C.	10	—	3	—	1	14
Dallas	13	1	—	—	—	14
Seattle	5	—	9	—	—	14
All other	41	13	29	40	1	124
Total	376	201	364	101	38	1080

Source

Subcommittee on Financial Institutions Supervision, Regulation, and Insurance, *Task Force Report on the International Competitiveness of U.S. Financial Institutions*, 1991, p. 42.

manufacturer, a computer disk maker, a semiconductor- and wafer-fabricating facility, a big-screen television plant, the Rockefeller Center, and an options trading venture.

The current trend of Japanese banking in the United States is to seek more profitable transactions in the middle market, that is, medium-size corporations. Of course, this is the same corporate market that U.S. banks have targeted for future growth. This implies a trend of increasing competition between U.S. and Japanese banks in the United States.

The general focus on international banking is not limited to Japanese banks. Exhibit 1-11 shows the extent of international activity among the banking systems with the largest international portfolios. International investments are the smallest percentage of total assets for U.S. banks at 8.6 percent. The highest percentages are Luxembourg and Belgium at 96.1 and 54.2 percent, respectively. These data help to illustrate the outward focus of other banking systems relative to the United States.

This trend is changing the nature of commercial lending in this country. Foreign banks now account for 36 percent of all commercial loans in the United States.[2] This situation is directly attributable to the retrenching of U.S. banks from international operations. U.S. manufacturers turn increasingly to export markets for sales growth. The supply of export finance that is available through indigenous U.S. banks does not meet the increasing demand. Although exact figures are not available because the transactions involve proprietary information, it has been estimated that affiliates of foreign banks provide over half the commercial trade finance in the United States. Often the vehicle used for this purpose is a letter of credit. Basic letter of credit transactions can be more easily carried out between branches of the same international bank—one in the exporting country, the other in the importing country.

In addition, industrial companies sometimes require financing of their continuing overseas operations that is difficult to obtain from U.S. banks. For example, Charles Machine Works, Inc., a manufacturer of construction equipment in the United States, recently looked to establish a banking relationship to finance its inventory for its European dealers. The company has $150 million in annual sales, a

EXHIBIT 1-11

INTERNATIONAL INVESTMENTS BY BANKS:
A CROSS-COUNTRY COMPARISON

Country	%[1]
Belgium	54.2%
Canada	13.4
France	40.4
Germany	16.3
Japan	13.9
Luxembourg	96.1
Netherlands	36.2
Switzerland	26.2
United Kingdom	45.0
United States	8.6

[1] Foreign assets of depository institutions (excluding monetary authorities) as a percentage of total assets in 1990.

Source

Author's calculations based on data from:
International Monetary Fund, *International Financial Statistics*, May 1991.

solid balance sheet, and a trenching-digging machine that was recently included on *Fortune* magazine's list of 100 products that America makes best. Charles Machine Works is an ideal example of a middle-market company with strong international growth potential. But because U.S. banks (which have traditionally served such companies) do not have meaningful overseas operations or connections, this company is forced to look for European banks—one country at a time—that will provide the necessary financing. These industrial firms represent strong growth potential in U.S. commercial banking. Foreign banks in the United States will continue to gain ground in this market if indigenous banks do not work to gain and keep a competitive advantage.

CONCLUSION

Traditional banking services can be obtained now from any number of financial institutions, including investment companies, insurance companies, pension funds, and finance companies. Competition between domestic and foreign institutions is becoming much keener. From a relatively small foreign presence less than three decades ago, international interests now control as much as 25 percent of U.S. banking assets and 36 percent of loans to commercial and industrial firms. The economies of the world clearly are becoming more integrated. If anything is a constant in the changing financial services industry, it may be the continuing trend toward integration of institutions, markets, and economies. U.S. commercial banks must rise to the challenge of international competitiveness.

SELECTED REFERENCES

Barth, James R., R. Dan Brumbaugh, Jr., and Robert E. Litan. *Banking Industry in Turmoil: A Report on the Condition of the U.S. Banking Industry and the Bank Insurance Fund.* U.S. Government Printing Office, Washington, D.C., December 1990.

Board of Governors of the Federal Reserve System. *Flow of Funds Accounts: Financial Assets and Liabilities, Washington, D.C.*

Casey, Robert W. "Foreign Lenders Piling Up Gains in U.S." *United States Banker,* April 1993, pp. 30–32,71.

Chandler, Clay. "Japanese Bid to Bail Out Banks Weighed Down by Conflicts, Concern about Using Public Funds." *Asian Wall Street Journal,* October 19, 1992.

Federal Deposit Insurance Corporation. *FDIC Quarterly Banking Profile.* Washington, D.C.

Hardy, Quentin. "Bank of Tokyo Unit to Buy 28 Branches of Bank America." *Asian Wall Street Journal,* March 9, 1992.

Holstein, William J., James Treece, Stan Crock, and Larry Armstrong. "Hands across America: The Rise of Mitsubishi." *Business Week,* September 24, 1990, pp. 102–107.

Krarr, Louis. "How Americans Win in Asia." *Fortune*, vol. 124, no. 8 (October 7, 1991), p. 140.

Leung, Julia. "Bank of America Unveils Asia Plan in Wake of Merger." *Asian Wall Street Journal*, April 27, 1992.

Leung, Julia. "U.S. Banks Are Poised for Further Expansion in Asia This Year As Demand for Services Grows." *Asian Wall Street Journal*, February 24, 1992.

Liner, Doug. "Some Trends in Export Financing." *Export Today*, May 1993, pp. 39–41.

Lorch, Donatella. "Banks Follow Immigrants to Flushing." *New York Times*, August 7, 1991, pp. B1–B2.

Task Force on the International Competitiveness of U.S. Financial Institutions. *Report of the Subcommittee on Financial Institutions Supervision, Regulation, and Insurance.* U.S. Government Printing Office, Washington, D.C., October 1990.

U.S. Department of Commerce, Bureau of Economic Analysis. *Business Statistics 1961–1988. Washington, D.C.*

U.S. Department of Commerce, Bureau of Economic Analysis. *Survey of Current Business, April 1991. Washington, D.C.*

ENDNOTES

1. There are four general forms of business organizations through which a bank may conduct overseas operations. The *representative office* is the most restricted of the four. Representative offices may *not* accept deposits, make loans, or conduct any banking services. They are simply points of contact between parent banks and their clients. *Agencies* have somewhat more authority. They may accept predetermined payments in connection with international trade or deliver undisbursed portions of loans made by the parent bank. However, deposit-taking or fiduciary activities (such as portfolio management) are strictly prohibited. Essentially, no credit decisions are made by agencies. Agencies may only execute credit decisions made by the parent. *Branches* and *subsidiaries* perform all normal banking functions. In the United States, a foreign *branch* must be licensed by either the state in which it is located or by the federal government. Technically, the results of operations are not

distinguished from those of the parent bank. As a result, its lending limits are tied to the capital and surplus of the parent. Laws and regulations of the home country govern branch activities. *Subsidiaries* are separate legal entities, incorporated by the government of the country in which they operate. Each has its own capital base. However, it is not uncommon for the parent bank to own 100 percent of the subsidiary's stock. Generally, laws of the host country govern the operation of overseas subsidiaries. The choice of organizational form will depend upon a number of circumstances. If the bank has a large number of clients in the overseas location or a small number of major clients, a full service bank (branch or subsidiary) may be preferable. On the other hand, a representative office is a cost-effective way to explore a new geographical market before setting up more extensive operations.

2. The earlier analyses referred to total loans, including, but not limited to, commercial loans.

2   An International Comparison of Bank Systems and Powers

INTRODUCTION

Commercial banks in all industrialized countries share certain common features. Each banking system is involved in the payments mechanism, in the provision of consumer services, and in financial support of industrial firms. There are differences, however, in the form of these services and the extent to which the pace of technological change has transformed the services themselves. U.S. banks are generally smaller than their counterparts in other countries and frequently have a more narrow scope of bank powers. At the same time, U.S. banks are pushing the frontier of permitted services and developing technology-based financial specialties.

BANKING HERE AND ABROAD

Of the world's 1,000 largest commercial banks in 1993, 45 percent were in Europe, 13 percent in North America, and 39 percent in Asia, with the rest of the world accounting for only 3 percent. Together, the top 1,000 banks control assets of roughly $25 trillion. With approximately $12 trillion in assets, the banking systems of the United States, Canada, the United Kingdom, Germany, France, Switzerland, and Japan control a large share of the world's banking assets.

The United States

Unlike banking systems in other countries, the United States has a large number of both state-chartered and national commercial banks. The number peaked at 30,000 in 1920, but because of failures and mergers is now less than 12,000. One-third of these are nationally chartered, hold 60 percent of U.S. bank assets, and control 53 percent of U.S. bank offices. Thus, national banks are large with ample branch networks. In terms of number of separate banks, however, the largest group is non-Federal Reserve member state institutions, representing about 60 percent of all commercial bank charters. These smaller institutions represent only 24 percent of bank assets and 35 percent of bank offices. The smallest group in terms of number of charters, Federal Reserve member state banks, hold roughly 8 percent of bank charters, but 16 percent of assets and 12 percent of offices.

As a result, national banks have average total assets of about $470 million, state-chartered Federal Reserve member banks $520 million, and non-Fed member state-chartered banks $100 million. Across all banks, the average size is $260 million. While New York is often described as the U.S. money center because the country's largest banks are headquartered there, the structure of the U.S. banking system is essentially a diverse collection of institutions with limited geographical service areas. Among industrialized countries, the United States is unusual in this regard. Even when regional banks operate in other countries, a strong system of banks that branch nationwide is the rule rather than the exception.

Exhibit 2-1 shows the growth of U.S. bank assets during the 1980s. In 1981 U.S. bank assets totaled $2 trillion. By the end of the decade, the total stood at $3.3 trillion, representing an annual increase of 6.2 percent.[1] The assets of commercial banks expanded rapidly during the 1980s because of a general expansion in the U.S. money supply. Capital levels, however, did not keep pace and, by the early 1990s, expansion of bank assets slowed as bank regulators

EXHIBIT 2-1

U.S. BANK ASSETS

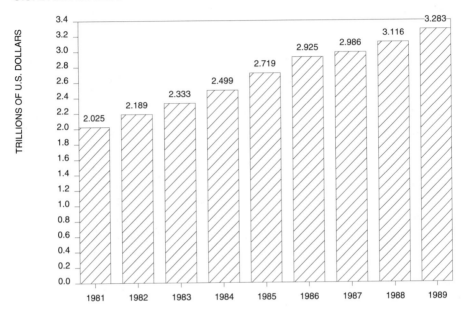

Sources

Author's calculations and graphic based on data from:
1. *Bank Profitability: Statistical Supplement, Financial Statements of Banks 1981–1989,*
   Organisation for Economic Co-operation and Development, 1991.
2. *International Financial Statistics,* International Monetary Fund, Yearbook 1990.

placed more emphasis on building capital levels, a policy position observed in many industrialized countries.

The United Kingdom

Prior to 1914, London was recognized as the world's center for international finance. The pound sterling was the major currency of the world because London has historically provided significant amounts of long-term investment capital and short-term trade finance. Furthermore, the government of the United Kingdom has a long tradition of facilitating domestic and international trade.

For centuries, the Bank of England—a private bank with certain government privileges—oversaw all banking operations and monetary policy. After being nationalized in 1946, the bank received the power to give directives to other banks, a power that it did not exercise. Instead, its quasi-official status and its ability to affect the liquidity of other commercial banks, just as the Federal Reserve does in the United States, made it possible for the Bank of England to achieve its desired results through requests. In general, the banking system of the United Kingdom is based on convention and mutual understanding between government, the Bank of England, and other institutions.

Clearing banks in the United Kingdom perform the same functions as commercial banks in the United States. In particular, clearing banks provide the nation's primary payments mechanism (checks and other forms of payment) and short-term liquidity to industrial firms through extensive overdrafts.[2] Unlike U.S. banks, British clearing banks branch nationwide. This system has resulted in a relatively small number of clearing banks that process 80 percent of all check and credit card transactions. Among these, the largest are:

- Barclays Bank

- National Westminster Bank

- Midland Bank

- Lloyds Bank

Secondary banks, also known as *merchant banks*, offer primarily time, rather than demand, deposits. Competition among secondary banks is aggressive and the banks use interest rates to attract large, wholesale deposits. To match the average maturity of deposits and loans, secondary banks generally make longer-term loans, frequently to non-British enterprises.

Both clearing and merchant banks use discount houses to adjust their liquidity levels. Discount houses are intermediaries between the government and the clearing banks. These private firms absorb the entire weekly U.K. Treasury Bill offering, can borrow from the Bank of England, are active dealers in short-term government securities, and make a secondary market with merchant banks in negotiable CDs and acceptances. The Bank of England does not make direct loans to, nor conduct open market operations with banks, as the Federal Reserve does in the United States. Instead, the Bank of England conducts these transactions with discount houses; in turn, the discount houses deal directly with the banks.

Exhibit 2-2 shows the growth in assets of the 47 clearing and secondary banks in the United Kingdom. From slightly over $300 billion in 1981, the total assets of U.K. banks increased at an average rate of 11 percent per year to reach $731 billion by the end of the decade. In terms of total assets, the size of the U.K. banking system is thus less than one-quarter the size of the U.S. system, but the average size (total system assets divided by number of banks) of a U.K. bank is $15 billion, much larger than the average U.S. bank.

Canada

The Canadian banking system is a blend of the U.S. and U.K. systems. Structurally, it resembles the U.K. system in that banks branch nationwide, but its monetary policy implementation is similar to that of the United States, with the Canadian central bank having direct relations with the commercial banks.

The Bank of Montreal, the first true bank, began operations in 1817 and received a charter in 1822. The bank's charter contained provisions that illustrate the strong governmental influence over Canadian banks. The original charter was granted for only 10 years, prohibited the bank from owning real estate other than bank promises and from making loans collateralized by real estate, required annual reports to shareholders with specified information, and placed a ceiling of 6 percent on loan interest rates. In the United States, in contrast, strict government supervision of commercial banks did not begin until enactment of the National Bank Act of 1863.

The Finance Ministry of Canada implements both fiscal and monetary policy. The original Bank Act was passed in 1871 and subsequent amendments to the act have shaped the financial system over time. The Bank Act amendment of 1924 established the Office of

EXHIBIT 2-2

U.K. BANK ASSETS

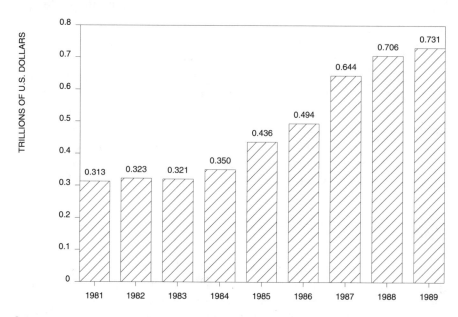

Sources

Author's calculations and graphic based on data from:
1. *Bank Profitability: Statistical Supplement, Financial Statements of Banks 1981–1989*, Organisation for Economic Co-operation and Development, 1991.
2. *International Financial Statistics*, International Monetary Fund, Yearbook 1990.

the Inspector General of Banks, Canada's primary bank examiner. The Canadian central bank, the Bank of Canada, was created by a 1934 amendment to the Bank Act.

Restrictions of bank operations have eased over time. Residential mortgage loans with a 15 percent government guarantee have been permitted since 1936. In the mid-1940s, the government began to guarantee short- and intermediate-term bank loans to farmers and veterans. Also, the government lifted loan interest rate ceilings in 1967 (13 years before the major deregulatory thrust in the United States), allowed banks to offer discount brokerage services in the early 1980s, and permitted banks to own securities firms in the late 1980s (a practice permitted for only a few commercial banks in the United States).

Generally, there has been a good relationship between government and the banking industry. Canadian banks have been permitted to expand lending powers as desired and have enjoyed virtually complete freedom to offer a variety of deposits. This contrasts with the U.S. experience in which expansion of banking powers has been permitted primarily by bank regulators, rather than by legislators, because of the reluctance of legislators to pass further bank liberalization laws.

The Canadian equivalent of commercial banks is *chartered banks.* Between 1820 and 1970, 157 charters were granted. Sixty of these, however, were never used; 45 banks either failed or ceased operation for some other reason; and there were a number of bank mergers. These factors have caused the number of Canadian banks to be much smaller than the number of U.S. banks. Five chartered banks control roughly 90 percent of Canadian bank assets:

- The Royal Bank of Canada

- The Bank of Montreal

- The Bank of Nova Scotia

- The Toronto-Dominion Bank

- The Canadian Imperial Bank of Commerce

Unlike U.S. money-center banks, these five operate branching networks throughout Canada, a practice prohibited for U.S. banks.

Exhibit 2-3 shows the growth of total Canadian bank assets in U.S. dollars during the 1980s—on average growing 4 percent per year during this period. The slump in growth in the early 1980s is attributable primarily to the strength of the U.S. dollar versus the Canadian dollar at that time. In general the size of the Canadian banking system is 12 percent the size of the U.S. banking system. Because there are only 10 banks, however, the average size of a Canadian bank is $39.5 billion.

EXHIBIT 2-3

CANADIAN BANK ASSETS

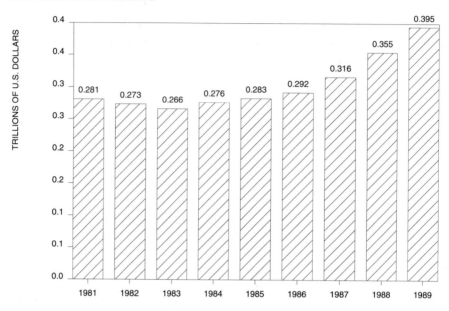

Sources

Author's calculations and graphic based on data from:
1 *Bank Profitability: Statistical Supplement, Financial Statements of Banks 1981–1989*, Organisation for Economic Co-operation and Development, 1991.
2. *International Financial Statistics*, International Monetary Fund, Yearbook 1990.

Germany

Commercial banks in Germany have even greater operational free-dom than Canadian banks. Past abuses of power by the government have resulted in a general disdain for government intervention in the banking system.[3]

Moreover, individual states in Germany have a long history of regional strength and independence from the central government, resulting in several cities with significant economic influence. Bonn and Berlin are the political centers; Hamburg is the busiest port and second largest city; Dusseldorf is a major manufacturing site; and

Frankfort is the financial center. In this respect, German banking is comparable to U.S. banking, with a large number of state and regional banks.

In contrast to the U.S. system, however, the Deutsche Bundesbank, the German central bank, does not restrict the scope of bank activities. German banks offer corporate underwriting services and hold the common stock of their clients as investments. Because of this wide range of bank services, German banks are called *universal* banks. The central bank does, however, perform customary roles of lender of last resort and facilitator of monetary policy. The German banking system has operated in this way since shortly after the end of World War II.

In addition to the state and regional banks, there are three big banks in Germany:

- Deutsche Bank

- Dresdner Bank

- Commerzbank

With assets of over $400 billion, these three banks control half of all German bank assets and branches and, like Canadian banks, operate nationwide.

Exhibit 2-4 shows the strong growth in German banking assets in the 1980s. From $271 billion in 1981, total assets increased at an annual rate of 12 percent to reach $670 billion by the end of the decade. Part of this is attributable to the depreciation of the U.S. dollar in the second half of the decade, but even in German deutsche marks, bank assets increased at an average rate of 8 percent a year. Total assets in the German banking system are 11 percent of the U.S. total, but because there are only 264 banks in that system, the average size of a German bank is $2.5 billion, ten times the U.S. average.

France

Before World War I, Paris was second only to London as an international financial center. Although France was ravaged by both World Wars, Paris has since regained much of its former status in world

EXHIBIT 2-4

GERMAN BANK ASSETS

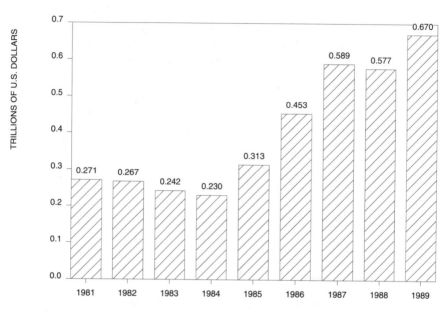

Sources

Author's calculations and graphic based on data from:
1. *Bank Profitability: Statistical Supplement, Financial Statements of Banks 1981–1989*, Organisation for Economic Co-operation and Development, 1991.
2. *International Financial Statistics*, International Monetary Fund, Yearbook 1990.

finance. In 1945, the four largest deposit banks were nationalized and all banks were required to assume one of three forms: *banque de dépôts* or deposit bank (accepting deposits and granting loans), *banque d'affaires* or investment bank (granting loans and taking equity positions), or *banque de crédit à long et moyen terme* or medium- to long-term credit bank. Deposit banks receive demand deposits or any deposits repayable within two years. Business banks underwrite new securities issues. Medium- to long-term credit banks offer loans and accept time deposits that have a longer term than the deposit bank instruments. Subsequently, the remaining deposit banks were also nationalized.[4]

In 1966, however, the distinction between deposit banks and business banks was weakened in a move toward bank deregulation. In 1984, the distinctions were completely eliminated when the *établissement de crédit* and its functions replaced the former three categories of institutions. Currently, French deposit banks offer a full line of financial services, including short- and medium-term loans, demand and time deposits, and securities dealing and underwriting.

Like Germany, France has a number of large banks that dominate the industry. The top three French banks control 80 percent of all bank deposits versus 20 percent for the top three banks in the United States. The largest French banks are:

- Banque Nationale de Paris

- Crédit Lyonnais

- Societé Générale

- Banque Paribus

- Banque Indosuez

- Credit Commercial de France

Exhibit 2-5 shows that the eight big banks of France are larger than the 47 British, 10 Canadian, or 264 German banks described thus far. Assets of these French banks increased at an average rate of 12 percent from $410 billion in 1981 to over $1 trillion by the end of the decade.[5] With average assets of $129 billion, these large now-universal banks play a major role in European finance.

Switzerland

Swiss commercial banks operate in an environment of privacy that is unmatched in the rest of the world. The 1934 Banking Law, the first federal banking law in that country, contained provisions that protected depositors in Swiss banks. Banks are prohibited from revealing details of financial transactions to outsiders unless an illegal act, according to Swiss law, is involved. This secrecy provision was partially motivated by attempts of agents of Nazi Germany to determine

EXHIBIT 2-5

FRENCH BANK ASSETS

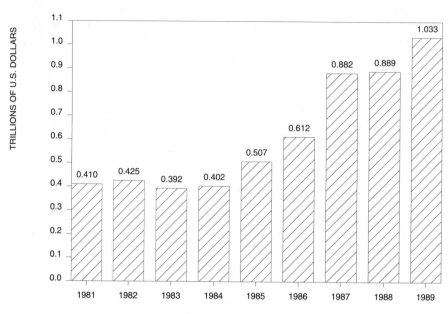

Sources

Author's calculations and graphic based on data from:
1. *Bank Profitability: Statistical Supplement, Financial Statements of Banks 1981–1989*, Organisation for Economic Co-operation and Development, 1991.
2. *International Financial Statistics*, International Monetary Fund, Yearbook 1990.

the nature and amount of Swiss deposits owned by German citizens. The bank secrecy law protected private citizens from the misguided whims of government by allowing depositors to use accounts identified with numbers only, the so-called "numbered accounts," and by preventing transactions disclosure.

The provisions of the 1934 act have, nevertheless, created some tensions between the governments of Switzerland and other countries. Tax evasion and insider stock trading, for example, are considered criminal acts in the United States, but are prosecuted administratively (in civil proceedings) in Switzerland. Because they are civil offenses in Switzerland, these acts do not override the bank secrecy law. In the interest of good international relations, however, the Swiss government has cooperated with the United States in some cases involving insider trading violations. Along these same lines, beginning in 1991, the actual owner of all Swiss bank accounts, not a lawyer or other agent for the depositor, must be known by at least two bank officials.

Switzerland has had a favorable financial climate for other reasons. The Swiss people themselves have long been ardent savers, with the result that the country has consistently been a net exporter of capital. Consistent with its respect for privacy, Switzerland has remained politically neutral, avoiding burdensome expenses of war. Stability of the Swiss franc and the Swiss banking system after World War I contributed to its reputation of a safe haven for funds. As a result, during the 1920s and 1930s, the country's commercial banks received large deposits, primarily from Germany.

Over time, Switzerland's economic stability, political neutrality, and bank secrecy law have attracted capital worldwide. Foreign banks have likewise been attracted to Switzerland's stable financial markets.

Liechtenstein is a sovereign state approximately one hour's drive from Zurich and shares its currency, legal structure, and customs with Switzerland. Because of these shared characteristics, Liechtenstein has also become involved in the world of international banking.

Like German banks, the major banks in Switzerland are also universal banks. The five largest institutions control almost 50 percent of all Swiss bank assets and $72 billion each on average. The "big three" are:

- Union Bank of Switzerland

- Swiss Bank Corporation

- Crédit Suisse Bank

Swiss banks are heavily involved in capital markets and equity investments in industrial firms.

Cantonal banks are publicly owned and restricted to the geographical areas in which they are located. While these 29 institutions are considered banks, they tend to specialize in savings deposits and mortgage loans but also offer financial services to local industry. Controlling roughly one-quarter of bank assets, cantonal banks are the second most important group of banks.

Foreign banks represent the third largest presence in Switzerland, greater than domestic savings banks and credit cooperatives. With over 100 foreign institutions, Switzerland is one of the world's largest international financial centers.

Exhibit 2-6 shows the assets of big banks and cantonal banks in Switzerland. Growing at 14 percent a year, Swiss bank assets totaled $491 billion by 1987. The appreciation of the Swiss franc accounted for a portion of the high rate of growth, but banking system assets in Swiss francs grew at an average rate of 8 percent per year. The 34 big and cantonal banks have average total assets of $14 billion, over 50 times the amount for the average U.S. bank.

Japan

Exceeding the size of Canadian and European banks, Japanese banks are currently the world's largest, primarily because of Japan's large trade surpluses and the strength of the Japanese yen. This was not always the case, however. The 1868 Meiji Restoration was an early turning point in the economic development of Japan, replacing the prior feudal system that had generated little economic progress for the country.

The Meiji government established the Osaka Mint in 1871 and passed the New Currency Act. The 1872 National Bank Act established national banks, similar to those in the United States. The objectives of these acts were to create a stable currency and to mobilize funds for needed development. Although there were 153 national banks by 1879, the individual savings rate was quite low, most loans were agricultural, and there was limited availability of small business loans.

Rapid expansion of the money supply through the new national banks led to widespread inflation in 1877 through 1880. In turn, the inflation necessitated an amendment of the National Bank Act that created Japan's central bank to facilitate industrial finance, lower interest rates, and increase the resources available to financial institu-

EXHIBIT 2-6

SWISS BANK ASSETS

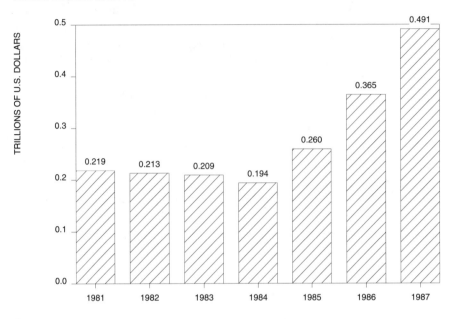

Sources

Author's calculations and graphic based on data from:
1. *Bank Profitability: Statistical Supplement, Financial Statements of Banks 1981–1989*, Organisation for Economic Co-operation and Development, 1991.
2. *International Financial Statistics*, International Monetary Fund, Yearbook 1990.

tions. The Bank of Japan began operations in 1882 and was given sole note-issuing power after 1899. All other banks were reorganized as ordinary banks.

The ordinary bank classification is composed of *city banks* and *regional banks*. City banks are large, nationwide organizations that target major industrial firms, while regional banks cater to the needs of smaller businesses and individuals. The activities of regional banks are typically limited to one prefecture or state.

Prior to World War II, Japanese banks were often members of large industrial combinations called *zaibatsu*. Through this mechanism, strong ties between banks and industrial firms were formed with the largest *zaibatsu* banks, Sumitomo, Mitsui, and Mitsubishi, being particularly instrumental in Japan's economic development.

After World War II, *zaibatsu* were dismantled and *keiretsu*, or industrial groups with interlocking ownership, formed. Former *zaibatsu* banks still provided the majority of debt financing to their *keiretsu* affiliates. Although the regional banks channeled their savings deposits to the *keiretsu* city banks through interbank loans, until the 1970s city banks were consistently overloaned. Overlending is the situation in which a bank's loan demand consistently exceeds available deposits and capital.

The Bank of Japan relieved the overlending by making loans to the city banks. The Bank of Japan encouraged loans to high priority industries by offering its loans to city banks at favorable interest rates, which were then reflected in favorable interest rates to industrial firms. Overlending ended after the 1970s when Japan became a net capital exporter because of large trade surpluses. While industrial firms are now less dependent on their *keiretsu* banks, they still maintain close relationships.

In the late 1920s, there were approximately 1,000 ordinary banks in Japan. During World War II, many were liquidated or consolidated so that by 1945, only 61 ordinary banks remained. Today, the 13 city banks hold almost 70 percent of total bank assets. With nationwide branch networks, these 13 institutions control over 20 percent of all bank offices. The largest include:

- Dai-Ichi Kangyo Bank

- Sumitomo Bank

- Fuji Bank

- Sakura Bank (formerly Mitsui Bank and Taiyo Kobe Bank)

- Sanwa Bank

- Mitsubishi Bank

The average asset base of a city bank is $273 billion, more than twice as large as the average French big bank.

Exhibit 2-7 illustrates the rapid growth of Japanese bank assets for all ordinary banks. From a total of $1.2 trillion dollars in 1981

EXHIBIT 2-7

JAPANESE BANK ASSETS

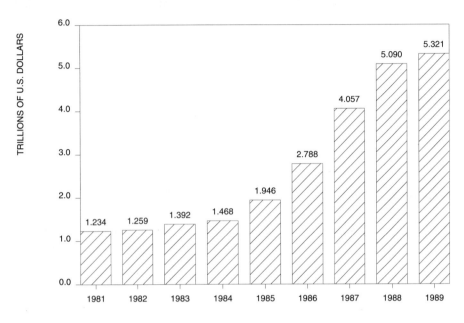

Sources

Author's calculations and graphic based on data from:

1. *Bank Profitability: Statistical Supplement, Financial Statements of Banks 1981–1989*, Organisation for Economic Co-operation and Development, 1991.

2. *International Financial Statistics*, International Monetary Fund, Yearbook 1990.

Japanese bank assets increased at the rate of 20 percent a year to reach $5.3 trillion by the end of the decade, more than 1.5 times as large as the total assets of all U.S. banks. Part of this increase is attributable to the appreciation of the Japanese yen, but even in yen terms, Japanese bank assets grew at almost 14 percent per year during the 1980s. The average assets for these 145 banks is $37 billion. There is no question that Japanese trade surpluses have moved these banks to the forefront of international finance, as indicated in Exhibit 2-8.

THE STRUCTURAL DIFFERENCES

When the banking system of the United States is compared to the systems in other industrialized countries, the contrasts are striking. Several points are clear:

- The amount of total assets in the U.S. banking system is smaller than the Japanese but larger than the others in the comparison.

- The average bank size in the United States is smaller than in any other country analyzed.

- The growth rate of U.S. bank assets is slower than that of other countries.

Asset Base

Exhibit 2-9 shows the relative proportions of bank assets in the seven countries discussed above. Japanese bank assets alone are almost half the total and the United States represents over 25 percent. The other shares range from 3.3 percent to 8.7 percent. Taken in the aggregate, the U.S. banking system is the second largest banking system in the world.

Size

Even with a large share of total banking assets, U.S. banks operate at a competitive disadvantage because their average size is so much smaller. Consider the following breakdown of average bank size for these countries in 1989.

	# of banks	Assets ($ billions)
United States	12,689	$ 0.26
United Kingdom	47	15.55
Canada	10	39.50
Germany	264	2.54
France	8	129.13
Switzerland	34	14.44
Japan	145	36.69

EXHIBIT 2-8

THE WORLD'S TOP 20 BANKS RANKED BY ASSET SIZE—1991
($ Billions)

Rank		Assets
1	Dai-Ichi Kangyo Bank, Japan	$475.8
2	Sumitomo Bank, Japan	464.1
3	Fuji Bank, Japan	455.4
4	Sakura Bank, Japan	448.3
5	Sanwa Bank, Japan	445.0
6	Mitsubishi Bank, Japan	432.0
7	Industrial Bank of Japan	333.3
8	Norinchukin Bank, Japan	331.0
9	Crédit Agricole, France	306.3
10	Crédit Lyonnais, France	305.4
11	Deutsche Bank, Germany	295.4
12	Banque National de Paris, France	275.1
13	Tokai Bank, Japan	271.0
14	Mitsubishi Trust & Banking, Japan	261.6
15	Barclays Bank	257.7
16	Long-Term Credit Bank of Japan	255.7
17	Bank of Tokyo, Japan	247.2
18	ABN Amro Holding, Netherlands	242.4
19	Sumitomo Trust & Banking, Japan	234.9
20	Société Général, France	234.1

Source

Alan Chai, Alta Campbell, and Patrick J. Spain, editors, *Hoover's Handbook of World Business 1993*, p. 68.

EXHIBIT 2-9

COMPARISON OF BANKING SYSTEM ASSETS—1989

Country	Assets[1]	%[2]
Japan	$ 5,321	44.6
United States	3,283	27.5
France	1,030	8.7
United Kingdom	731	6.1
Germany	670	5.6
Switzerland	491	4.1
Canada	395	3.3
	$11,921	100.0%

[1] Billions of U.S. dollars.
[2] Percentage of total banking assets for the group of seven countries included in the analysis.

Note: Data for Switzerland is for 1987.

Sources

Author's calculations based on data from:
1. *Bank Profitability: Statistical Supplement, Financial Statements of Banks 1981–1989,* Organisation for Economic Co-operation and Development, 1991.
2. *International Financial Statistics,* International Monetary Fund, Yearbook 1990.

The average size of U.S. banks is 10 percent the size of the average German bank, 0.2 percent the size of the average French bank, and somewhere in between these percentages for the banks in the other countries. This significant size difference is important because an increasing number of foreign banks operate in the United States and compete directly with U.S. domestic banks. To the extent that U.S. banks are smaller and less able to offer a full range of services, domestic banks will continue to lose market share on their own turf.[6]

The size difference is important also because industrial firms operate increasingly in a global environment. The future international competitiveness of the United States will depend in large measure on the ability of small- and medium-size firms to sell their goods and services abroad. Just as the large *zaibatsu* banks helped Japanese industrial firms to compete and to expand internationally, so too can U.S. banks assist U.S. firms. The assistance can be limited by the size of the bank, however, because a smaller bank's loan portfolio can more easily become overly concentrated in one industry. Furthermore, it is not certain that foreign banks will have the same kind of commitment to U.S. firms that U.S. banks have.

Growth Rate

The competitive pressures on U.S. banks domestically and internationally are partially reflected in the growth rate of U.S. bank assets. The annual growth rates of bank assets during the 1980s in the seven industrialized countries included here are:

	(in local currency)	(in U.S. dollars)
United States	6.2%	6.2%
United Kingdom	13.6	11.2
Canada	4.0	4.4
Germany	8.1	12.0
France	12.4	12.2
Switzerland	8.1	14.4
Japan	13.8	20.0

The U.S. growth rate was lower than any other country, except Canada. U.S. bank regulators are now emphasizing higher capital ratios, leading some banks to reduce their overall size in order to boost the capital ratio. But the Basel Accord on capital standards applies to international banks in all these countries.[7] Thus, regulators are emphasizing capital standards in all the industrialized countries.

The fact remains that U.S. bank assets are not growing at the same pace as those in other major trading partners. All other things being equal, this means that the competitive disadvantage of smaller U.S. banks will only be compounded in the future. It will be difficult for the large number of banks to all increase in size and market share, particularly given a slow rate of growth within the U.S. domestic economy. The problem can be alleviated, however, if banks are allowed to branch nationwide and to merge and consolidate freely across state lines. Permitting U.S. banks to compete in other forms of financial services, such as securities underwriting, can also add to bank profitability and growth potential. Given the current regulatory constraints within which they must operate, however, U.S. banks are seeking niches in which they can extend their client base and increase profitability.

COMPARATIVE BANK SERVICES

Payment Mechanisms

Checks in the United States. Historically, *checks* have been the second most preferred method of payment in the United States, with *cash* representing the greatest number of transactions—70 percent of all transactions. Yet in terms of dollar volume, checks represent a much larger amount of payments. It is estimated that 80 percent of total legal payments in the United States are made in the form of checks— 2 billion checks per day.

Individuals write the greatest number of checks in the United States (over 50 percent). The payees of these checks are primarily businesses, with governments and other individuals receiving less than 10 percent of them. The next most frequent check writers are businesses, making payments to other businesses (23 percent), to individuals (16 percent), and to governments (1 percent). Governmental bodies write about 5 percent of checks.

To clear these checks, banks rely on check-clearing systems. The system can either be a local clearinghouse, or a Federal Reserve clearing system if the banks are not in the same area. Fedwire is operated by the Federal Reserve and is the official network for clearing domestic checks. This system is also used for market transactions between the Treasury Department and the Federal Reserve.

With the volume of checks that is processed each day, financial transactions would be delayed considerably if each bank waited to determine its overall cash position before paying those checks drawn on it. The net result of this clearing activity is that total interbank deposit accounts (those accounts that banks have with other banks) can be as much as $100 billion out of balance. These temporary imbalances necessitate borrowing in short-term money markets such as overnight loans (called federal funds) and repurchase agreements (involving Treasury and other marketable securities).

Many of these money market transactions are recorded on bank-owned electronic networks. Clearinghouse Interbank Payments System, or CHIPS, processes large payments between banks and even banks and their clients. Bankwire, a smaller bank-owned network, typically gets the overflow from Fedwire and CHIPS.

In the past, some payee banks placed holds on checks until they cleared payor banks. If the payees were not advised of these "holds," they could write checks that exceeded their *available balance*, that is, that portion of the account balance that may be withdrawn immediately. In some cases, banks would not pay interest on the deposit until the end of the predetermined "hold period," even if the deposited check cleared before that time.

To correct these problems, Congress passed the Expedited Funds Availability Act of 1987. The act did not prohibit holds because banks have a legitimate need to protect themselves against check fraud or forgery. Instead, the law set a maximum hold period on specific accounts. The law states when interest on the deposit must begin accruing and requires that the bank tell its customers when funds will be available.

Not all accounts are covered by the legislation. Only transaction accounts are subject to the law. This includes demand deposits and NOW (negotiable order of withdrawal) accounts. No holds may be placed on U.S. Treasury checks or U.S. Postal Service money orders. For other checks, the hold period depends on whether payee and payor banks are in the same Federal Reserve check-processing zone. If they are in the same zone, the maximum hold is one business day. If they are not, the maximum is four business days. The Federal Reserve is responsible for implementing this law. Federal Reserve regulation CC is the enforcement regulation.

Notwithstanding the time limits imposed by Regulation CC, it can take six to ten days for an out-of-town check go through the system and the advice be returned to the payee bank. If such a check was drawn on an account with insufficient funds, the payee bank would have already released the funds to its customer. This possibility has encouraged the development of more efficient clearing systems.

An example of a more efficient clearing system is Electronic Check Presentment or ECP. The basic principle underlying ECP is that the information on a check may be shared electronically much faster than the physical check can be shipped. The bank in which a check is deposited scans the magnetic ink character recognition (MICR) line. This information is wired to the bank upon which the check is drawn. If there are insufficient funds for the check, the check is flagged overnight instead of a week later.

ECP standards and practices are being developed through the Electronic Check Clearing House Organization (ECCHO), with member banks including Citicorp, Bank of America, Chase Manhattan, Chemical Bank, and NationsBank. The procedure is being tested in the states of Michigan and California. Approximately 1,000 banks currently have the computer capacity to receive some sort of electronic check information.

While there are obvious benefits, the cost of ECP is also substantial. A bank that wishes to send checks electronically must invest $50,000 and applicable training costs. A bank that wishes to receive checks electronically should expect to invest an additional $200,000 to $300,000. However, the availability of such timely information can be turned into a fee-generating operation. For example, a corporate bank customer that has deposited a check for goods can be advised if the check will not be honored before any merchandise is shipped. Also, ECP can eliminate many of the delays associated with check processing for small, remote banks that have correspondent relationships with large banks. Part of the cost of ECP systems can be deferred by charging fees for the advance information that the system generates. In any event, as ECP applications become more common, the cost will undoubtedly decline.

Check Writing in Other Countries. The check-writing habit is also well developed in Canada, but the clearing function is much different. Five major banks control the vast majority of total bank assets: the Royal Bank of Canada, the Bank of Montreal, the Bank of Nova

Scotia, the Toronto-Dominion Bank, and the Canadian Imperial Bank of Commerce. Reciprocal agreements among them have all but eliminated payor float, that is, the time that elapses between the payee's receipt of a check and the corresponding reduction in the payor's account. Consumer checks are paid on a same-day basis, despite the fact that actual settlement occurs the next day. Writers of checks in denominations of $50,000 or more (business transactions) are assessed any float costs that accrue. Of course, this system is possible because there is a high degree of concentration in the Canadian banking system. In addition, nationwide branching of the five major banks has resulted in distributed locations and comparable market share.

In Europe, most countries have a *giro system* that performs the function of checking accounts in the U.S. A giro system is a nonbank payments system (frequently at the post office) that transfers funds from one account to another on a same-day basis. Because payments are effected at a centralized location, there is no payor float. The bank transaction in the United States that is most similar to a giro transfer is an "on-us" check, that is, a check deposited in the same bank on which it is drawn.

Interestingly, the giro system of the United Kingdom is not used as frequently as its continental European counterparts. This is partially because the U.K. Post Office giro system was not introduced until 1968. More fundamentally, however, British clearing banks have long emphasized personal banking services, branching nationwide and encouraging the use of checks. The four major U.K. clearing banks dominate the retail banking market, controlling the majority of all personal bank accounts. They are Barclays, Lloyds, Midland, and National Westminster.

In contrast, in Japan, checks and giro transactions originate almost exclusively in the business sector. Japanese payments are much more frequently in the form of cash or electronic transfer. The Japanese postal savings system has no parallel in the United States. The system accumulates savings from individuals and small businesses. It is a popular outlet for savings because the interest income was tax-exempt for deposits up to ¥3 million until 1988 and because there are over 20,000 locations, compared to approximately 10,000 bank branches. Currently, accounts may be maintained with balances up to ¥5 million. While interest income on these accounts is no longer tax-exempt, the interest rate is attractive as compared to other alternatives. Also, the postal system is extremely convenient. Through the postal savings system, wire transfers are easily done.[8] Transfers are possible not only to all domestic locations, but also to 82 other countries that have agreements between their postal authorities and Japan's.

Automation has clearly affected the payment mechanisms. The impact of automation on payments exceeds beyond check clearing and cash transfers, however.

Credit Cards in the United States and Abroad. As compared to cash and checks, credit cards are a relatively new means of payment that has become extremely popular. The first cards were introduced in the 1950s, at which time, card payees manually telephoned to receive authorization for each transaction. The current technology uses plastic cards with magnetic strips on the back. The magnetic strip enables payees to verify cards electronically before accepting them as payment. This verification is via a communications network set up over telephone lines. Credit cards are convenient and reduce the need to carry cash. Because card verification is now so streamlined, many retail establishments frequently accept credit cards more readily than checks.

For banks, credit cards are a profitable product line because income is realized in several ways. In every case, the payee accepting the credit card for payment does not receive the full amount shown on the *credit card draft*, that is, the sales slip created in a credit card transaction, showing amount, payee, payor, credit card issuer, and payor signature. The draft is an instruction by the payor to the credit card issuer to pay the amount shown to the payee. However, when the draft is presented to the credit card issuer, it is discounted by 3 to 5 percent. The *discount* is a source of income for commercial banks that issue credit cards.

If the bank charges an *annual fee* to cardholders (usually $25 to $50), these fees are also income for the bank. The payor receives a monthly statement from the bank that lists the transactions for that month. Typically, if the cardholder pays the bank for these transactions before the specified due date, no interest is charged. If not, the bank earns *interest income* on unpaid balances. The interest rate on credit card loans is higher than other forms of consumer lending, often in excess of 18 percent. Because of this high rate, the discounts, and annual fees, credit card operations can be quite profitable. Of course, there is also a relatively higher probability of uncollectible loans since most credit cards are unsecured.

Credit card business is concentrated among the largest banks in the United States. As of year-end 1992, the 380 banks with assets in excess of $1 billion represented 3 percent of all FDIC-insured banks, 71 percent of total U.S. bank assets, but more than 87 percent of credit card loans outstanding. Citicorp is the largest bank credit card issuer, with over 25 million accounts nationwide. Its MasterCard and VISA accounts are only a portion of its credit card businesses. The corporation also owns Diner's Club and Carte Blanche travel and expense cards.

Originally, Citicorp began card operations in New York state, subject to a 12 percent usury law loan rate ceiling. Subsequently, the state of South Dakota relaxed entry requirements for bank holding companies and eliminated interest rate ceilings. Citicorp transferred all of its credit card operations to a bank in Sioux Falls where loans and receivables are subject to no interest rate ceilings. This strategic move is but one of many innovative techniques that Citicorp, the largest bank holding company in the United States, has employed to maintain a competitive advantage with respect to retail banking.

In addition, Citicorp has designed private label credit cards for retail merchandisers such as Goodyear and Tandy Radio Shack. A private label credit card program is one in which a financial institution manages the credit card operation of a retailer, including promotion, credit evaluations, billing, and accounting—all in the retailer's name.

The credit card networks of Visa and MasterCard have introduced innovations in an effort to differentiate themselves. For example, Visa is introducing a "procurement card" that can be used for small corporate purchases under $5,000. The card will incorporate internal controls that limit the type and amount of purchases for which the user can receive authorization. In addition, the corporate card owner can take advantage of flexible billing arrangements, including centralized billing procedures and reporting at multiple levels.

MasterCard is offering a very upscale version of the gold card. Members of Louis Rukeyser's Wall Street Club, 400,000 investors who subscribe to his newsletter, may sign up for lines of credit up to $25,000 and an initial interest rate of 5.9 percent for the first six months. After this period, the rate goes to 2.9 percentage points above prime—still a bargain by most accounts. In addition, the cardholder is entitled to discounts on stock brokerage services, stock research, and quotations. The card will be closely watched by others in the industry as the first experiment in an affinity card that is linked with a high-profile personality.

Because of the healthy spread (difference between cost of funds and loan rate) that typically is available through credit cards, commercial banks face vigorous competition from outside their industry. Retailers such as Sears and even AT&T, the telecommunications giant, have credit cards that compete directly with bank-issued cards. But finance companies represent perhaps the strongest competing industry with many services that are directly comparable to those offered by commercial banks. For example, General Electric Capital Corporation (GECC) owns a credit card bank called Monogram Bank USA. A credit card bank is not subject to the same regulatory constraints as a commercial bank because it is designated to conduct primarily credit card business. GECC has issued over 35 million private label credit cards for major retailers such as the Macy's department store chain. Banks will no doubt continue to face mounting competition in this lucrative segment of the U.S. system of payments.

Travel and entertainment cards have been available in Europe for some time. However, bank credit cards are a recent innovation. With widespread acceptance and issuance of bank cards in the United States, American banks have turned to Europe for possible market expansion. In Germany, where bankers rely heavily upon their clients' presence in bank offices to cross-sell a number of products, the bank credit card received a cool reception.

To the displeasure of German banks, American Express purchased a Frankfurt bank through which insurance and other services were sold via credit card. Attempts to block this activity with regulatory intervention and with agreements among German banks for nonparticipation in the card venture proved unsuccessful. Unable to stop the introduction of the bank card, German banks joined with their own version, the Eurocard. In 1987, retailers announced plans to issue their own cards. The introduction of credit cards by American firms has facilitated market expansion. As a result, German residents now enjoy a broader range of financial services.

In the United Kingdom, the Barclaycard was the first. In some ways, the innovative spirit of Barclays is similar to that of Citicorp. Barclays is also the largest of Britain's clearing banks, with 5,000 branches worldwide, more than any other British bank.

In general, consumer banking services have been slower to evolve in Japan than in the United States or the United Kingdom. This is primarily because the 13 larger city banks have historically focused on large corporate clients. The 64 regional banks that did cater to individuals had neither comparable nationwide networks nor management. However, at the urging of the Ministry of Finance and certain political factions, city banks began to issue credit cards in the 1960s. The Japan Credit Bureau (JCB) is the most widely distributed. Initiated in 1961, the JCB is offered by Sanwa, Mitsui, Kyowa, Daiwa, Hokkaido Takushoku, and Taiyo Kobe.[9]

The Union Credit card, the second most popular, is also jointly operated by Fuji, Dai-Ichi Kangyo, Saitama, and Sakura. Sumitomo, Mitsubishi, and Tokai have each independently marketed their own credit cards. As consumer credit is developed in Japan, credit cards and related services should be considered a growth industry in that country.

It should be noted that there may still be considerable payor float involved with credit card transactions. In this case, the float is the time necessary to process, invoice, and collect the sales drafts. In essence, card-issuing banks are compensated for this sometimes considerable float through the discount.

Telecommunications technology has enhanced the use of bank credits as a part of the payments system in the United States and abroad. In a similar way, the use of direct electronic payments has increased.

Electronic Payments. Electronic payments may take several forms. The *automated clearinghouse (ACH)* is similar to the European giro system in that both account balances change on the same day, with no payor float. In an ACH, a written agreement documents the transactions that will be covered by the service in which one party is entitled to initiate a transaction with another party. With one or two days notice to the bank, a given transaction is effected with hardcopy detail of the transaction following. The most common examples are payroll direct deposit, U.S. government payments, and recurring payments such as insurance premiums. The Federal Reserve processes most ACH transactions in the United States.

These transfers were the first electronic link between banks, an indirect connection. Large volume, regular payments are recorded by a bank for its customer (for example, a utility company) on a magnetic tape. The clearinghouse computer simply sorts the transactions on the tape, creating a new separate tape for each bank on the other side of the transfers. Output tapes are then used to adjust interbank balances.

Wire transfers eliminate the need for magnetic tapes and are more direct electronic links. Through Fedwire (Federal Reserve), CHIPS (Clearing House Interbank Payment, New York), SWIFT (Society for Worldwide Interbank Financial Telecommunications), or Cashwire (international, regional, and national private sector firms), large interbank transactions are settled on a same-day basis. Wire transfers are an extension of the special handling for important transactions such as money market purchases or sales. Currently, immediately available funds can be transferred to any other party almost instantaneously. The volume of interbank transfers on such networks, including check clearing activities, can easily amount to $2 trillion in a single day.

Point of sale (POS) electronic links theoretically accomplish the same objective as wire transfers. However, while wire transfers typically involve large denominations, POS is geared to the smaller high volume retail market, for example, grocery stores and service stations. In this context, *convenience* and *cost* are important considerations.

In order to be convenient, a standardized system with adequate distribution is necessary. Standardization may be achieved with plastic *debit cards* with magnetic strips containing information about the payor's account. Use of a debit card results in reduction of the payor's bank account balance, that is, a "debit" to the deposit account of that payor. The offsetting "credit" is to the payee's deposit account, or, alternatively, to the deposit account of the payee's bank. Telecommunications equipment that connects the records of participating banks makes it possible to simultaneously reduce the account balance of the payor by the amount of the retail transaction and increase the balance of the retailer.

However, unless the number of banks and retailers in the area is relatively small, coordination of all systems involved can become complicated and make it difficult to distribute the service. For example, an early POS experiment in Los Angeles was discontinued because there were multiple competing banks and no single grocery store enjoyed even a 10 percent market share.

Cost considerations are both in terms of out-of-pocket expense and security. Required hardware and software development can entail substantial initial investment. These fixed expenditures require a high volume of transactions to bring per-unit cost within a reasonable range. However, high volume will at least partially depend on public acceptance of this means of payment. From the consumers' perspective, the greatest benefit is the reduced need to carry cash. Yet checking accounts serve virtually the same function. Switching from checks to debit cards requires that consumers relinquish payor float. So, unless participating banks can price POS services in such a way that they are competitive with checks, the immediate advantages for consumers are not clear.

Aside from out-of-pocket expense, banks participating in the on-line arrangement described above must open their records to access by a system over which they do not exercise complete control. The more secure alternative of off-line transactions (perhaps through ACH) increases the probability of loss through use of invalid cards. The considerations of cost and security can be significant deterrents in the implementation of POS technology.

Cash dispensers (CDs) were the first applications of automation in retail banking. These early machines usually dispensed a fixed amount of currency in a single denomination and most were off-line. Fairly rapid advances have made it possible to receive larger amounts of currency and to perform other functions, such as loan payments, deposits, transfers between accounts owned by the customer, and payments to third parties. The later generations are referred to as *automated teller machines (ATMs)*.

Some ATMs are positioned in an outside wall of the bank building to provide 24-hour access to bank services. Others are located in the lobby of the bank or in separate, adjoining lobbies. The enclosed ATMs provide greater customer security while using an ATM. Increasingly, ATMs are on-line operations, particularly in the United States.

Shared ATMs away from bank branches enable several banks to establish a "branch" in high density areas such as factories, hospitals, universities, and airports. Generally, banks have been reluctant to share ATMs on their own premises. Banks in various geographical regions have agreed to such arrangements in order to provide convenient service for traveling customers.

It is estimated that 4.1 billion U.S. bank transactions will be made through ATMs in 1993, while 6.2 billion will take place at the teller window inside the bank. Clearly, the ATM has an established position in the provision of bank services. Moreover, the rate of growth of ATM transactions is 12 percent per year—3 times the growth rate for in-bank teller transactions.

ATMs have been well received both in the United States and abroad. Full-service machines tend to be more common in the United States. However, universally, customers use ATMs primarily as cash dispensers often in connection with a credit or debit card.

In general, on-line debit cards have not been marketed as aggressively as credit cards, which are generally considered more profitable. There are 8 million locations worldwide that accept credit and off-line debit cards, but only 100,000 debit card terminals (on-line machines). In this regard, commercial banks are not fully capitalizing on the portion of the payments system that still remains almost entirely within the banking industry—the debit card system.

In most cases, customer fees are based on actual transactions using the card. However, there is growing sentiment that the availability of the debit card itself should generate revenue for the issuing bank, just as in the case of credit cards. Before such charges become industry norm it will probably be necessary to increase the perceived value of the card. This may include increasing on-line retail or ATM locations at which the card may be used and adding other attractive features. For example, the technology currently exists to increase withdrawal limits for customers with high checking account balances. Also, prestige card holders can be offered insurance protection or buyer protection plans that are now only associated with credit cards. Only a few brokerage firms have issued Visa Debit cards that give consumers access to their mutual fund accounts. The field remains wide open for commercial banks to develop with relatively little competition.

An innovative experiment with debit cards is the stored-value feature. Previously, stored-value cards were used for only one application—perhaps train rides or public copy machines. CoreStates Bank in Philadelphia has initiated an expanded test program with its 3,000 employees. Users of the MoneyPass card can load $1, $5, $10, or $20 on the cards using machines in the bank building and at ATMs. The cards can then be used at the company-owned cafeteria, vending machines, postal service, gift shops, and pay telephones. MoneyPass card users are generating almost 160,000 prepaid transactions a month and CoreStates plans to offer the service to colleges and client corporations. Since more than 6.3 billion transactions of $20 or less are generated each year in the Northeast quadrant of the United States, existing stored-value card applications have barely begun to scratch the surface.

Expanding Technology. It is safe to say that banks now compete in large measure based on their technological edge. This extends beyond credit or debit cards to marketing services to customers and managing customer information. If the loan system does not communicate with the deposit system, for example, valuable customer-profile information can be lost. If systems procedures in various departments are significantly different, customers can get the impression that they are working with several different banks.

A solution to this problem is the use of client/server technology. The server is designed to be the host system or central system. The client refers to the user—a bank employee. The server manages the functions for the entire organization. It can be mainframe, a minicomputer, or a larger personal computer (PC). Each user performs his or her own proprietary functions, usually on a PC. This arrangement has gained popularity because it gives each user greater control over data and the computing process.

Whichever approach is taken, however, the trend is toward better management of technology. The basic steps to realizing the full benefit from technology are:

- *Defining what the bank wants to achieve with its technology.* Systems will have the two general components of (1) operation or transactions processing and (2) management information analysis, such as asset/liability information. The exact combination of these two components will depend on the system. The bank should decide which proportions are appropriate for its applications.

- *Identifying the bank's existing technology.* In some cases, hardware or software that the bank already owns could increase efficiency if it were fully utilized.

- *Integrating the technology.* If transactions information and management information technology are integrated, it is possible to identify customer profiles, analyze client segment profitability, and to produce better data for asset/liability management.

With the increased use of computer-based products, such as credit, debit, and stored-value cards, the bank that is to remain competitive must keep abreast of the developments in the field of bank technology.

Corporate Services

In the past, U.S. commercial banks fostered relationships with corporate clients such that one bank provided a number of services for a given firm. Loan pricing was a function of all the other services and their respective profitability. More recently, however, surplus corporate cash is more frequently invested in money market instruments, instead of bank deposits. Corporate loan pricing must now be competitive with commercial paper rates for large, creditworthy clients. Thus, performance and profitability measurement of individual services is critical.

Because of the diversity of clients, corporate services are often custom-tailored. In fact, banks engage in corporate banking to varying degrees. While Citicorp management places heavy emphasis on retail banking, other money center banks have tended to specialize in corporate accounts. J.P. Morgan, the holding company of Morgan Guaranty, is an example of this. Morgan Guaranty's management has shaped the organization into a wholesale operation, with only 2 percent of the New York Metropolitan area branches of Citibank. The holding company also owns, partially or completely, subsidiaries engaged in trust, real estate, investment, international, and merchant banking activities.[10]

The Shrinking Top-Tier Corporate Clientele. Whatever the degree of emphasis on corporate services, certain trends are undeniable. Historically, commercial banks have earned substantial spreads by assuming credit risks of their corporate clients and financing these loans with relatively inexpensive deposit funds (demand or savings deposits). The cost of deposit funds has become more volatile since the 1980s. Further, larger corporations more frequently use commercial paper financing at more favorable interest rates. Thus, traditional spreads are no longer available on loans to major corporations.

During the early 1990s, low short-term interest rates made investments in long-term government securities extremely attractive for commercial banks. Also, the Basel Accord capital guidelines have encouraged investment in government securities by placing a zero risk-weight on this category. This means that there is no capital requirement for these instruments. On the other hand, commercial and industrial loans are assigned a 100 percent risk-weight, that is, must be backed by a full 8 percent of capital. The effect of market forces and regulatory requirements is reflected in changes in bank portfolios during 1992. Commercial and industrial loans decreased by $22.5 billion to $536.3 billion—a 4 percent decline. During the same year, securities portfolios grew by $81.4 billion to $772.8 billion—a 12 percent increase.

One consequence of this situation is that small- and medium-sized firms represent a market segment with significant future growth potential. Because these corporations have relatively less access to money and capital markets, they must necessarily depend more heavily upon commercial banks and other financial intermediaries. To cultivate a new client in this category, it may be necessary to employ direct mail, telemarketing, calling officers, seminars, or special events. This can be a relatively expensive process (perhaps as much as 300 basis points) if the resulting loan or deposit balance is in the $50,000 to $100,000 range—as can easily be the case for a smaller firm. Also, smaller firms are more likely to fail within two to three years, preventing the bank from recovering the cost of account acquisition through interest and fees.

Nevertheless, the market is large, with an estimated 10 million small businesses in the United States. In a recent survey by the Bank of Montreal, it was shown that 80 percent of small businesses have only one account with a given bank and 60 percent have an account with more than one bank. At the same time, the most profitable small business clients maintain multiple relationships with a given bank. The key to enhancing bank profitability in the middle market will be to integrate information about existing clients and to provide them with a wider range of bank services.

Emphasis on Fee Income. Another consequence of the thinner spreads available on loans to larger corporate customers is that fee income has become a much more important part of bank profitability. Thus, conventional services such as checking accounts and associated activities (e.g., stop payment orders and items returned for insufficient funds) are now important fee income generators.

However, there are some fee-generating segments that are not being exploited. Letters of credit for U.S. exporters is one of these. In 1992, $440 billion in merchandise was exported, with letters of credit and bills of exchange used as common vehicles to finance these transactions. Unfortunately, U.S. banks are losing ground to U.S. offices of foreign banks that are more willing and, in some cases, able to provide this form of trade finance. Sometimes foreign banks have an advantage because they may be knowledgeable about their home markets or have long-time relationships in specific areas of the world. In addition, other foreign banks specialize in dealing with public and privately supplied export credit insurance for use on short-term exports of less than $100,000 or in selling foreign trade receivables.

Nevertheless, a U.S. bank can generate fees at several levels in assisting exporters with letters of credit (L/Cs). Consider a transaction in which a U.S. exporter requests an L/C from the foreign buyer. When the L/C from the overseas bank is sent to the United States, it is received by a U.S. bank that acts as an *advising* bank, that is, the bank that assures the authenticity of the L/C. The advising fee is generally $50 to $150. If the U.S. bank agrees to *confirm* the L/C, that is, to guarantee payment (even if the foreign bank does not pay), the fee is 12.5 to 300 basis points based on the amount of the L/C. Finally, when the merchandise has been shipped, the L/C is *negotiated*, that is, the exporter is paid. This generates another 12.5 to 50 basis points based on the amount of the L/C. Thus, a U.S. bank that advises, confirms, and negotiates a $100,000 L/C can realize as much as $3,650 in fee income ($150 + (.035 x 100,000)).

In addition to traditional lines of business, commercial banks have begun to offer other services, many of which produce fee income:

- foreign exchange and treasury services
- data processing
- highly leveraged loans
- a greater volume of commercial real estate loans
- off-balance-sheet commitments

Multinational clients with domestic and international telecommunications networks can contract with the bank for worldwide cash flow information. With the assistance of the bank, receipts and disbursements can be more readily offset, often reducing the required number of foreign currency transactions. The bank performs all the required transactions, sometimes including risk management techniques that compensate for the multinationals' total exposure in specific currencies. To the extent that bank cash management techniques and technology are more advanced than those of its client, the client is more likely to contract with its bank.

Smaller corporate clients will not usually require such assistance. Instead, payroll or general ledger maintenance may be an appealing and appropriate service. This arrangement generally involves little or no incremental cost for the bank but enables it to sell unused time on its computer system. Since the bank already has cash flow details in connection with its clients' deposit and loan accounts, it has a comparative advantage over other data processing services.

Increased Risk in the Commercial Loan Portfolio. In other cases, banks have become involved in *leveraged buyouts* (*LBOs*), particularly in the 1980s. A leveraged buyout is the purchase of the common stock of a firm with borrowed funds. The objective for an LBO is to gain control of the company. Presumably, the group that gains control will be able to manage the firm more effectively than was the case before the LBO. The assets of the firm form the basis for the transaction and are sometimes at least partially sold to repay the borrowing. When bonds are used to raise the money to buy the stock, they are often referred to as junk bonds because the credit rating is not investment grade. When bank loans are used to raise the money, these loans are referred to as highly leveraged transactions (HLTs).

These HLTs carry an attractive interest rate, but they are also risky. In an economic downturn, companies have difficulty paying the high rates of interest on relatively large amounts of debt. This, of course, puts the lender at risk of default. In 1991, HLTs amounted to $150 billion, roughly 20 percent of all commercial and industrial loans by U.S. banks.

Commercial real estate loans have also offered attractive returns to help replace the blue-chip commercial borrowers that have turned to the commercial paper market. But this market is also risky. In 1992, commercial real estate loans totaled $364 billion, or 18 percent of *total* bank loans.

Both HLTs and commercial real estate loans have reduced the safety of the banking system as a whole. In the early 1990s, these high levels of risky loans caused regulators considerable concern and they required banks to set aside large loan loss provisions. This, together with the need to meet the 8 percent capital ratio target of the Basel Accord by 1992, created a tense regulatory climate. Commercial banks responded by severely reducing their lending activity. The "credit crunch" that resulted was at least partially blamed for the slow recovery from the 1991 economic recession in the United States.

It may be true that the banks were overly aggressive in the 1980s. But the profit pressures were no less real. The high cost of deposits and borrowed funds motivated banks to search for high-yielding loans and additional sources of fee income. Many *off-balance-sheet* activities are good sources of fee income. An off-balance-sheet activity is an activity or service that does not appear on the bank's financial statements, that is, a contingent obligation or an obligation to provide service in the future. Examples of off-balance-sheet activities include:

- commitments to make or purchase loans
- futures and forward contracts
- letters of credit
- standby letters of credit
- commitments to purchase foreign currencies
- interest rate swaps

In 1984, the dollar value of these contingencies and commitments was just under 60 percent of those liabilities recorded on the balance sheet. By 1989, this percentage had grown to almost 120 percent. The growth in these activities is clear evidence of the emphasis on fee income.

At the same time, unchecked growth in contingent liabilities is not necessarily the best way to boost earnings. Besides which, the 1992 Basel Accord capital requirements stipulate that banks must provide capital to cover these contingencies and commitments.

Securities Operations

Other possible fee income generators remain at least partially off-limits for U.S. commercial banks. Since 1933, when the Banking Act (Glass-Steagall) was passed by Congress, U.S. banks have been restricted with respect to investment banking activities. The act required that commercial banks divest themselves of investment banking affiliates. No national bank or state bank that was a member of the Federal Reserve could *directly* deal in, underwrite, or purchase securities. Further, no entity engaged in the business of issuing, underwriting, selling, or distributing securities could accept deposits. While Glass-Steagall *did* permit national banks to buy and sell securities without recourse as agents for their customers, subsequent rulings by the Comptroller of the Currency prohibited commercial banks from engaging in brokerage activities.

Until recently, most securities activities continued to be off-limits. Exceptions to this general rule were transactions involving fixed-income, investment-grade securities, such as federal government securities and general obligations of state and local governments. Glass-Steagall allowed national banks to own, deal in, and underwrite these instruments in U.S. markets and to engage in private placements.

Full-scale underwriting activities by U.S. banks are permitted in overseas markets. The net result of this regulatory difference is that only those banks that are large enough to maintain substantial overseas operations have been able to enter the securities business to any meaningful extent. At least in this respect, small- to medium-sized banks have found themselves at a competitive disadvantage as compared to larger institutions.

While U.S. commercial banks are not permitted to engage in securities underwriting in the United States, foreign banks have long been permitted to do so. This is because, before 1978, foreign banks operating in the United States were not subject to Glass-Steagall. The *International Banking Act of 1978* had the effect of prohibiting foreign banks from engaging in securities underwriting. However, 17 foreign banks were grandfathered, that is, permitted to continue to operate existing securities affiliates in the United States. Among these, there are eight German firms, three French, three Swiss, and one Japanese. Of course, the ability of these firms to do securities underwriting places domestic firms at a competitive disadvantage.

Federal legislators have thus far not been responsive to these apparent competitive inequities. While recent banking laws have served to remove interest rate ceilings and to provide for more attractive deposit instruments (e.g., NOW accounts, small-saver certificates, and money market deposit accounts), they have *not* relaxed prohibitions against securities operations. In 1991, the Secretary of the Treasury Department proposed, among other things, that commercial banks in sound financial condition be permitted to engage in securities transactions through a separate affiliate. To date, there has been no congressional action on this recommendation.

In the absence of legislative measures, U.S. bank regulators have granted expanded powers with respect to securities activities. During the 1980s, the Federal Reserve Board and the Comptroller of the Currency permitted bank holding companies and national banks to:

- underwrite commercial paper, mortgage-backed securities, municipal revenue bonds, and consumer-related receivables through subsidiaries that underwrite U.S. government securities

- place commercial paper without recourse for the account of customers

- transfer the commercial paper to a holding company subsidiary

- issue, underwrite, and deal in collateralized mortgage obligations through finance subsidiaries

- offer securities brokerage and investment advisory services to institutions

- offer and sell units in a unit investment trust solely on the order and for the account of the bank's customer through a bank or bank holding company subsidiary

- make limited investments in an investment bank

- create and sell interests in a publicly offered common trust fund for individual retirement account assets

Beginning in 1987, the Federal Reserve interpreted the Glass-Steagall Act in such a way as to permit banks to engage *indirectly* in securities activities. Section 20 of the Glass-Steagall Act prohibits Federal Reserve member banks from affiliating with any organization "engaged principally" in the issue, flotation, underwriting, public sale, or distribution of securities. (Other provisions of the act prohibit a bank from participating in these activities *directly*.) The Federal Reserve interpreted Section 20 as permitting a bank to affiliate with a firm engaged in securities transactions as long as securities transactions are not the principal business of the firm.

The Federal Reserve gave bank holding companies the right to establish nonbank subsidiaries that earn up to 10 percent of revenue from otherwise prohibited securities transactions. These transactions include underwriting of and dealing in:

- commercial paper

- mortgage-backed securities

- municipal revenue bonds

- securitized assets

- corporate bonds

- corporate equities

To ensure that the affiliation with banks is truly indirect, "firewalls" must be constructed and maintained. These firewalls limit transactions between the Section 20 subsidiary and the bank so as to limit risk to the bank, limit bank subsidies to the Section 20 sub, and prevent conflicts of interest between the two.

Generally speaking, commercial banks are moving more toward securities transactions for their own accounts as well as for clients, especially the larger banks. In 1992, the 50 large banks that are monitored by Salomon Brothers earned $3.2 billion from trading activities as compared to $1.4 billion in 1988. Typically, regional banks are less involved in trading activities because of the potential volatility in earnings. Recently, investment funds that make it possible for all banks to participate in securities trading are appearing. For example, Farrell Capital Management (FCM) has operated since 1988 with this objective. The primary fund is Globe Map I, for which FCM is the registered investment advisor. In 1992, the fund had $27 million under management with investors that included two U.S. banks, two Mexican banks (Nacional Financiera and GBM Atlantico), and two U.S. pension funds. This is a new area for many smaller banks, but one that promises to grow as banks become more involved in securities transactions.

It should be noted that state, nonmember banks are not subject to Section 20 of the Glass-Steagall Act. That is, while state nonmembers may not engage *directly* in securities transactions, the law is silent with regard to their affiliation with securities firms.

Exhibit 2-10 provides a list of Section 20 subsidiaries that were authorized as of July 1993. Of the total 31 securities subsidiaries, 12 are in the New York district. Of these 12, seven are foreign banks. When the four foreign banks in the Chicago and San Francisco districts are included, the total number of foreign Section 20 subs is 11 and the number of domestic 20. When the 17 foreign banks that were grandfathered under the International Banking Act of 1978 are considered, foreign bank securities operations in the United States outnumber those of domestic, Federal Reserve member banks.

Even so, the U.S. securities industry has challenged these developments, but these attempts have generally been unsuccessful. It is more likely that Congress will validate these powers and further expand the scope of banking activities. While it is not likely that U.S. bank powers will expand to this extent, the German banking system presents an interesting case of commercial bank involvement in industrial finance.

While U.S. banks attempt to provide a wider range of fee-generating services to corporate clients in order to bolster profitability, German banks have long enjoyed a much broader scope of corporate activity. German banks underwrite corporate securities and hold large portfolios of stock. As long as a German bank is adequately capitalized, there is virtually no regulatory limit on equity investments or other involvement in nonbank corporations.

EXHIBIT 2-10

COMMERCIAL BANK SECURITIES (SECTION 20) SUBSIDIARIES[1] AS OF JULY 1993

Banking Organization	Date Authorized
Boston District:	October 1988
Fleet/Norstar Financial Corporation	
New York District:	
The Bank of Nova-Scotia[3]	April 1990
Bankers Trust N.Y. Corp.[3]	April 1987
Barclays Bank PLC[2]	January 1990
Canadian Imperial Bank of Commerce[3]	January 1990
Chase Manhattan Corporation[2]	May 1987
Chemical N.Y. Corp.[2]	May 1987
Citicorp[2]	April 1987
Deutsche Bank AG[3]	December 1992
The Long-Term Credit Bank of Japan, Ltd.	May 1990
J.P. Morgan & Co.[3]	April 1987
The Royal Bank of Canada[3]	January 1990
The Toronto—Dominion Bank	May 1990
Philadelphia District:	
Dauphin Deposit Corporation[3]	June 1991
Cleveland District:	
Banc One Corporation	July 1990
Huntington Bancshares, Inc.	November 1988
PNC Financial Corp.	July 1987
Richmond District:	
First Union Corp.	August 1989
NationsBank[2]	May 1989
Atlanta District:	
Bank South Corporation	May 1993
Barnett Banks	January 1989
SouthTrust Corp.	July 1989
Synovus Financial Corporation	September 1991

EXHIBIT 2-10

COMMERCIAL BANK SECURITIES (SECTION 20) SUBSIDIARIES[1]
AS OF JULY 1993 (Continued)

Banking Organization	Date Authorized
Chicago District:	
Amsterdam-Rotterdam Bank N.V.	June 1990
The Bank of Montreal	May 1988
First Chicago Corporation	August 1988
St. Louis District:	
Liberty National Bancorporation	April 1990
Minneapolis District:	
Norwest Corporation	December 1989
San Francisco District:	
BankAmerica Corporation	March 1992
Dai-Ichi Kangyo Bank, Ltd.	January 1991
The Sanwa Bank, Ltd.	May 1990

[1] Authorized to underwrite and deal in certain municipal revenue bonds, mortgage-related securities, commercial paper, and consumer-receivable related securities.
[2] Also has corporate debt securities powers.
[3] Also has corporate debt and equity securities powers.

Source

Board of Governors of the Federal Reserve System, August 1993.

In addition to their own equity positions, German banks are major depositories for individual shareholders. These individuals may authorize their depository bank to vote their shares during annual shareholder meetings. Because most agree with their bank's policy position with respect to a given industrial firm, bank influence over the corporate sector is even further enhanced.

Thus, it is common for bank representatives to hold seats on corporate boards of directors. Since German banks (1) hold significant shares in their own accounts, (2) represent most of the votes of shares deposited with them, and (3) provide the bulk of debt finance to industry, corporations also seek bank financial advisory service. Firms generally have a "house bank" that exercises significant influence over managerial decision making.

The house bank has close day-to-day contact with its corporate client, not simply as a cash manager or arms-length third party, but as an industry specialist, a readily accessible research facility, and a confidant. While French and Japanese banks also have close working relationships with their corporate clients, the German model is, perhaps, the *best* example of the extent to which bank/industry relations can be developed to facilitate industrial development. In contrast, in the United States relationships have not been permitted to evolve to this extent.

In 1983, the Federal Reserve Board permitted BankAmerica Corporation to purchase Charles Schwab Corporation. Since then more than 2,000 banks and bank holding companies in the U.S. have begun to offer discount brokerage services.

During the early 1980s, stock market participation by individual investors increased significantly, largely because of strong, broadly based stock price increases. The Dow Jones Industrial Average (an index of 30 blue-chip stocks in the United States) rose from 836 at the end of 1979 to 2,225 in October 1987, or at an average rate of 13 percent per year. During the same period, the annual inflation rate (as measured by changes in the consumer price index) averaged 5 percent. The 8 percent average real rate of return (13 percent–5 percent) available in the early and mid-1980s lured many individual investors into the stock market. The subsequent stock market crash in October 1987 discouraged many individuals and caused this segment of the market to contract. But in the meantime, discount brokerage firms grew faster than more traditional, full-service brokers. This phenomenon is also due to demographic factors. As the "baby boom" generation (born shortly after World War II) ages, its members have more time to analyze their investments, that is, are less dependent on the *advice* of brokers. For these investors, convenient, low-cost transactions are an appealing alternative.

Beyond demographic considerations, individual investors are becoming more sophisticated with respect to investment opportunities. A consequence of this heightened awareness is interest rate and price sensitivity. This sensitivity helps to account for the growth in interest-sensitive bank deposits and the discount brokerage business.

Within the discount industry, bank brokerages appear to have enjoyed particularly strong growth. One of the most popular vehicles has been the fixed annuity contract. These are rather straightforward, tax-deferred investments that are typically offered through an insurance company. With the current low level of interest rates, these contracts have lost much of their appeal, however. A more recent trend is the sale of variable annuities, also available from insurance companies, that perform more like mutual funds. In fact, the variable annuity is a combination of a mutual fund and an annuity. The attractions of a variable annuity over a mutual fund are tax deferral and guarantee of principal. The bank earns a commission on the sale from the issuing insurance company. Some banks that offer proprietary mutual funds, contract with insurance companies to wrap the insurance protection around the mutual fund and create the equivalent of a variable annuity. In either case, the variable annuity market is considered a strong candidate for future growth in the banking industry.[11]

In general, commercial banks possess certain comparative advantages in the discount brokerage business. The name recognition of the bank is a strong marketing tool, in that *confidence* in the brokerage firm is easier to establish. Also, bank clients are already familiar with the institution, making it possible to incur less *advertising* expense. Lastly, existing bank customers are ideal *prospects* for brokerage services. Thus, while nonbank discounters have had to rely on television and newspaper advertising, bank brokerages have been able to successfully use less costly advertising such as direct mail and bank statement enclosures.

The securities industries, both corporate services and retail brokerage, have substantial growth potential for commercial banks. As the conventional intermediation functions of accepting deposits and making loans continue to be challenged by nonbank competition and shrinking spreads, banks will seek these and other avenues to diversify their product mix. The insurance industry also holds promise.

Insurance

When the office of the U.S. Treasury Secretary recommended in 1991 that well-capitalized banks be permitted to engage in securities activities, it was also proposed that full-service insurance activities be permitted. The National Bank Act (1863) permits national banks to engage only in underwriting and brokerage of insurance that is incidental to banking. This includes credit life, accident, and health insurance. The Bank Holding Company Act (1956) and the Garn-St. Germain Act (1982) prohibit bank holding companies (companies that own banks) from engaging in *any* insurance activity. However, existing insurance operations were grandfathered when the legislation was passed. Also, national banks and bank holding companies in towns of fewer than 5,000 persons are exempted from the prohibitions.

The banking industry has long taken the position that banks should be allowed a more active role in the insurance industry. Arguably, insurance is quite similar to banking in that:

- Banks accept deposits; insurance companies accept premiums.
- Both types of institutions invest the money in order to generate a profit.
- Eventually both depositors and policyholders are repaid.

If a bank were permitted to perform these functions in the insurance industry it would be an *insurance underwriter*, that is, the company that assumes full responsibility of paying the benefits promised in an insurance policy.

Because insurance underwriting can give rise to large liabilities associated with benefit payments, the U.S. Treasury recommended that any bank-run insurance operations be confined to a separate insurance affiliate and that "firewalls" be constructed around the bank. This is similar to the Treasury recommendation for a separate securities affiliate for those banks on sound financial footing. A separate affiliate with bank firewalls limits risk to the bank.

Even if a bank does not engage in full underwriting activities, a bank-run *insurance agency* can increase noninterest income significantly. An insurance agency is a company that sells insurance policies for an insurance underwriter. Since the insurance underwriter bears the ultimate burden of paying insurance claims, the commissions earned by an insurance agent are also riskless income. Also, banks could provide cost-effective "packages" of:

- mortgage loans and mortgage insurance (insurance that repays the mortgage in the event of death or disability of borrower)

- auto loans and auto insurance

- small business loans and "key individual" insurance (insurance that covers those people who are most important to the operations of the business)

- corporate loans and corporate life or property/casualty insurance (insurance that covers all employees and property of the corporation)

As is true in the case of securities operations, federal regulators have attempted to liberalize national bank powers. The Office of the Comptroller of the Currency (which charters national banks) has given permission to national banks to underwrite and sell title insurance (protecting the buyer of real estate property from ownership claims of previous owners) and property insurance related to loan collateral. National banks have also been granted the right to broker fixed-rate annuities (insurance policies that pay a stream of fixed payments rather than a lump sum).

Federal regulators have attempted to liberalize bank powers within the framework of existing federal law that relates to national banks, state banks that are members of the Federal Reserve, and bank holding companies. Only U.S. congressional action can change the federal law. Meanwhile, state-chartered banks that are not members of the Federal Reserve are not subject to many of these existing laws.

More than half of all bank charters belong to state-chartered non-members. The expansion of bank powers is much more pronounced within this group.

State-Chartered Banks

Exhibit 2-11 is a summary, by state, of the activities in which state-chartered banks may participate. National banks and bank holding companies are precluded from operating in these areas. The general categories are insurance, real estate, and securities. Twenty-one states allow banks to underwrite securities and five permit insurance underwriting. Brokerages in securities and insurance are allowed in 23 and 16 states, respectively. In 25 states, state-chartered banks may engage in real estate development and project ownership. Real estate brokerage is allowed in nine states.

Real estate activity is the most frequently noted expanded power among these. Real estate involvement has also been the source of many of the recent loan losses in the banking industry. This has essentially placed federal regulators in the position of insuring operations over which they have relatively little authority. The 1991 U.S. Treasury recommendations also included a provision to limit these state-granted powers. Specifically, the recommendations with respect to state banks were:

1. Prohibit *direct equity investment* in *real estate* and other commercial ventures.

2. *Limit* state bank activities to those permitted to *national banks* unless:

   a. The bank is fully capitalized and

   b. The FDIC verifies that the activities do not create a substantial risk of loss to the insurance fund.

The proposed restrictions do not apply to agency activities, that is, those for which the bank does not assume the ultimate risk of loss, for example, an insurance agency.

These recommendations are aimed at protecting the Bank Insurance Fund (BIF) under supervision of the FDIC. The rationale is that,

EXHIBIT 2-11

STATE-CHARTERED BANKS: EXPANDED POWERS

State	Insurance		Real Estate			Securities	
	U	B	EP	DEV	B	U	B/no U
Alabama		X					
Alaska							
Arizona			X	X		X	X
Arkansas			X	X			
California		X	X	X		X^8	
Colorado			X	X			
Connecticut			X	X			X
Delaware	X	X				X	X
Dist. of Col.							
Florida			X	X		X	X
Georgia			X	X	X		X
Hawaii							
Idaho	X	X				X	X
Illinois							
Indiana		X^2				X^9	X^{16}
Iowa		X^3			X	X	X
Kansas						X^{10}	X
Kentucky			X	X			
Louisiana							
Maine			X	X	X^7	X	X
Maryland							
Massachusetts			X	X	X	X	
Michigan				X		X	X
Minnesota							X
Mississippi							
Missouri			X	X		X^{11}	
Montana						X^{12}	
Nebraska		X				X^{13}	X
Nevada			X	X			
New Hampshire			X	X			
New Jersey		X	X	X	X	X	X
New Mexico							
New York							X
North Carolina	X	X	X	X	X	X^{14}	X
North Dakota							
Ohio			X	X			
Oklahoma							

Exhibit continues

EXHIBIT 2-11

STATE-CHARTERED BANKS: EXPANDED POWERS (Continued)

State	Insurance U	Insurance B	Real Estate EP	Real Estate DEV	Real Estate B	Securities U	Securities B/no U
Oregon		X		X	X		
Pennsylvania		X				X^{15}	X^{7}
Rhode Island		X		X			
South Carolina		X					
South Dakota	X	X	X	X			
Tennessee			X^{5}			X	X
Texas							X
Utah	X^{1}	X	X	X	X	X	X
Vermont							X
Virginia			X	X			
Washington		X^{4}	X	X		X	
West Virginia			X	X		X	X
Wisconsin		X	X^{6}	X^{6}	X		
Wyoming		X					

U	Underwriting
B	Brokerage
Dev	Development
B/no U	Brokerage, no underwriting

1	Grandfathered institutions
2	Cannot broker life insurance, all other types permitted
3	Property and casualty only
4	Banks in small towns may engage in insurance activity without geographic limitation.
5	Banks may not be active partners in real estate development.
6	As of May 1986, Commissioner of Banking may establish rules under which state banks may engage in activities authorized for other financial institutions in the state.
7	May own or operate brokerage firm to dispose of bank-owned property.
8	May underwrite mutual funds.
9	May underwrite municipal revenue bonds, money market mutual funds, and mortgage-backed securities.
10	May underwrite municipal bonds
11	May underwrite mutual funds and may underwrite securities up to state legal loan limit.
12	May underwrite bonds only.
13	May underwrite U.S. government securities.
14	May underwrite U.S. government, federal farm loan act, and general obligation municipal bonds.
15	May underwrite municipal and mortgage-related securities.
16	May conduct discount brokerage.

Source

U.S. Department of the Treasury, *Modernizing the Financial System: Recommendations for Safer, More Competitive Banks*, 1991.

if state banks are not allowed to participate in activities prohibited to national banks, there will be less risk of state bank failure, failure that necessarily results in losses that must be covered by the BIF and the U.S. taxpayer if BIF resources prove inadequate. Of course, the irony is that state banks have also been the most innovative and the closest approximation of banks in other countries with which the United States competes internationally.

Canada, Germany, Japan, and the United Kingdom

Exhibit 2-12 is a comparison of the bank powers in the United States and four of its major trading partners: Canada, Germany, Japan, and the United Kingdom. The powers indicated for the United States are for national banks as permitted by federal law.

Among these, the Japanese system is most similar to the U.S. One major difference is that Japanese banks are permitted to invest in equities, or stocks. It is through these equity investments that Japanese banks maintain their close relationships with industry, many as part of *keiretsu* arrangements, that is, cross-holdings of stock among companies in the same group.

The banks in Canada, Germany, and the United Kingdom all have a much broader range of powers than those in the United States. It is also true that these systems are much more concentrated with a few banks controlling from 50 percent (Germany) to 90 percent (Canada) of bank assets. This high degree of concentration makes it relatively easy for regulators to oversee the operations of banks. In contrast, in the United States, there are close to 12,000 banks, and bank supervision is complicated by this large number.

Yet this does not change the reality that, according to federal law, U.S. national banks cannot offer the same range of services as banks in other developed countries. Removing the expanded powers of state-chartered banks would only make these inequities worse.

CONCLUSION

Commercial banks are an integral part of the economy in all industrialized countries. In the United States, commercial banks serve a rela-

EXHIBIT 2-12

BANK POWERS: A CROSS-COUNTRY COMPARISON

	Canada	Germany	Japan	United Kingdom	United States
Insurance:					
Brokerage	N	Y	N	Y	N*
Underwriting	N	Y*	N	Y*	N
Equities:					
Brokerage	Y*	Y	N	Y	Y
Underwriting	Y*	Y	N	Y*	N
Investment	Y	Y	Y	Y*	N
Other underwriting:					
Government debt	Y	Y	N	Y*	Y
Private debt	Y*	Y	N	Y*	N
Mutual funds:					
Brokerage	Y	Y	N	Y	N
Management	Y*	Y	N	Y	N
Real estate:					
Brokerage	N	Y	N	Y	N*
Investment	Y	Y	N	Y	N
Other brokerage:					
Government debt	Y	Y	Y	Y	Y
Private debt	Y	Y	Y	Y	Y

Y Yes
Y* Yes, but not directly by the bank.
N No
N* No, with exceptions.

Source

U.S. Department of the Treasury, *Modernizing the Financial System: Recommendations for Safer, More Competitive Banks*, 1991.

tively small geographic area because nationwide branching is not permitted. In other major trading partners of the United States, there is no such prohibition. One of the consequences of this is that U.S. banks are on average much smaller than banks in other industrialized countries. Furthermore, the large trade surpluses of Japan have led to that country's banks dominating the ranks of the world's largest. The competitive position of U.S. banks could be improved, however, if the number of banks was reduced through consolidation and nationwide branching were permitted.

Universal functions of commercial banks are accepting deposits and making loans. In most cases, these deposits represent a significant part of a country's money supply. However, technological advances have led to changes in both the delivering and form of payments services. Credit cards and the use of ATMs now frequently substitute for check-writing. Point-of-sale facilities are also operational. Commercial banks can maintain part of their competitive advantage in the payments system by introducing wider uses for debit and stored-value cards.

Greater access to money and capital markets by large corporate bank clients has meant thinner margins in corporate lending activities. As a result, banks have turned increasingly to fee-generating services and to the middle segment of the corporate market. Cash management, data processing, commercial paper underwriting, and provision of discount brokerage facilities are some of the services being emphasized.

Regulatory barriers to other services are being challenged. Section 20 subsidiaries have been authorized by the Federal Reserve to permit bank affiliates to engage in securities transactions to a limited extent. State banking authorities allow state-chartered banks a much wider range of functions including securities, insurance, and real estate participation. Even so, the United States has a more restrictive regulatory structure than other countries in the developed West.

The U.S. banking industry is involved in radical change. Many of these changes are necessary to first maintain and then improve bank profitability. A conflict between bankers and legislators (and at times, regulators) arises because the need of bankers to compete effectively must be balanced with the need to maintain a safe, stable banking system in the United States.

SELECTED REFERENCES

The Banker 1000. Special issue of *The Banker*, July 1993.

Bank Profitability: Statistical Supplement, Financial Statements of Banks 1981–1989. Organisation for Economic Co-operation and Development, Paris, 1991.

Bayliss, B. T., and A. A. S. Butt Philip. *Capital Markets and Industrial Investment in Germany and France: Lessons for the U.K.* Saxon House, Westmead, England, 1980.

Bean, Randall. "Banks' Big Opportunities in Small Business." *Bankers Monthly*, January 1993, pp. 35–36.

Beckwith, Burnham P. "Eight Forecasts for U.S. Banking." *The Futurist*, vol. 23, no. 2 (March-April 1989), pp. 27–33.

Boreham, Gordon F. "Canadian and U.S. Banking Systems: Some Comparisons." *Canadian Banker*, vol. 94, no. 3 (1987), pp. 6–14.

Borowsky, Mark. "Banks Are Betting on Electronic Presentment." *Bank Management*, April 1993, pp. 26–28.

Bronte, Stephen. *Japanese France: Markets and Institutions.* Germany Publications, London, 1982.

Chai, Alan, Alta Campbell, and Patrick J. Spain, Editors. *Hoover's Handbook of World Business 1993.* The Reference Press, Austin, Texas, 1993.

Coler, Mark, and Ellis Ratner. *Financial Services: Insiders' Views of the Future.* New York Institute of Finance, New York, 1988.

Compton, Eric N. *The New World of Commercial Banking.* Lexington Books, Lexington, Massachusetts, 1987.

Davies, Michael S. "Exploiting Opportunities in Small-Business Lending," *Journal of Retail Banking*, vol. 15, no. 1 (Spring 1993), pp. 33–37.

Federal Deposit Insurance Corporation. "Quarterly Banking Profile." First Quarter 1993.

Federal Deposit Insurance Corporation. *FDIC Statistics on Banking 1992.* Washington, D.C., 1993.

Gart, Alan. *Banks, Thrifts, and Insurance Companies: Surviving the 1980s.* Lexington Books, Lexington, Massachusetts, 1985.

Giesen, Lauri. "Debit Cards Get Some Respect—Finally." *Bank Management,* January 1993, pp. 47–51.

Gillis, M. Arthur. "Unscrambling the Jargon: A Glossary of Terms in the Technology Arena." *Independent Banker,* vol. 43, no. 4 (April 1993), pp. 26–27.

Grady, John, and Martin Weale. *British Banking 1960–85.* St. Martin's Press, New York, 1986.

Hay, Tony. *A Guide to European Financial Centres.* St. James Press, Chicago, 1990.

Horne, James. *Japan's Financial Markets.* George Allen and Unwin, North Sydney, Australia, 1985.

International Financial Statistics. International Monetary Fund, Washington, D.C., Yearbook 1990.

King, Mary L. *The Great American Snafu.* Lexington Books, Lexington, Massachusetts, 1985.

Kurtzman, Joel. *The Death of Money: How the Electronic Economy Has Destabilized the World's Markets and Created Financial Chaos.* Simon & Schuster, New York, 1993.

Lawrence, Colin, and Robert P. Shay. *Technological Innovation, Regulations, and the Monetary Economy.* Ballinger Publishing Company, Cambridge, Massachusetts, 1986.

Lees, Francis A., and Maximo Eng. *International Financial Markets: Development of the Present System and Future Prospects.* Praeger Publishers, New York, 1975.

Liner, Doug. "Some Trends in Export Financing." *Export Today,* May 1993, pp. 39–41.

Marshall, Jeffrey. "Variable Annuities: Hope or Hype?" *United States Banker,* June 1993, pp. 25–26.

McRae, Hamish, and Frances Cairncross. *Capital City: London as a Financial Centre.* Methuen, London, 1984.

Milligan, John W. "Who's Afraid of Proprietary Trading?" *United States Banker*, July 1993, pp. 12–14.

Mitchell, Richard, and Robert Kazel. "Finding New Uses for Debit Cards." *Bank Management*, January 1993, pp. 52–55.

Mullineux, Andrew. *International Banking and Financial Systems: A Comparison*. Graham and Trotman, London, 1987.

Mullineux, A. W. *U.K. Banking after Deregulation*. Croom Helm, London, 1987.

Neufeld, E. P. *The Financial System of Canada*. Macmillan Company of Canada, Toronto, Canada, 1972.

Pecchioli, R. M. *Prudential Supervision in Banking*. Organisation for Economic Co-operation and Development, Paris, 1987.

Pressnell, L.S. *Money and Banking in Japan*. St. Martin's Press, New York, 1973.

Radigan, Joseph. "Can Branch Automation Deliver the Goods?" *United States Banker*, May 1993, pp. 65–67.

Rehberg, Virginia J. "Letters of Credit: Cracking the Code." *Export Today*, September 1991, pp. 21–23.

Revell, J. R. S. *Banking and Electronic Fund Transfers*. Organization for Economic Co-operation and Development, Paris, 1983.

Revell, Jack. *The British Financial System*. Macmillan Press, Ltd., London, 1973.

Rosenbluth, Frances McCall. *Financial Politics in Contemporary Japan*. Cornell University Press, Ithaca, New York, 1989.

Skully, Michael T. *Financial Institutions and Markets in the Far East: A Study of China, Hong Kong, Japan, South Korea, and Taiwan*. St. Martin's Press, New York, 1982.

Spong, Kenneth. *Banking Regulation: Its Purposes, Implementation, and Effects*, 3rd edition. Federal Reserve Bank of Kansas City, 1990.

Subcommittee on Financial Institutions Supervision, Regulation, and Insurance. *Report of the Task Force on the International Competitiveness of U.S. Financial Institutions*. U.S. House of Representatives, Committee on Banking, Finance, and Urban Affairs, Washington, D.C., 1991.

Suzuki, Yoshio. *The Japanese Financial System*. Oxford University Press, New York, 1987.

Suzuki, Yoshio. *Money and Banking in Contemporary Japan*. Yale University Press, London, 1980.

U.S. Department of the Treasury. *Modernizing the Financial System: Recommendations for Safer, More Competitive Banks*. Washington, D.C., 1991.

Viner, Aron. *Inside Japanese Financial Markets*. Dow Jones-Irwin, Homewood, Illinois, 1988.

"Visa's Corporate Card Push," *United States Banker*, August 1993, pp. 46–47.

"Wall Street Cache." *United States Banker*, August 1993, p. 47.

Weiner, Jerry. "Your Technology: It May Be Better Than You Think." *Independent Banker*, vol. 43, no. 4 (April 1993), pp. 24–25.

Wilson, J. S. G. *Banking Policy and Structure: A Comparative Analysis*. Croom Helm, London, 1986.

ENDNOTES

1. As of year-end 1992, the total was $3.5 trillion.

2. An overdraft is a check written for which there are insufficient bank funds that the bank honors, effectively granting the check writer a short-term loan.

3. Germany suffered hyperinflation after World War I and, again, during World War II as a result of the abandonment of sound central banking principles by the Reichbank (central bank prior to creation of the Bundesbank). Extensive credit created for use by the German government severely devalued the country's currency and destabilized the entire economy.

4. In 1986, Société Générale was returned to private ownership among companies that were friendly to the French government.

5. Fluctuations in the value of the French franc played no role in the increase, as there was a 12 percent increase in bank assets in French franc terms as well.

6. See Chapter 1 for a description of the increasing trend of foreign bank loans as a percentage of total bank loans in the United States.

7. Effective 1993, the international banks of OECD countries must comply with uniform capital requirements. The total of Tier I capital (primarily common equity and disclosed reserves) and Tier II capital (primarily subordinated debt and revaluation reserves) must equal at least 8 percent of risk-weighted assets, with Tier I capital representing at least 4 percent of risk-weighted assets.

8. This and other forms of electronic payment are discussed in the section "Electronic Payments" that follows.

9. Subsequently, Mitsui and Taiyo Kobe merged to form Sakura Bank.

10. See Chapter 5 for a discussion of management strategies of U.S. banks.

11. In order to offer variable annuity contracts, the seller must have a Series 6 (permitting sales of mutual funds) or Series 7 (permitting sales of stocks and bonds) securities license as well as a current life insurance license for the applicable state. In some states, a specific variable annuity license may be required. In contrast, sellers of fixed annuity contracts need only a life insurance license.

3 The Forces of Change

INTRODUCTION

The financial markets of the world are evolving into high-technology networks over which billions of dollars, marks, yen, and francs are traded each day. The forces that are driving this evolution include the development of offshore financial markets that are subject to little, if any, regulation; the move toward deregulation within national boundaries; and the creation of a harmonized financial system within Europe.

Euromarkets, where home-currency instruments are traded outside national borders, provide alternative financing vehicles and investment opportunities. Eurocurrencies, particularly Eurodollars, have proved effective in correcting international liquidity imbalances for banks, industrial firms, and sovereign governments. Eurocurrency markets that started in London are now found in other European cities, and in Singapore, Hong Kong, Tokyo, the Cayman Islands, and the Bahamas, while London is still the site of most Eurobond issues and active secondary trading. Eurocommercial paper, Euronotes, and Euroequities have all grown rapidly.

Within national boundaries, limits on the scope of activities of depository institutions in the presence of volatile interest rates threatened the continued existence of many financial institutions in the

United States. Movements toward deregulation have put in motion a force that will forever change the nature of commercial banking in the United States and other countries. The 12-nation European Community continues to move toward a full integration of the markets for goods and services, including financial services. The Single European Market represents a landmark event in the growth of cross-border financial investments.

EUROMARKETS

Euromarkets are financial markets that involve instruments either denominated in a currency that is not the local domestic currency, or denominated in the domestic currency but sold in nondomestic markets, or distributed by a international syndicate of investment bankers or merchant banks. This is a comprehensive definition that describes a multitude of financial instruments and arrangements. These activities can be found in four general market classifications:

- currency markets
- bond markets
- commercial paper markets
- equity markets

Currency Markets

Eurodollars form the core of international money market transactions. Eurodollars are deposits denominated in U.S. dollars issued by banks outside the U.S. Even if the bank's home office is in the U.S., the deposit is considered a Eurodollar deposit. These markets developed as the result of a number of factors.

In the late 1950s and 1960s, banks in Western Europe, the Middle East, the Far East, and elsewhere began actively to trade U.S. dollars for reasons having to do with international trade and U.S. legislation.

In 1957, Great Britain severely restricted non-British borrowing and lending in British pounds. At about the same time, countries in

Western Europe liberalized bank trading in U.S. dollars to facilitate formation of the European Common Market.

During the 1960s, U.S. exports of goods and services exceeded imports by $40 billion, which created a net international demand for dollars to pay for the American goods. The supply of dollars came primarily from capital outflows of $52 billion from the United States for large investments in foreign capital assets as U.S. firms established international operations.

These large holdings abroad of U.S. dollars (still convertible into gold) and the accompanying conversions strained the nation's gold reserves and shook international faith in the soundness of the dollar. The U.S. government reacted with several pieces of legislation to restrict capital outflows. The *Interest Equalization Tax (IET)* of 1964 discouraged the issuance of foreign securities in the United States by effectively increasing by 1 percent the cost of financing for foreigners. When evidence showed that the IET merely encouraged more bank financing, bank loans were subsequently included in IET provisions.

The *Voluntary Foreign Credit Restraint Program (VFCRP)* of 1965 recommended limitation of the amount of foreign lending and investment by commercial banks, insurance companies, and pension funds. The program also asked industrial firms to improve their individual capital flows either by exporting more goods and services, by postponing marginal foreign direct investment, or by raising more funds abroad.

The 1968 *Foreign Direct Investment Program (FDIP)* placed mandatory restrictions on direct investment to advanced European economies, Australia, and South Africa. More liberal ceilings applied to developing countries.

The net effect of these regulations was to put pressure on the multinational customers of U.S. commercial banks to fund their foreign operations outside U.S. markets. Moreover, loan rates that banks could offer foreign borrowers were not as competitive as they would have been otherwise. U.S. industrial firms found it difficult to turn to their domestic banks for financing, and foreign borrowers found significant disincentives to borrow from U.S. banks. These factors combined to significantly reduce demand for bank loans in the United States.

At the same time, U.S. commercial banks were subject to Regulation Q (Reg Q) of the Federal Reserve, which placed ceilings on deposit interest rates. When, in 1966, Reg Q ceilings for negotiable certificates of deposit (NCDs) were below market rates, banks responded by offering more competitive NCD rates in their foreign offices, offices in which they were not subject to Reg Q. The overseas NCDs, known as *Eurodollar CDs*, became a significant source of funds for U.S. commercial banks, especially because they were not subject to costly reserve requirements and deposit insurance premiums.

Investment of the proceeds from Eurodollar CD sales was, likewise, not subject to the IET, VFCRP, or the FDIP. Thus, Eurodollars provided banks with liquidity to finance the foreign operations of U.S. multinational firms. Even after the Reg Q ceiling on domestic NCDs was removed in 1970 and the capital outflow legislation was abolished in 1974, the Eurodollar market continued to flourish, primarily because of the absence of reserve requirements and deposit insurance premiums.

London became the most important Eurodollar financial center because of its long tradition as an international financial center with well-developed money, interbank, and discount markets. Equally important is the absence of strict regulations with respect to foreign currency transactions by non-British financial institutions. As a result, banks from other countries have been able to establish a virtually unregulated presence in London.

Paris is the second largest Eurodollar market, although its transactions volume is much less than that of London. Frankfurt, Amsterdam, Zurich, Basel, Geneva, Milan, and Vienna also maintain Eurodollar operations. The Cayman Islands and the Bahamas have become major Eurodollar markets primarily because of tax advantages.

Since 1968, when the withholding tax on interest payments made to nonresidents was removed, Singapore has been an important center for U.S. dollar deposits. Both Hong Kong and Tokyo are now also designated *Asiandollar* financial centers. Singapore has generally dominated Hong Kong and Tokyo, because its tax environment has been the most favorable and foreign exchange controls have been almost nonexistent. Dollar deposits even in Asia are frequently referred to as Eurodollar deposits. In fact, the "Euro" designation applies to any transaction made outside the home country of the currency involved.

While the U.S. dollar has dominated Euromarkets, deposits in other currencies are also traded. Notice in Exhibit 3-1, that the U.S. dollar represented almost 83 percent of 1983 Eurocurrency deposits, which totaled $1.615 trillion. Together, the other currencies shown accounted for 15 percent. The European Currency Unit (ECU), a basket of currencies created in 1979 as part of the European Monetary System, which serves as a settlement currency among central banks of the European Community, in 1983 represented less than one-half of 1 percent of Eurocurrency deposits.

EXHIBIT 3-1

EUROCURRENCY DEPOSITS

	1983		1987	
	Amount[1]	%	Amount[1]	%
U.S. dollar	$1,337.2	82.8	$2,210.6	68.9
Deutsche mark	113.5	7.0	338.8	10.6
Swiss franc	63.9	4.0	181.5	5.7
Japanese yen	21.7	1.3	137.2	4.3
British pound	14.6	0.9	67.0	2.1
French franc	11.3	0.7	35.0	1.1
Dutch guilder	11.4	0.7	22.6	0.7
ECU	7.0	0.4	69.4	2.2
Other	34.3	2.1	144.8	4.5
Total	$1,614.9		$3,206.9	

[1] In billions of U.S. dollars.

Sources

Amounts: *Comparative Economic and Financial Statistics: Japan and Other Major Countries 1988*, Bank of Japan.

Percentages: Author's calculations.

By 1987 Eurocurrency deposits had grown at an average annual rate of 19 percent to $3.207 trillion, while the U.S. dollar share had dropped to 69 percent. This decline in relative importance is attributable at least partially to the decline in the U.S. dollar value that began in 1985, but currency appreciation alone does not explain the increased market shares of other currencies. The most graphic example of this is Japan. From fourth quarter 1982 to the same period in 1986, the yen appreciated 62 percent. Yet the share of yen-denominated Eurocurrency deposits more than doubled from 1983 to 1987. As domestic financial markets of other countries are deregulated, the dollar will likely continue to have less prominence in international markets.

Currency traders are often located in one large room at a bank, where each trader has access to several telephones, video screens, and news tapes. A trader generally specializes in one or a small number of currencies, communicating with other traders at banks around the world. Interbank transactions are in wholesale denominations of $1 million or more. An unusually large currency exchange may be facilitated by a broker working on a commission basis with several banks. Long-standing relationships and preestablished lines of credit allow both sides of a trade to make firm commitments over the telephone.

The currency markets operate 24 hours a day in different time zones around the world. When the New York market closes at 5 p.m., the San Francisco market is still open. At 8 p.m., New York time, the San Francisco market closes, and the Tokyo market opens. An hour later (9 p.m., New York time), the Hong Kong and Singapore markets open. At 3 a.m., Tokyo closes but Frankfurt opens. An hour later (4 a.m., New York time), Hong Kong and Singapore close, and London opens. This continuous operation and almost instantaneous, firm commitments via telephone make the foreign currency markets the most efficient in the world.

The volume of trading in currency markets ranges from $640 to $800 billion per day. Historically, most of this trading was controlled by banks. More recently, however, fund managers have become important participants in currency market trading. Many currency funds have institutional investors and may trade as much as $1 billion in a given currency in one day. Banks that operate in Eurocurrency markets should be aware of the potential losses that can arise from a practice by fund managers that is known as being "lined up." For example, a fund manager may instruct its traders to sell $300 million in a currency. The order is divided into six separate orders for $50 million each. The first dealer receives a sell order for $50 million, and, in rapid succession, five other dealers are contacted. By the time the first dealer tries to sell his $50 million in the currency, the market may have moved significantly, creating an automatic loss on the trade.

Banks that act as currency dealers can protect themselves from this practice by asking the trader to reveal the size of their transactions before quoting an exchange rate. If the trader declines to reveal the size, the bank has the alternative of adjusting the rate to compensate for a potentially automatic loss as the result of being lined up.

Bond Markets

As robust as the Eurocurrency market is, growth has been even stronger in the longer-term market for Eurobonds. International bonds are either Eurobonds or foreign bonds. The major currency in the international bond market is the U.S. dollar, with growing participation in other currencies. Eurobonds developed after the Eurocurrency markets. Eurobonds are bonds that are issued by parties outside their domestic capital markets, underwritten by an international investment banking syndicate, placed in at least two countries, and, perhaps, issued in more than one currency. The firms that underwrite Eurobonds generally maintain offices in New York, London, Tokyo, and other Euromarket centers. An international underwriting syndicate and multinational placement distinguish Eurobonds from other international issues. Eurobond issuer and investor need not *necessarily* be in different countries. For example, a U.S. firm may issue a Eurobond and sell part of it to a U.S. insurance company.

In the case of foreign bonds, though, the country of origin of foreign bond issuers is *not* the same as that of the investor. Foreign bonds are issued by entities outside their own domestic capital markets in a foreign market, underwritten by a firm that is domestic to that foreign market, usually denominated in the currency of the market in which they are issued, but occasionally denominated in another currency. Foreign bonds are sometimes referred to as *traditional* international bonds because they existed long before Eurobonds. *Yankee bonds* are foreign bonds issued in the United States. Foreign bonds issued in the United Kingdom are called *Bulldog bonds*, while those issued in Japan are known as *Samurai bonds*.

Immediately after World War II, the United States was the primary market for foreign bonds, but the interest rate disincentive of the Interest Equalization Tax caused much of the dollar-denominated borrowing to move to the Eurobond market. More recent trends in international bond issuance continue to favor Euromarkets.

Exhibits 3-2 and 3-3 show that, as recently as 1980, issuances in the Eurobond and foreign bond markets were roughly equivalent, at $20 billion and $18 billion, respectively. By 1986, however, Eurobond issuances had far outpaced new foreign bonds. Foreign bond issuances grew during the period at an annual rate of 14 percent to $39 billion, while Eurobond issuances expanded at an annual rate of 45 percent to $187 billion.

Switzerland, which has historically prohibited Eurobond issues, dominated the foreign bond market in 1980 with 42 percent of all issuances. Its dominance grew to 61 percent in 1986. The United States and Japan were a distant second and third.

Eurobonds denominated in dollars continue to represent the majority of issuances, even though the share has slipped somewhat. A gradual decline in the relative importance of the dollar is linked to several factors. Depreciation of the dollar and uncertainty about its future stability have contributed to the use of other currencies. Liberalization of regulations in the United Kingdom, Japan, Germany, and France have made international bond issuance easier. Lastly, the popularity of currency swaps has made it possible to issue Eurobonds in one currency and swap the proceeds for another currency.

Exhibit 3-4 graphs the relative growth of Eurobonds and foreign bonds during the 1980s. From 1980 to 1989 new issues of foreign bonds more than doubled from $18 billion to $42 billion. In 1989 the value of Eurobond issues at $212 billion was ten times the 1980 value.

EXHIBIT 3-2

CURRENCIES USED IN EUROBOND ISSUES

	1980		1986	
	Amount[1]	%	Amount[1]	%
U.S. dollar	$13.6	66.7	$117.2	62.6
Deutsche mark	3.5	17.2	16.9	9.0
Japanese yen	0.3	1.5	18.7	10.0
British pound	1.0	4.9	10.5	5.6
ECU	—	—	7.0	3.7
Other	2.0	9.8	16.8	9.0
Total	$20.4		$187.1	

[1]   In billions of U.S. dollars.

Source

U.S. Securities and Exchange Commission, *Internationalization of the Securities Markets.*

EXHIBIT 3-3

FOREIGN BOND ISSUES: COUNTRY OF ISSUE

	1980		1986	
	Amount[1]	%	Amount[1]	%
United States	$ 2.7	15.0	$ 6.1	15.8
Germany	5.0	27.8	—	—
Japan	1.5	8.3	4.8	12.4
United Kingdom	0.2	1.1	0.5	1.3
Switzerland	7.5	41.7	23.4	60.6
Netherlands	0.3	1.7	1.8	4.7
Other	0.8	4.4	2.0	5.2
Total	$18.0		$38.6	

[1]   In billions of U.S. dollars.

Source

U.S. Securities and Exchange Commission, *Internationalization of the Securities Markets.*

EXHIBIT 3-4

INTERNATIONAL BOND ISSUES

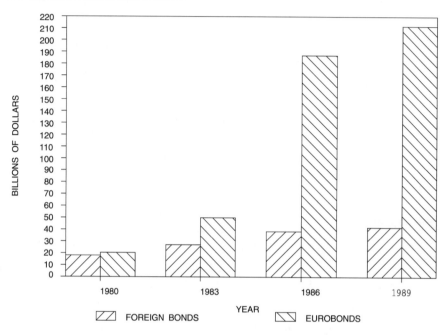

Sources

Author's graphics based on data from:
1. U.S. Securities and Exchange Commission, *Internationalization of the Securities Markets.*
2. International Monetary Fund, *International Capital Markets: Developments and Prospects,* April 1989 and April 1990.

The currency composition of new international bonds (including both Eurobonds and foreign bonds) continues to become more diverse. Exhibit 3-5 shows that 50 percent of the value of new international bonds was denominated in U.S. dollars. The Japanese yen, Swiss franc, Deutsche mark, ECU, British pound, and Canadian dollar made up 40 percent of the total in roughly equivalent proportions.

Perhaps surprisingly, these countries were not so evenly represented among the ranks of bond issuers in 1989. Exhibit 3-6 shows that just under 39 percent of the new bonds were issued by Japanese

EXHIBIT 3-5

INTERNATIONAL BOND ISSUES BY CURRENCY—1989

NEW ISSUES = $251.2 BILLION

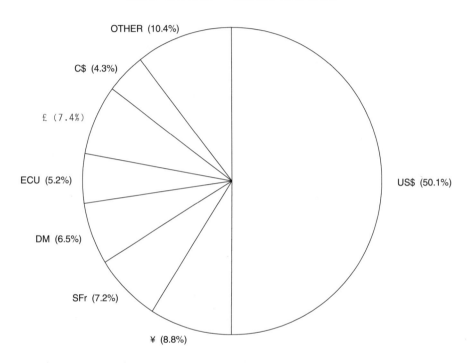

Legend:

US$ United States dollar
¥   Japanese yen
SFr   Swiss franc
DM   Deutsche mark
ECU   European Currency Unit
£   British pound
C$ Canadian dollar

Source

Author's calculations and graphic based on data from:
International Monetary Fund, *International Capital Markets: Developments and Prospects*,
April 1990.

EXHIBIT 3-6

INTERNATIONAL BOND ISSUES BY COUNTRY OF BORROWER—1989

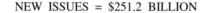

NEW ISSUES = $251.2 BILLION

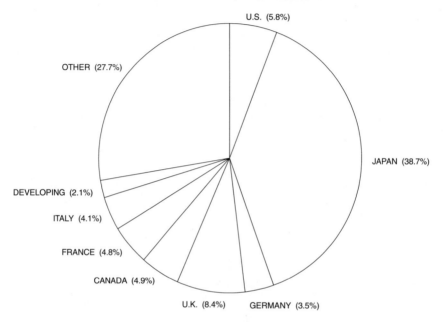

Source

Author's calculations and graphic based on data from:
International Monetary Fund, *International Capital Markets: Developments and Prospects*,
April 1990.

concerns. The next largest share belonged to British issuers (8.4 percent). All other individual countries, including the United States, issued less than 6 percent of the total.

Japanese issuers are increasingly prominent in the international
bond market. This may be partially explained by Japan's large international trade surpluses, much of which is tied to trade with the
United States. The magnitude of this dollar-denominated trade gives
Japan easy access to long-term and short-term international financial
markets.

A new form of the Eurobond has emerged recently as the *global bond*. To qualify as a global bond, an issue must be offered in the three main geographical centers—London, New York, and Tokyo—with no restrictions. The first global bond issue was in 1989 for the World Bank. Recently, the instrument gained more acceptance as a way of raising funds for highly rated sovereign borrowers. The first such application was a $2 billion five-year issue for the Republic of Ireland in November 1992. The market apparently viewed the issue favorably, pricing it only 52 basis points over Treasuries. The second sovereign global bond issue was that of the Kingdom of Sweden, a $2 billion 10-year flotation in February 1993. The Province of Ontario has also participated with a $2 billion issue in May 1992 led by J.P. Morgan and Salomon Brothers International.

The global bond market accelerated in 1992 (rather than 1989—after the first World Bank entry) primarily because sovereign borrowers needed to raise large amounts of capital. This interest is expected to continue because Sweden, Italy, and Finland have large budget deficits to finance. In fact, Italy emerges as the most likely candidate since its government hopes to raise $10 to $15 billion in foreign currency. Because of that country's political and economic problems, including a recent downgrading of its credit rating to A1 by Moody's, bankers have suggested that a large, dollar-denominated global issue may be the best alternative.

Global bonds appear to have an enhanced liquidity because there are more investors which, in turn, create greater demand. For example, in April 1993, two global issues of the World Bank and Ireland were the most actively traded. Part of this larger market, of course, is in the United States. U.S. regulations with respect to Eurobonds have an impact on the way global bond syndicates are typically structured. U.S. investors are allowed to purchase Eurobonds only after a 40-day waiting period, unless the borrower qualifies for an exemption. The waiting period is waived if:

- The borrower does not have a substantial market interest in the United States, that is, its debt is not held by more than 300 U.S. persons, *and*

- More than $1 billion and 20 percent of the outstanding debt of the borrower is not held in the United States.

U.S. investors that reside outside the United States are not subject to the rule. Thus, as many as 25 U.S. investment funds have overseas offices through which they buy Eurobonds. Nevertheless, the participation by U.S. investors is greatly enhanced when the bond is also issued in the United States, as is the case with a global bond.

To facilitate issuance in the United States, a U.S. institution is almost always retained to assist in the Securities and Exchange Commission (SEC) registration. Not infrequently, the issue is denominated in U.S. dollars and this has become a point of contention. On one hand, U.S. institutions take the position that the global bond is a way to create a kind of international currency. On the other hand, European banks consider the global bond to be a ploy on the part of U.S. institutions to break into European markets. The continued debate should prove interesting particularly since the World Bank and Crédit Local de France plan to issue global issues denominated in deutsche marks and French francs, respectively.

The stakes are high. In the year ended June 1993, new issuances totaled $51 billion in Euro-deutsche mark bonds and $34 billion in Euro-French franc bonds. At this point, domestic houses continue to dominate, with Deutsche Bank and Dresdner Bank alone accounting for 76 percent of these Euro-deutsche mark flotations and the top five French banks 94 percent of the Euro-French franc issues.

Nevertheless, the U.S. institutions have made an impressive showing in the global bond arena. In the 18 months ended May 1993, the top ten lead managers in global bond issues include 6 U.S. firms:

Firm	Value of issues (billions)
Goldman Sachs	$6.2
Merrill Lynch	5.9
Salomon Brothers	3.5
Nomura	3.0
J.P. Morgan	2.6
Industrial Bank of Japan	2.5
Scotia McLeod	1.9

Firm	Value of issues (billions)
Morgan Stanley	1.6
Lehman Brothers	1.0
Deutsche Bank	0.8

It is commonly believed that a global bond issue is appropriate for at least a $1 billion issue with perhaps an upper bound of $5 billion. However, it is possible that the vehicle could be used for smaller issues as well. For example, the World Bank has been successful with a New Zealand dollar bond in the amount of NZ$ 250 million (U.S.$ 135 million). The bond trades in the U.S. market, the Euromarket, and the home market. As such it is highly liquid.

The global bond promises to be an interesting component of the Euromarkets for large and small borrowers. It also represents another opportunity for U.S. institutions both to capitalize on their large domestic market and to position themselves in international finance.

Commercial Paper Market

A relatively new short-term instrument in the international arena is *Eurocommercial paper*, another offshoot of the Eurocurrency markets. Eurocommercial paper is short-term unsecured notes issued by firms in markets outside their domestic markets. This instrument is one of the more recent to develop in Euromarkets. Throughout the 1970s and early 1980s, both U.S. and foreign borrowers relied heavily on the U.S. commercial paper market. Even though the first issue of Eurocommercial paper was in 1970 by an American firm, this form of financing did not gain widespread acceptance until 1985.

Arrangements that permit an issuer to request immediate sale of the paper or that allow a securities dealer to solicit an issue when the timing is most advantageous have made the market more appealing as an alternative to short-term bank loans. Advances in communications technology have made precise timing of the issues possible. In addition, commercial paper interest rates compare favorably with other sources of financing.

The structure of Eurocommercial paper is not exactly the same as U.S. commercial paper. While U.S. commercial paper ranges in maturity from 25 to 270 days, Eurocommercial paper usually has an original maturity of six months. U.S. commercial paper is a simple instrument that is backed by a bank line of credit. Eurocommercial paper is a more complex financial contract with no comparable guarantee. Lastly, U.S. commercial paper is typically a physical document. But Eurocommercial paper is increasingly issued in book-entry form, that is, with electronic record-keeping only.

Euronotes are similar to Eurocommercial paper except that they include an additional agreement, a *Euronote facility*, by an underwriter to place the issuer's notes, when issued, for a specified period of time. This makes a Euronote facility a medium-term credit arrangement.

Floating rate notes (FRNs) are long-term obligations with a variable interest rate. The interest rate is usually tied to LIBOR, the London Interbank Offering Rate, but most FRNs guarantee a minimum rate of return.

During the 1980s, this market expanded rapidly. After its acceptance in 1985, Eurocommercial paper grew to an almost $60 billion industry one year later, more than double the size of Euronote issues. Exhibit 3-7 shows the composition of the market from 1983 through 1989. Note that the Eurocommercial paper market contracted during the second half of the 1980s. A factor contributing to this decline is the default of several Eurocommercial paper issuers. Another is adoption of international capital standards for commercial banks that penalize the off-balance-sheet commitments they make to back up Euronotes or to swap currencies upon issue. Also, the liberalization of certain domestic markets has made commercial paper more accessible. For example, the yen market developed in 1987 and quickly became the world's second largest domestic commercial paper market. The Deutsche mark market was established in 1991 and also experienced rapid growth.

Equities

Another segment of international financial markets that experienced rapid growth followed by contraction during the 1980s is the *Euroequities* market, where common and preferred stocks are offered out-

EXHIBIT 3-7

EUROCOMMERCIAL PAPER AND EURONOTE ISSUES

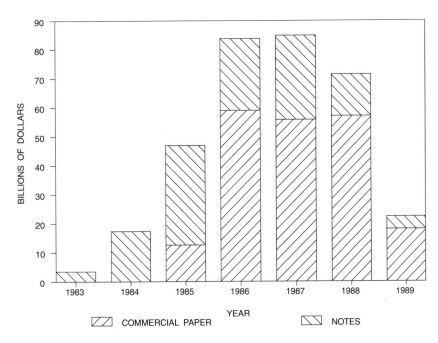

Source

Author's graphic based on data from:
International Monetary Fund, *International Capital Markets: Developments and Prospects*,
April 1989 and April 1990.

side the issuer's domestic capital market in one or more foreign markets and underwritten by an international syndicate. Issuing equities outside the home country market is not a new practice; firms have often floated stock issues in other countries when their domestic market was too small to absorb a large issue. In many cases, firms have issued stock in London or other major capital markets.

Euroequities are differentiated from these more traditional international issues by the nature of the underwriting syndicate. The same network of investment firms and banks that has been active in the

Eurobond market is now underwriting equity issues. To the extent that an issue or a portion of an issue is offered through such an international syndicate, it is a Euroequity issue. As is true with other Euromarkets, the home of the Euroequity market is London.

Frequently, large corporations issue two or more *tranches*, that is, groups of identical or similar securities, each offered under slightly different terms and conditions or being distributed in different ways. A multinational firm may offer domestic and international tranches, for example, with the international tranche distributed through a Euromarket syndicate, thereby qualifying as a Euroequity.

The best candidates for this form of distribution are firms that have an international product market, so that name recognition abroad will help ensure adequate investor interest. International placement helps issuing firms receive a price that is determined by worldwide market conditions and to diversify across a wider shareholder base. Firms from Germany, the United Kingdom, Italy, Switzerland, the United States, and France represent almost 90 percent of Euroequities issued.

Exhibit 3-8 shows international issues of $11.8 billion in common and preferred stock in 1986. In 1987, this amount increased to $18.2 billion, of which 44 percent was Euroequities. The stock market collapse in October 1987 put a damper on the market in 1988, with issues amounting to only $7.7 billion. Even so, the average annual growth rate of international equity issues from 1984 (when the total was $300 million) to 1988 was 125 percent.

Historically, the Euroequity market has been a primary market, with most secondary trading occurring in the domestic market of the issuer. The volume of secondary market trades outside the home market is increasing, however. Exhibit 3-8 shows that the trading volume of international equity (the value of secondary market transactions) was barely interrupted by the 1987 stock market crash. The 1988 total of $1.2 trillion was not far behind the $1.3 trillion in 1987. This strong trading pattern indicates acceptance of the benefit of international diversification in managing investment portfolio risk.

The existence and operation of Euromarkets is changing the fundamental nature of banking. No longer can commercial banks consider their competition to be other domestic institutions. Increasingly,

EXHIBIT 3-8
INTERNATIONAL EQUITY ISSUES AND TRADING VOLUME

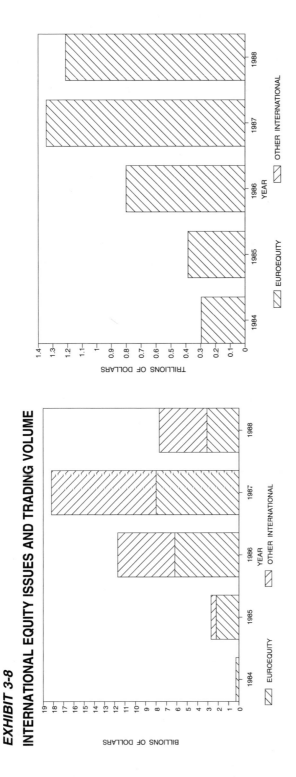

Source

Author's graphics based on data from:
International Monetary Fund, *International Capital Markets: Developments and Prospects*, April 1990.

the quality of their service and the pricing of their products is being held to international standards. The internationalization of banking standards and practices has been an important influence in the deregulation of the banking industry in the United States and abroad.

DEREGULATION

In the wake of the high and volatile interest rates of the 1970s, commercial banks and other depository institutions found themselves at a competitive disadvantage in financial services markets. As market interest rates rose and mutual funds and securities firms began to compete with commercial banks and savings and loan associations, the flow of funds to depository institutions declined.

The Need for Change

Money market mutual funds offer small savers market rates of interest for a substantially smaller investment than once required. The funds then pool these small investments to purchase Treasury securities, large bank certificates of deposit (not subject to interest rate ceilings after 1970), commercial paper, and bankers' acceptances. Individual investors not only earned high rates of return but also received limited check writing privileges. In 1974, money market funds controlled roughly $2 billion in assets; by 1980, the total was $200 billion.[1] The growth of these funds was one of the major motivations behind elimination of deposit interest rate regulation.

Securities firms too offered transactions accounts in direct competition with bank checking accounts. Besides earning interest on their accounts, clients received a full range of brokerage services. Competition from these two sources resulted in *disintermediation*, that is, the withdrawal of funds from depository institutions for the purpose of investing in other vehicles. Two government studies analyzed the problems of depository institutions and made specific recommendations to address them.

In 1971, the *President's Commission on Financial Structure and Regulation (the Hunt Commission)* suggested that savings and loan associations, credit unions, and mutual savings banks be permitted to offer transactions accounts. The Hunt Commission also recommended that deposit interest rate ceilings (Regulation Q) be eliminated after a phase-out period and reinstated only if necessary.

Of course, eliminating ceilings was feasible only if investment powers were also expanded. Institutions had to have the power to make investments that would earn high enough rates of return to provide a reasonable margin over deregulated deposit interest rates. In order to put all depository institutions on an equal footing, the commission suggested instituting uniform reserve requirements and giving the Federal Reserve regulatory authority over all such institutions.

In 1975, the House Banking Committee conducted the *Financial Institutions and the Nation's Economy (FINE) Study*. Several of its recommendations coincided with those of the Hunt Commission:

- Thrift institutions (savings and loan associations and mutual savings banks) should receive broader investment powers.

- Reserve requirements should be uniform.

- Deposit interest rate ceilings should be eliminated.

The study suggested furthermore that regulatory and insurance functions be consolidated. Even with this unanimity of opinion, federal legislation was not enacted for several years after these studies.

In 1979 inflation had been fueled by Federal Reserve monetary policy that kept interest rates low. Even so, stagnant economic growth persisted. The Federal Reserve shifted its emphasis from interest rate control toward control of monetary aggregates to discourage further expansion of the money supply. This forced depository institutions to operate in a regulatory environment that was out of step with the rest of the market. Maintaining deposit interest rate ceilings, as other market interest rates found their natural level, was inconsistent policy. Competitive pressures mounted until depository institutions were essentially in crisis.

Commercial banks withdrew from Federal Reserve membership at an unprecedented rate. Nonmember state banks had the advantages of often lower reserve requirements and the freedom to invest reserves in interest-bearing investments (unlike those held at Federal Reserve banks). The Federal Reserve became concerned that such wholesale defection would impair its ability to implement monetary policy.

The Federal Home Loan Bank Board, then the chief regulator of savings and loan associations, also pressed for reform. The deposit instruments S&Ls could offer were hardly competitive under the circumstances. Individual S&L managers also sought expanded deposit and investment powers.

Even consumer groups lobbied for deregulation. They argued that Regulation Q discriminated against small investors. Since 1970, the deposit rate ceilings for certificates of deposit in excess of $100,000 had been eliminated. Only rates paid to small depositors were still maintained at artificially low levels.

At the state level, mutual savings banks had won the right to offer NOW (negotiable order of withdrawal) accounts that were in fact interest-bearing checking accounts. However, such permission had been won primarily in the Northeast, the region in which mutual savings banks are concentrated; NOW accounts were not available nationwide. The U.S. Congress had little alternative. In 1980, the first major legislative overhaul of depository institutions since the 1930s was carried out.

Legislative Changes

The *Depository Institutions Deregulation and Monetary Control Act of 1980*, DIDMCA, provided for expanded asset and liability powers and, simultaneously, increased the authority of the Federal Reserve.[2] Its main features are listed below:

1. New reserve requirements for both member and nonmember commercial banks were set. This provision virtually eliminates the motivation to withdraw from the Federal Reserve. (See Exhibit 3-9.)

2. The Federal Reserve was instructed to provide services to *all* depository institutions, including access to the discount window.

EXHIBIT 3-9

RESERVE REQUIREMENTS IN THE DIDMCA OF 1980

Type of Deposit	Percentage
Transactions Accounts	
$0 = $26.3 million[1]	3%
Over $26.3 million	12
Nonpersonal time deposits[2]	
Less than 1.5 years	3
1.5 years or more	0
Eurocurrency liabilities	3

[1] This amount is adjusted each year by 80% of the change in total transactions accounts for all depository institutions, e.g., the 1988 base amount was $41.5 million.

[2] By original maturity

Source

S. Kerry Cooper and Donald R. Fraser, *Banking Deregulation and the New Competition in Financial Services*, 1984, p. 117.

---

3. The reserve requirements applicable to commercial banks were applied to other depository institutions. Savings and loans associations, mutual savings banks, and credit unions are now subject to uniform reserve requirements.

4. The Federal Reserve was instructed to establish a schedule of fees for services. Prior to DIDMCA, there were generally no fees.

5. The Depository Institutions Deregulation Committee (DIDC) was created to oversee the phase-out of Regulation Q deposit interest rate ceilings over a six-year period. Voting members of the DIDC were the Secretary of the Treasury and the chairs of the Federal Reserve, the Federal Deposit Insurance Corporation, the Federal Home Loan Bank Board, and the National Credit Union Administration. The Comptroller of the Currency was a nonvoting member.

6. Interest-bearing transactions accounts became legal products for all depository institutions. All banks and thrifts could offer negotiable order of withdrawal (NOW) accounts. Credit unions were permitted to offer share drafts. Only individuals and nonprofit organizations, however, could take advantage of NOW accounts and the interest rate was set at slightly over 5 percent.

7. The limit of insurance for accounts in depository institutions was raised from $40,000 to $100,000.

8. S&Ls could now offer credit cards and were permitted to make commercial real estate loans and consumer loans, each up to 20 percent of total assets.

9. Mutual savings banks could make business loans and offer demand accounts to business clients.

10. State usury laws were effectively eliminated for mortgage, business, and agricultural loans.

With the DIDMCA, the scope of Federal Reserve authority has been expanded from state bank members to *all* depository institutions. Depository institutions are more competitive in that they may now offer interest-bearing checking accounts. The legislation mandated the phased-out elimination of all deposit interest rate ceilings and allowed S&Ls and mutual savings banks to move into more diversified and profitable, albeit more risky, lines of business. At the same time, the deposit insurance ceiling increased by 150 percent. In other words, as more potential risk was introduced into depository institutions, the government safety net expanded—a dangerous combination.

Problems in the thrift industry did not completely disappear, of course. Moreover, both commercial banks and thrifts continued to operate at a competitive disadvantage vis-à-vis money market mutual funds, whose rates of return to investors were not constrained in any way. Legislation in 1982 attempted to correct these deficiencies.

The *Garn-St. Germain Depository Institutions Act of 1982* sought to expand financial institutions' powers still more and to facilitate the rescue of failing institutions. Its major provisions are:

1. The money market deposit account (MMDA) was legalized for depository institutions. MMDAs could compete directly with money market mutual funds. If the accounts were owned by individuals, there were no reserve requirements. A 3 percent reserve requirement was stipulated for business accounts.

2. Federal, state, and local governments were permitted to own NOW accounts.

3. Federally chartered S&Ls were empowered to offer demand accounts to persons or organizations with whom they had business relationships.

4. The DIDC was instructed to eliminate (Regulation A) deposit rate differentials between commercial banks and thrifts.

5. Savings and loan associations were permitted to diversify asset portfolios further, up to certain percentages of total assets:

a.	commercial real estate loans	40%
b.	secured and unsecured commercial loans	5%
c.	commercial leasing	10%
d.	consumer loans	30%

6. Savings and loan associations could add state and local government revenue bonds to their asset portfolios. Before 1982, only investments in general obligation bonds were allowed.

7. Federal regulators received more financial and geographic flexibility for rescuing thrifts, making it possible for financial and nonfinancial firms to purchase thrifts on more favorable terms for the buyers.

8. The percentage of capital that a national bank could lend to a single borrower was increased from 10 percent to 15 percent,

plus an additional 10 percent for loans collateralized by readily marketable assets.

9. National banks were permitted to form bank service companies and to invest in export trading firms. These provisions gave national banks more operational flexibility.

10. The transfer of assets (excluding low-quality assets) between bank holding companies and affiliated banks was substantially liberalized.

11. The Federal Deposit Insurance Corporation (FDIC), the Federal Savings and Loan Insurance Corporation (FSLIC), and the National Credit Union Administration (NCUA) were instructed to study the federal deposit insurance system and to identify and evaluate possible alternatives.

The Garn-St. Germain Act made it easier for regulators to close failing thrift institutions. Under the act, depository institutions can now compete directly with money market funds, by offering a similar instrument *with* deposit insurance coverage. For commercial banks, lending limits to individual customers were increased and the scope of activities expanded. S&Ls' powers were so transformed that, at least in terms of statutory powers, it became difficult to distinguish S&Ls from commercial banks.

Even these expanded powers did not bring an end to the problems in the savings and loan and commercial banking industries. In fact, the 1980s would witness bank and S&L failure rates that had not been seen since the 1930s.

The Deposit Insurance Crisis

In 1989, Congress was compelled to restructure the deposit insurance system and make major changes in regulatory oversight. The federal deposit insurance agencies that were created in the early 1930s have only recently been seriously challenged. During the 37 years from 1943 through 1979, only 210 banks failed. But in the six-year period ended 1985, 300 failed. Another 769 failed between 1986 and 1989.

Thus, in the 1980s, over 1,000 banks failed, five times the number of failures in the previous four decades. Contraction of the savings and loan industry has been even more severe. S&Ls numbered over 5,000 in 1979. By 1989, only 3,000 remained and currently the number is closer to 2,000.

Not all the bank failures have been handled in the same way. When the troubled bank is large, it is more likely that all depositors and creditors will be paid by the FDIC. The controversial arrangement for large banks is attributed to the "too big to fail" theory of deposit insurance. In essence, it means that depositors in large institutions have implicit insurance on all deposits, including those with balances in excess of $100,000, and that general creditors (without the status of deposits) will also face no loss. The concept is controversial because it:

- involves differential treatment of bank depositors by a government agency

- discourages depositors in large banks from forcing market discipline on those banks, as the depositors remain confident that their investments are safe regardless of bank behavior

- causes depositors to have less confidence in small banks, thereby making them less competitive

- greatly increases the exposure of FDIC to loss, thereby indirectly exposing the U.S. taxpayers to greater loss

The FDIC's reason for handling large troubled banks in this way is the potential effect to the banking system as a whole should a large bank fail. A large bank failure could bring systemwide instability and bank runs. The cost of this instability is thought to be greater than the cost of an unconditional bank bailout.

The first instance of this special treatment was Continental Illinois National Bank in 1984, with liabilities of $33 billion, of which only $3 billion were insured. All claims of depositors and creditors were completely guaranteed by the government. To rescue the bank, the coordinated efforts of the FDIC, the Federal Reserve, and a private bank syndicate were necessary.

The Bank of New England was allowed to fail, but FDIC was there with the same spirit of assistance as in the case of Continental. In the two years before it collapsed in January 1991, the Bank of New England lost $600 million. The bank was pulled down by the region's downward economic spiral, bankrupt companies, and vacant real estate. The prospects for the Bank of New England were so dismal that only three bidders participated in the auction—Fleet Financial Group, Bank of America, and Bank of Boston. Fleet won with its $625 million bid.

Since then, Fleet's earnings have skyrocketed. The company reported third-quarter 1992 earnings of $72 million, of which Bank of New England contributed $31 million. Fleet forecasts that the recent acquisition may contribute as much as $200 million to Fleet's 1993 earnings. Furthermore, with this acquisition, Fleet is now the largest bank in New England, moving up from fourth position.

While low interest rates and aggressive cost-cutting have contributed to this turnaround, it also was facilitated by the FDIC. The agency agreed to absorb any losses attributable to Bank of New England's troubled loans, set up a special "bad bank" to hold these loans, and paid Fleet to liquidate them. The FDIC may not step in every case to this extent, but it is clear that certain larger banks will always warrant special treatment to minimize the market disruption that may be associated with their failure.

In the savings and loan industry, there are no institutions that are too big too fail. In fact, most operate with relatively little regulatory oversight. The new powers of the 1980 and 1982 legislation combined with higher deposit insurance, were tailor-made for abuse in a lax regulatory climate. Many S&Ls attracted *brokered deposits*, large certificates of deposit (CDs) sold through securities brokers. Since the CDs were completely insured as long as the deposit did not exceed $100,000, investors were confident that their money was safe and asked few questions about the soundness of the S&L. The S&L had a ready source of cash then to invest in new activities permitted to it, including junk bonds, commercial loans, commercial real estate loans, and direct real estate investments. The originally conservative residential mortgage finance industry was transformed into a freewheeling, high risk money machine, completely insured by the federal government.

The failure rate became so high that the *Financial Institutions Reform, Recovery, and Enforcement Act* (FIRREA) was passed in August 1989. Under the strain of widespread failures, the Federal Savings and Loan Insurance Corporation (FSLIC) was declared insolvent and absorbed by the FDIC. The fund that insures savings and loan associations is still maintained separately from the bank insurance fund. Under the FDIC, the S&L fund is designated the Savings Association Insurance Fund (SAIF).

But FDIC resources had also been strained. Bank failures had accelerated because of Third World bank loans and domestic loans in the oil and gas and commercial real estate sectors. The Bank Insurance Fund (BIF—the renamed FDIC fund), which stood at $18 billion at the beginning of 1988, fell to $11.4 as of June 1990. The FDIC Assessment Rate Act of 1990 gave the FDIC board broad authority to set premiums in order to maintain desired reserves to deposit ratios for the BIF and SAIF. By 1991, the fund balance was down to $8.4 billion and in danger of being depleted if not for injection of new capital. The FDIC Improvement Act of 1991 gave the FDIC the power to borrow $70 billion from the Treasury Department and from member banks.

In 1989 FIRREA had mandated that the FDIC adjust insurance premiums so that the fund balance be maintained at an amount between 1.25 percent and 1.40 percent of estimated insured deposits. At the end of 1989, the ratio of insurance fund balance to insured deposits was only 0.70 percent. By June 1990, the ratio stood even lower at 0.57 percent.

To reverse this trend, deposit insurance premiums have gone from 0.083 percent of deposits before FIRREA to 0.195 percent of deposits in 1991 and, according to provisions in FIRREA, could go as high as 0.325 percent. The FDIC Improvement Act also stipulated that the weighted average bank assessment may not fall below .23 percent for deposits until the ratio of fund balance to insured deposits reached 1.25 percent. It is apparent, however, that increased insurance premiums may not be sufficient to restore the fund and that federal government assistance may still be necessary. As of year-end 1992, the FDIC fund balance was in deficit and represented –.01 percent of insured deposits. The burden of insurance premiums promises to be continually debated until this issue is resolved.

At the same time that FSLIC was absorbed by FDIC, the Federal Home Loan Bank Board, once essentially an independent agency, was converted into the Office of Thrift Supervision (OTS) and brought under the authority of the Treasury Department.

Those S&Ls that had been closed by federal regulators and others, in unstable financial condition but still open because FSLIC lacked the funds to close them, became the responsibility of the Resolution Trust Corporation (RTC), created by FIRREA to liquidate failed savings institutions. As of August 1989, RTC held over 250 institutions with assets of over $100 billion in conservatorship. The chairperson and the director of FDIC each serve the same function in RTC. The RTC Oversight Board, the policy-making body, includes the Secretary of the Treasury (as chairperson), the Chair of the Federal Reserve, and the Secretary of Housing and Urban Development. With such a far-flung policy-making board, the RTC is a cumbersome structure in terms of making timing decisions about asset liquidation and has been criticized because of this. FIRREA mandates that the RTC will operate only until December 31, 1996.

FIRREA attempts to correct some of the excesses of the early 1980s legislation by requiring higher capital levels and more prudent investment policies for thrifts, shoring up the federal insurance fund, and limiting the use of brokered deposits. Exhibit 3-10 outlines the major provisions of this legislation.

While there are no definite amounts identified as the total cost of cleaning up the S&L industry, estimates range from $150 billion to $500 billion. How the bailout is to be financed is the subject of much debate. The federal budget deficit is a stubborn financial problem, even before considering the savings and loan issue. Current commercial bank failures, moreover, although not as widespread as S&L failures, do not bode well for the long-term solvency of the FDIC.

The liabilities of institutions that have already been closed and the even worse *potential* exposure of the U.S. government have brought the concept of federal deposit insurance under scrutiny.

EXHIBIT 3-10

FIRREA

The major provisions of the Financial Institutions Reform, Recovery, and Enforcement Act of 1989 are:

- The Office of Thrift Supervision (within the Treasury Department) became the chief regulator, replacing the Federal Home Loan Bank Board. The FDIC took over the insurance function from the Federal Savings and Loan Insurance Corporation, now maintaining two funds: the Bank Insurance Fund (BIF) and the Savings Association Insurance Fund (SAIF).

- To complete the liquidation of failed savings and loan associations (S&Ls), the Resolution Funding Corporation was created to raise the necessary funds, with Resolution Trust Corporation (RTC) overseeing the liquidations.

- Insurance premiums for S&Ls and banks were increased. FIRREA also gave FDIC the right to increase the rates in either fund, if necessary, to ensure solvency of SAIF and BIF. Premiums may not exceed 32.5 cents per $100 of deposits or be raised by more than 7.5 cents per year.

- With respect to community reinvestment, the Community Reinvestment Act of 1977 was amended to require public disclosure of a depository institution's regulatory rating. In addition, member institutions of Federal Home Loan Banks were to establish special funds to help finance home purchases, housing rehabilitation, and economic development for low- and moderate-income families.

- For S&Ls, minimum tangible capital was set at 1.5 percent of total assets.[1] Minimum core capital was set at 3 percent of total assets. By the end of December 1992, thrifts are required to meet the same capital requirements as commercial banks (prescribed by the Office of the Comptroller of the Currency).

- Brokered deposits could no longer be accepted by any insured depository institution that does not meet minimum capital requirements.[2]

- Savings institutions may no longer invest in bonds that are not rated investment grade. All holdings of such "junk" bonds must be sold as soon as possible, but no later than 1994.

- The penalties for bank fraud were stiffened. The maximum fine increased from $5,000 to $1 million and the maximum prison term increased from 10 years to 20 years.

Exhibit continues

EXHIBIT 3-10
FIRREA (Continued)

Source

Dianne Meyer and Sandra A. Ballard, "Issues in Lending: A Guide to FIRREA," *Journal of Commercial Bank Lending*, Vol. 72 (January 1990), pp. 11–23.

1   Tangible capital includes common stock equity, noncumulative preferred stock, nonwithdrawable deposit accounts, pledged deposits, and minority interest in consolidated subsidiaries. Core capital is tangible capital plus qualifying intangibles, including goodwill (the premium paid by an investor when purchasing a troubled thrift institution.

2   Brokered deposits are placed with a depository institution through a third party, typically a securities broker. The broker tries to find the highest rate of return available in an institution that is federally insured. Previously, troubled institutions could attract large amounts of brokered deposits by offering high interest rates, putting even more pressure on profits.

Future Deposit Insurance Reforms

FIRREA also instructed the Treasury Department to conduct major studies on the issue of federal deposit insurance and in fact the current deposit insurance system has sometimes been cited as a significant cause of the instability in the banking industry. The rationale for this argument is that the government guarantee encourages excessive risk taking by managers of financial institutions. The incentive is said to be strong because any failure of risky investments to pay off as originally anticipated will not hurt depositors; the federal government will assume the deposit liabilities. The converse is that if these risky investments *do* pay off, the bank and its managers will prosper. This situation is often referred to as a *moral hazard*: investing with all the attendant benefits, but passing the costs along to another party. Possible reforms to the deposit insurance system involve:

- abolition of federal deposit insurance
- modifying insurance coverage
- charging risk-adjusted premiums

Proponents of the proposal to *abolish* federal deposit insurance suggest that closer market scrutiny, not government oversight, will restore discipline to the market. Those opposed to the abolition of federal deposit insurance argue that its absence would destroy confidence in the system and lead to domino-effect bank runs. Proponents of abolition assert that the Federal Reserve *can* and *would* provide needed liquidity to shore up the system; it would not passively allow large-scale bank failures as it did in the 1930s.

Other alternatives involve *modification of insurance coverage*, rather than abolition of insurance. Sharing risk with the insured party is referred to as *co-insurance*. In one type of co-insurance plan, each depositor would be required to pay the first dollars of loss. A variation, *fixed proportional sharing*, requires the insured to pay a fixed percentage of every dollar of loss. Opponents of this type of modification argue that the current system is already co-insurance, because the government pays the first $100,000, and the depositor pays the remainder.

Another modification is to *lower the maximum coverage*. The relatively high $100,000 limit is 40 times the original limit of $2500, yet from 1934 to 1980 (when the higher limit was established), general price levels increased only seven times. A lower limit might reduce the moral hazard, as it would be more difficult for institutions to raise funds quickly by raising deposit rates; that is, several smaller insured deposits would be necessary to equal one $100,000 insured deposit. At the same time, small depositors would be completely protected, as the original 1933 legislation intended.

Risk-adjusted premiums are probably the most widely proposed alternative to the deposit insurance system. Such premiums are likely to impose a certain amount of discipline on the insured institution because more risky operations would cause its insurance premiums to rise. In fact, this is the practice in virtually all insurance arrangements other than those for depository institutions. From a practical standpoint, however, establishing appropriate premiums has been seen as a major obstacle. With risk-based capital requirements being established internationally, however, risk-based insurance premiums became much more feasible.

The FDIC Improvement Act of 1991 required the FDIC to develop regulations for a system of risk-based insurance assessment by January 1994. In response to this requirement, the FDIC instituted a sliding scale of premiums as of January 1993 with nine risk-based categories. The best-capitalized, best-managed banks are assessed at 23 basis points ($.23 per $100 of deposits), while the weakest institutions pay 31 basis points. Later in 1993, the FDIC introduced the concept of allowing the best-capitalized banks to be included in still another category of "minimal-risk institutions." These might be subject to assessments below 23 basis points. Also, the FDIC presented for comment the idea of more than nine categories, with assessments below 23 basis points and above 31. The rationale is that creating a wider range of premium levels may create more disincentive for allowing operating condition to deteriorate. A major consideration for such a plan must be the ability of the weaker banks to absorb the higher assessment and still remain viable.

Proper evaluation of portfolio risk has always been a challenge for federal regulators. This difficulty is compounded further by a traditional reluctance to disclose negative information about the regulated institutions. The usual justification for this stance has been that such disclosure could cause a lack of confidence in the institution that would result in bank runs. There are signs today that this protective attitude is giving way to more pressing concerns of restoring discipline to the industry.

Whatever the ultimate disposition of federal deposit insurance, it is safe to say that it has turned into one of the most critical issues in bank regulation in decades. Not since the bank failures of the Great Depression has the regulatory structure of the U.S. banking system faced so much scrutiny.[3]

Deregulation in Other Countries

While Swiss and German universal banks have long been permitted a full range of activities, the United Kingdom, Canada, and Japan have made significant strides in liberalizing their financial markets.[4] This trend toward deregulation will affect banking business for the foreseeable future.

EXHIBIT 3-11

A PROPOSAL FOR BANK REFORM

A plan for bank reform was proposed by Nicholas Brady, Treasury secretary in the Bush administration, in 1991. To date, it is the most comprensive plan for bank reform that has emerged. In essence, the proposal sought to allow well-capitalized banks more freedom of operation, to limit federal deposit insurance coverage, and to bring more market discipline to banking. The features of the plan include the following:

- Permit those banks that meet minimum capital requirements to branch nationwide and to engage in securities underwriting. (Those banks not meeting the capital requirements would be liquidated or absorbed by other institutions.)

- Limit insurance coverage to $100,000 per person per bank for regular banking purposes. Provide an additional $100,000 per person per bank for retirement accounts.

- Base deposit insurance premiums on the adequacy of bank capital, with strongly capitalized banks paying lower premiums.

- Eliminate insurance coverage of brokered deposits and nondeposit liabilities, frequently covered in large bank liquidations.

- Give bank regulators more authority to correct bank deficiencies sooner.

- Force banks to disclose the true market value of assets and liabilities.

- Permit nonbank financial firms and nonfinancial firms to own commercial banks through the holding company structure.

- Limit the ability of state-chartered banks to engage in activities not permitted for national banks to prevent the FDIC from being exposed to the risk of covering losses associated with these activities.

The proposals addressed important issues in U.S. banking and would help make banks more competitive and financially viable. U.S. Congress, however, has failed to enact necessary legislation to adopt the proposals.

Source

Modernizing the Financial System: Recommendations for Safer, More Competitive Banks, U.S. Department of the Treasury, 1991.

In the *United Kingdom*, the 1971 Competition and Credit Regulations of the Bank of England dismantled the interest rate cartel of clearing banks, with the primary objective of placing financial institutions on more equal footing. In a sense, these regulations were precursors of the 1980 U.S. Monetary Control Act. The Bank of England regulations have resulted in more vigorous competition among clearing banks and, in general, among *all* financial institutions. Banks are now permitted to operate as primary dealers in the market for Treasury securities.

The "Big Bang" of 1986 fundamentally changed the U.K. financial system in that banks were given the right to invest in securities firms. Mergers within the commercial and investment banking circles of London have created clearing banks that are becoming "universal" banks that offer a full range of financial services. Building societies (savings and loan associations) may sell mutual fund shares, offer credit cards, and compete in banking services. The shares of new and small companies may now trade on the London Stock Exchanges Third Market, created in 1987.

Competition among *Canadian* financial institutions has increased since 1967, as a result of the Canadian Bank Act. The act removed deposit rate ceilings and granted expanded lending powers to depository institutions. Chartered (commercial) banks began to offer deposits at market rates of interest and to cultivate mortgage and consumer loan business.

Foreign bank entry into the Canadian market had been difficult because of the high concentration of assets in the five largest banks and because of the close relationship of these five with the government. However, the 1980 Bank Act introduced a new type of bank, a Schedule B bank. Banks already existing were designated Schedule A banks. New Canadian-owned banks may be incorporated as Schedule A or Schedule B banks. No more than 10 percent of the shares of a Schedule A bank may be held by one party. On the other hand, as long as the capital of a Schedule B bank does not exceed $750 million, the 10 percent ownership restriction does not apply. This means that foreign banks may now enter the Canadian market under this Schedule B framework and establish a subsidiary that may remain closely held as long as capital does not exceed $750 million.

Like their U.S. counterparts, Canadian banks have also sought permission to engage in securities underwriting. In 1986 a plan for further deregulation included a provision that banks be permitted to engage in these activities. While all of the provisions have not been enacted, banks may now own securities firms in Canada. Eventually, this permission will be extended to all other types of financial services firms. Many Canadian banks have exercised this right by investing in existing securities firms. In this respect, Canadian deregulation is ahead of U.S. efforts.

The heavily regulated system of *Japan* has been liberalized, but not to the same extent. Previously denied access to money markets, commercial banks have enjoyed expanded powers since the late 1970s, notably the right to issue negotiable certificates of deposit (NCD). Banking reform in 1982 was the most comprehensive in over 50 years. Since 1982, Japanese banks have been permitted to purchase, sell, and underwrite government securities. Subsequent regulatory changes have allowed even more flexibility in banks' money market operations. From 1984 to 1985, the minimum denomination of NCDs was reduced from ¥500 million to ¥300 million to ¥100 million. The maximum maturity was extended from one month to three months. The Euroyen NCD was authorized in 1984 and the yen bankers' acceptance market permitted a year later. In 1985, banks were permitted to offer money market certificates with interest tied to money market rates. In the same year, interest rate ceilings were liberalized for deposits of ¥1 billion or more and then liberalized for deposits of ¥500 million in 1986. This deregulatory trend will most certainly continue.

Deregulation is a common theme in many financial markets today. As noted earlier, the increased interaction among markets makes these changes necessary to maintain and enhance competitive position. Deregulation in individual countries, however, ultimately will not have the same impact as the more sweeping implications of the Single European Market.

THE SINGLE EUROPEAN MARKET FOR FINANCIAL SERVICES

As evidenced by the emergence of Euromarkets, the barriers to free capital movement across national borders are being torn down. Perhaps the most significant instance of dissolution of capital barriers is the creation of a Single European Market among the countries of the European Community. The European Economic Community (EEC) Treaty of 1957, also called the Treaty of Rome, united Belgium, France, Italy, Luxembourg, the Netherlands, and Germany for the purpose of coordinating monetary policies and actions for their mutual benefit. In 1967 the EEC joined with two other European industrial associations—the European Coal and Steel Community (ECSC) and the European Atomic Energy Community (Euratom)—and the European Investment Bank (EIB) to become the European Community (EC). As early as the 1960s, the notion of even greater monetary integration began to gain support among its members.

The Concept

A framework for the monetary union is described in the 1970 Werner Report, which recommended that:

- EC members should pool their reserves and settle any deficits or surpluses internally.

- Members should agree to maintain their relative exchange rates within predetermined limits, or parities.

- Adjustments to these parities should become less and less frequent and the parities, eventually, should be fixed.

- The national currencies of the members should be replaced by one Community currency.

Implementation of these recommendations began during the 1970s and will continue through the 1990s.

Implementation

In 1979, the *European Monetary System* (EMS) was established. By this time, Denmark, Ireland, and the United Kingdom had joined the EC. It had four main results:

- The *European Currency Unit* (ECU) was created. The ECU is a GNP-weighted basket of member currencies, whose composition may change.[5] The ECU is used to denominate and settle central bank debts and claims of member countries.

- Short- and medium-term credit facilities were established for the members.

- Member countries agreed to maintain exchange rates within a band to be defined in terms of ECUs. The divergence indicator, a warning signal, would trigger action on the part of the EMS Council and the member country whose currency was involved. Presumably, members would intervene in the foreign exchange market to correct this divergence. This new arrangement is called the *Exchange Rate Mechanism (ERM)*.

- The European Monetary Cooperation Fund was established to issue ECUs against member country deposits of gold and foreign exchange.

The ECU serves several functions—both unit of account for the system and basis for the divergence indicator. The maximum variation of a member country currency rate is plus or minus 2.5 percent of its value in terms of ECUs, with the divergence indicator set at 75 percent of this maximum spread. Members of the ERM agreed to correct the exchange rate variation of their respective currencies whenever the divergence indicator was activated. This means that ERM members are obligated to intervene in currency markets in unlimited amounts to bring their currency values back in line.

To help accommodate any needed intervention of this nature, a short-term credit facility was initiated. Any ERM member required to enter the market in order to bring its currency value back within limits has been given automatic and unlimited access to this facility. The European Monetary System and the Exchange Rate Mechanism generally have reduced the amount of speculation in European currencies and have brought about more cooperation in the management of money supply within the ERM.

In 1981, Greece joined the EC and in 1985 Portugal and Spain were the last of the 15 countries to became part of the union. Also in 1985, a White Paper (position paper) was developed by the EC Commission (the EC body that makes policy proposals) and approved by the EC heads of government. The paper includes 300 proposed directives to unify EC markets further. The proposed measures fall into three main categories:

- liberalizing capital movements

- abolishing cross-border restrictions in the provision of financial services

- removing obstructions to the free movement of goods and services

To implement these recommendations, the Single European Act was adopted in 1986. According to this act, all barriers to the free movement of goods, persons, services, and capital were to be eliminated throughout the EC by December 31, 1992. The anticipated benefits of the unified market are given in Exhibit 3-12. The terms of the Single European Market have been and continue to be negotiated among the EC members in all areas of commerce.

In 1988, the decision was made to ask an EC committee to study the process of creating a unified European currency as suggested in the 1970 Werner Report. The resulting *Delors Committee Report*, accepted in 1989, recommends that conversion to a unified currency take place in three stages:

Stage 1

A period of closer coordination and full participation of EC members in the Exchange Rate Mechanism.

Stage 2

A transition phase during which (a) the central banks (monetary authorities) of EC countries would more closely coordinate monetary policy and (b) the framework for a European central bank, the *Eurofed*, would be established.

EXHIBIT 3-12

ADVANTAGES OF THE SINGLE EUROPEAN MARKET

The Single European Market of 1992 is intended to solve the problems within the European Community (EC) that arise because of the fragmentation of Europe into multiple markets with different laws and regulations. It is anticipated that efficiencies will be realized by reducing the following economic costs:

- Administrative costs of maintaining different bureaucratic requirements.

- Transportation costs related to formalities at national borders.

- Cost of relatively short production runs because final output is subject to different national product standards.

- Duplication in research and development efforts.

- Costs associated with inefficient and noncompetitive state-run enterprises.

- Costs incurred by consumers because of a lack of competition among firms, including narrow product selection and relatively high prices.

- Opportunity costs that are sustained by firms that cannot easily expand across national borders to realize full market potential.

Source

Task Force on the International Competitiveness of U.S. Financial Institutions, Committee on Banking, Finance, and Urban Affairs, U.S. House of Representatives, *Report of the Subcommittee on Financial Institutions Supervision, Regulation, and Insurance*, October 1990.

Stage 3

> The final point when the Eurofed assumes full control of European monetary policy and a single European currency circulates in lieu of existing national currencies.

The first stage was scheduled to end July 1990, but the United Kingdom joined the ERM only in October 1990 because of a philosophical struggle with the notion of relinquishing sovereign monetary control. Nevertheless, progress is being made in the Delors Report timetable. The second stage is due for completion by January 1994.

The objectives of monetary union were frustrated, however, when the United Kingdom and Denmark withdrew from the ERM in the fall of 1992. For reasons related to the German reunification of 1990, Germany has maintained high interest rates to both attract capital and to control inflation. This has caused the value of the Deutsche mark to remain high vis-à-vis other EC currencies. The cost of maintaining agreed-upon parities, in terms of both market intervention and maintenance of high interest rates, was too high and the United Kingdom and Denmark pulled out. For a period of time, currency exchange markets were in turmoil and serious doubts arose as to the feasibility of a true monetary union in Europe. Nevertheless, the process continues in the form of the Maastricht Treaty.

The Maastricht Treaty

In December 1991, the EC heads of state met in Maastricht (the Netherlands) and drafted an important framework in which monetary union would be accomplished. The Maastricht agreement is currently being ratified by each EC country. During Stage 2 of monetary union, the *European Monetary Institute* (EMI) will replace the existing Committee of Governors of EC Central Banks. Among other things, the EMI will:

- take over the administration of the European Monetary Co-operation Fund (which issues ECUs) and the accompanying financing mechanisms

- monitor the running of the EMS

- facilitate use of private ECU

- oversee development of the ECU clearing system

- be consulted by national authorities on monetary policy and help draft legislation on the eventual convergence of all currencies into the ECU

All EC central banks will be members of the EMI. The organization is intended to strengthen the coordination of the member states' monetary policies in preparation for Stage 3 of monetary union. Also during Stage 2, a *European System of Central Banks* (ESCB) will be formed, with the *European Central Bank* (ECB) as the principal new monetary institution. The formation of the new system will follow guidelines established by the Committee of Governors of EC Central Banks (predecessor of the European Monetary Institute).

The European System of Central Banks and the European Central Bank (Eurofed) will assume their full powers under Stage 3 and be responsible for issuing and managing the single currency—the ECU—that eventually will replace the national currencies. The United Kingdom and Denmark have reserved the right to not converge by the January 1999 date specified in the treaty, that is, to not automatically join Stage 3. For the remaining members, there are four convergence criteria. In order to join Stage 3, each member state must:

1. Achieve a high degree of price stability. The average one-year inflation rate before examination by EC authorities must not exceed by more than 1.5 percentage points the inflation rate of the three best performing EC members.

2. Demonstrate sustainability of its government financial position. An excessive government deficit can disqualify an EC country from convergence.

3. Observe the normal fluctuation margins provided by the Exchange Rate Mechanism for at least two years without devaluing its currency against the currency of another EC member.

4. Demonstrate adequate control of its interest rates. For one year prior to examination by EC authorities, the long-term government bond (or comparable) interest rate may not exceed by more than 2 percentage points the long-term government bond rate of the three best performing EC members.

Clearly, the criteria for convergence necessitate stable economic performance on the part of those EC members that are to join Stage 3. In the meantime, the growing acceptance of the ECU can be seen in the increase in ECU-denominated bond issues. Exhibit 3-13 shows that, from very modest beginnings in 1981, the value of the new

EXHIBIT 3-13
ECU BOND ISSUES

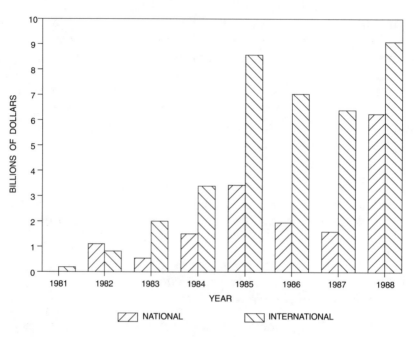

Source

Author's graphic based on data from:
International Monetary Fund. *The European Monetary System in the Context of the Integration of European Financial Markets*, October 1989.

issues (national and international) grew to over 15 billion ECUs by 1988.

Members of the EC are contributing to the acceptance of the ECU. Early in 1993, the United Kingdom issued Treasury notes amounting to ECU500 million and France raised ECU700 million in 10-year obligations. As part of the EC, the European Economic Community, the European Coal and Steel Community, and the European Atomic Energy Community raise funds in public capital markets for lending to others. The EEC lends to countries for the purpose of correcting balance of payments deficits (imports in excess of exports). Loans by

ECSC and Euratom are for coal, steel, and nuclear power purposes. In most cases, the EEC can raise funds more cheaply than those countries to which it lends. This is particularly true in the case of Eastern European nations. Moreover, a large percentage of these issues is denominated in ECUs. An important ECU issue by the EEC that has been approved recently by EC Parliament in the amount of ECU4 billion is for Italy, to cover its budget deficit and to replace reserves used by the Italian government to support the lira in currency markets.

The Single License

Economic integration of the European Community is clearly moving forward. There will soon be few impediments to trade throughout the EC. In the area of financial services, operations will be considerably simplified. A license in one country will entitle the holder to conduct its business throughout the EC. Banks and securities firms are expected to be major beneficiaries.

The First Banking Directive in 1977 established minimum legal requirements for credit institutions to be authorized in EC countries. The Second Banking Directive was adopted in 1989 and stipulated that an EC credit institution that has been licensed in the home country is allowed to conduct the same kinds of activities throughout the EC. Gone is the necessity to be licensed under 12 different sets of rules. The minimum capital requirement is a harmonized ECU5 million and risk-weighted capital standards associated with the Basel Accord apply.[6]

The Investment Services Directive (ISD) was agreed to by the EC in March 1993 and is very similar to the Second Banking Directive in that a firm receives a "single passport" to operate throughout the EC. Since there is no securities equivalent to the Basel capital standards for banks, the Capital Adequacy Directive (CAD) also was finalized in March. Both the ISD and the CAD become effective January 1996. Because of the diversity of capital standards, the CAD places responsibility for capital adequacy with the home country within the EC. This has raised some concerns that differing capital standards may place securities firms from some countries at a competitive disadvantage to firms from countries with less rigorous standards. Even more troublesome in the minds of some is the provision in the ISD that host countries may prevent or penalize irregularities committed in their territories. These irregularities may be actions that are contrary to legal or regulatory provisions "adopted in the interest of the general good." Such a provision could be used to prevent undue competition in the host country securities market. Confrontations concerning the implementation of both the ISD and the CAD could be forthcoming.

The Single European Community is perhaps the most dramatic example of financial market integration with single license banking and single passport securities operations. It is an integral part of the accelerating cross-border exchanges in all markets for currency, stocks, bonds, and other financial instruments.

CONCLUSION

The Euromarkets have grown from primarily wholesale money markets to a wide array of short-term and long-term financial services and instruments. In general, growth in Eurobonds has far outpaced the growth in traditional international bonds. Eurocommercial paper and Euronote issues expanded rapidly during the early 1980s, only to contract somewhat during the late 1980s. Primary issues in the international equity market were slowed considerably by the stock market crash of 1987, but secondary market trading has continued at a strong pace.

After the major bank legislation of the 1930s, the structure of the commercial bank system remained virtually unchanged until 1980, when depository institutions were deregulated in order to overcome competitive disadvantages vis-à-vis nondepository financial institutions. Thereafter, institutions failed at rates not seen since before the 1930s legislation. The federal agency responsible for savings and loan insurance (FSLIC) folded. Commercial bank failures accelerated, causing assets in the commercial bank insurance fund (FDIC) to decline for the first time since its inception. Without government assistance, the future of the FDIC is also questionable.

The 1980s brought significant change to the regulatory environment of depository institutions. Furthermore, with the remaining uncertainty that still surrounds the system, the 1990s will almost certainly witness additional changes.

Internationally, a major initiative in financial market liberalization and integration is the Single European Market. Financial firms that have been constrained by varying rules and regulations in the EC will be able to operate throughout the 12-nation region with a license from any one of them. Financial integration of Europe will be complete when an authoritative European Central Bank, or Eurofed, and a single European currency, the ECU, are fully operational by 1999.

SELECTED REFERENCES

Abrams, Richard K., Peter K. Cornelius, Per L. Hedfors, and Gunnar Tersman. *The Impact of the European Community's Internal Market on the EFTA.* International Monetary Fund, Washington, D.C., December 1990.

Bacon, Richard. "EC Finance Rules Face Fresh Obstacles." *Euromoney*, May 1993, pp. 50–55.

Benston, George J., and George G. Kaufman. *Risk and Solvency Regulation of Depository Institutions: Past Policies and Current Options.* Salomon Brothers Center for the Study of Financial Institutions at the Graduate School of Business Administration of New York University, New York, 1988.

Binhammer, H. H. *Money, Banking, and the Canadian Financial System.* Nelson Canada, Scarborough, Ontario, 1988.

Bronte, Stephen. *Japanese Finance: Markets and Institutions.* Euromoney Publications, London, 1982.

Comparative Economic and Financial Statistics: Japan and Other Major Countries 1988. Bank of Japan, Tokyo, 1988.

Cooper, S. Kerry, and Donald R. Fraser. *Banking Deregulation and the New Competition in Financial Services.* Ballinger Publishing Company, Cambridge, Massachusetts, 1984.

"Deposit Insurance, Redux." *United States Banker*, May 1993, p. 13.

Dyer, Geoff. "Global Bonds Aim to Broaden Their Scope," *Euromoney*, June 1993, pp. 84–88.

Economic and Monetary Union. Commission of the European Communities, Luxembourg, 1990.

Einzig, Paul, and Brian Scott Quinn. *The Eurodollar System: Practice and Theory of International Interest Rates*, 6th edition. St. Martin's Press, New York, 1977.

Europe 1992: The Facts. Department of Trade and Industry and the Central Office of Information, London, 1989.

European Economy: One Market, One Money: An Evaluation of the Potential Benefits and Costs of Forming an Economic and Monetary Union. Commission of the European Communities, Directorate-General for Economic and Financial Affairs, Brussels, October 1990.

Folkerts-Landau, David, and Donald J. Mathieson. *The European Monetary System in the Context of the Integration of European Financial Markets*. International Monetary Fund, Washington, D.C., October 1989.

Fraser, Donald R., and Peter S. Rose, Editors. *Financial Institutions and Markets in a Changing World*, 3rd edition. Business Publications, Inc., Plano, Texas, 1987.

Grady, John, and Martin Weale. *British Banking, 1960–85*. Macmillan Press, London, 1986.

Haggar, Euan. "How the EEC Can Save the ECU Market." *Euromoney*, February 1993.

Havrilesky, Thomas M., and Robert Schweitzer, Editors. *Contemporary Developments in Financial Institutions and Markets*. Harlan Davidson, Inc., Arlington Heights, Illinois, 1987.

Huat, Tan Chwee. *Financial Institutions in Singapore*. Singapore University Press, Singapore, 1981.

International Capital Markets: Developments and Prospects. International Monetary Fund, Washington, D.C., April 1989 and April 1990.

International Financial Statistics. International Monetary Fund, Washington, D.C., Yearbook 1990 and May 1991.

"The Maastricht Agreement on Economic and Monetary Union." *Bank of England Quarterly Bulletin*, February 1992, pp. 64–68.

Modernizing the Financial System: Recommendations for Safer, More Competitive Banks. U.S. Department of the Treasury, Washington, D.C.

Mullineux, Andrew. *International Banking and Financial Systems: A Comparison.* Graham and Trotman, London, 1987.

"Recent Developments in Overseas Commercial Paper Markets." *Bank of England Quarterly Bulletin*, November 1992, p. 405.

Roman, Monica. "The New Currency Gunslingers." *Global Finance*, vol. 6, no. 6 (June 1992), pp. 32–36.

Scott, Robert Haney, K.A. Wong, and Yan Ki Ho, Editors. *Hong Kong's Financial Institutions and Markets.* Oxford University Press, Hong Kong, 1986.

Smith, Geoffrey. "Fleet's Ship Comes In: Its Bank of New England Unit Has Earned Fat Profits Fast." *Business Week*, November 9, 1992, p. 104.

Subcommittee on Financial Institutions Supervision, Regulation, and Insurance. *Report of the Task Force on International Competitiveness of U.S. Financial Institutions.* U.S. House of Representatives Committee on Banking, Finance and Urban Affairs, Washington, D.C., 1990.

Tew, Brian. *The Evolution of the International Monetary System, 1945–81.* Hutchinson & Co., Ltd., London, 1982.

Ungerer, Horst, Juko J. Hauvonen, Augusto Lopez-Claros, and Thomas Mayer. *The European Monetary System: Developments and Prospectives.* International Monetary Fund, Washington, D.C., November 1990.

U.S. Securities and Exchange Commission. *Internationalization of Securities Market: Report to the Senate Committee on Banking, Housing, and Urban Affairs and the House Committee on Energy and Commerce.* Washington, D.C., 1987.

ENDNOTES

1. Currently, money market funds hold over $500 billion in assets.

2. The DIDMCA is also known as the Monetary Control Act of 1980 and as the Omnibus Banking Act.

3. The low, short-term interest rates of 1992–93 and the healthy rates available on long-term Treasury securities have helped bank profits rebound to, in some cases, record levels. However, future increases in short-term

rates will shrink these margins and once again reveal any structural deficiencies that remain.

4. See Chapter 2 for a discussion of powers of the Swiss and German banking systems.

5. In 1989, the ECU was composed of the Belgian franc (7.6 percent), Danish krone (2.4 percent), French franc (19.0 percent), Deutsche mark (30.1 percent), Irish pound (1.1 percent), Italian lira (10.1 percent), Luxemburg franc (0.3 percent), Netherlands guilder (9.4 percent), British sterling (13.0 percent), Greek drachma (0.8 percent), Spanish peseta (5.3 percent), and Portuguese escudo (0.8 percent).

6. See Chapter 4 for a discussion of risk-weighted capital standards.

4　The Regulators: Ours and Theirs

INTRODUCTION

Commercial banks in the United States are among the most strictly regulated institutions. Bank regulation appears reasonable since banks are such an important part of the payments system and provide basic financial services to consumers and businesses alike. To some extent, this is also true in other countries. U.S. and other regulators routinely limit the scope of activity of domestic banks in their overseas operations as well. However, in comparison to that in other countries, the relationship between U.S. banks and regulators is strained at best. In addition, in the United States, foreign banks were first ignored, then given preferential treatment, and lastly have been allowed to continue their protected activities under certain "grandfather" clauses in federal legislation.

THE NEED FOR REGULATION

It cannot be denied that bank regulation is necessary to maintain the safety and soundness of banking systems in all industrialized countries. As interest rates on deposits are being deregulated, many of the remaining regulations focus on the areas of liquidity standards, loan concentrations, and capital standards.

Liquidity Standards

The adequacy of bank liquidity is tied to solvency of the banking system. From a regulatory perspective, liquidity means a bank's ability to meet its obligations when they are due. Before the widespread use of liability management, liquidity was more easily measurable. Maintaining high-quality, liquid assets gave reassurance to both the public and the regulators.

The ability to convert these assets into cash meant that even heavy deposit withdrawal could be met. In turn, this situation led to confidence in the bank's solvency, so that runs were unlikely. However, it is not always possible to assess exactly the liquidity of certain assets. Municipal bonds are a good example. Large sales of municipals can depress their market value since secondary markets for municipals are not as well developed as markets for Treasury securities. Nevertheless, municipal bond yields frequently compare favorably with government bond yields (on an after-tax basis). From the bank's perspective, then, the less liquid municipal bonds may be preferable.

Another shortcoming of attempting to measure liquidity based on asset holdings is that this approach does not consider the dynamic aspect of banking. The use of active liability management began in 1961 when banks began to issue negotiable certificates of deposit as a means to more actively control funding sources. However, in 1966, regulated domestic deposit rates were not competitive with Treasury security rates. To circumvent the problem of low, noncompetitive rates, U.S. banks issued dollar-denominated negotiable CDs overseas. Since the rate ceilings did not apply to overseas deposits, competitive rates could be offered. Foreign branches raised funds that could not be raised domestically. These events gave birth to a much more active liability management and to the Eurodollar market.[1] In the case of the 1966 credit crunch, measuring liquid assets as a percentage of deposits would probably not have revealed the impending problem. That is, the balance sheet alone does not reflect the ease or difficulty that a bank may have in refinancing maturing deposits or other liabilities.

Because of these considerations, many regulators have moved more to a *cash flow* approach in assessing bank liquidity. In general, cash flow techniques attempt to measure any mismatch in the maturity structure of asset and liability portfolios.

The specific regulatory approach varies by country. Continental European countries still apply variations of specific liquidity measures. For example, Denmark has maintained a ratio of liquid assets to liabilities. The Netherlands and Switzerland vary required liquidity coefficients (coverage percentages) for specific balance sheet accounts (liabilities) based on type and maturity. In Germany, guidelines are established by law for maintenance of liquidity. However, German regulators reserve the right to impose stricter or more lenient ratios or guidelines as conditions warrant.

Some countries have fewer formal requirements. Instead, liquidity review is a part of the regular oversight process. In Canada, this is accomplished through informal monitoring of maturity mismatching. In the United Kingdom, cash flow over the next 12 months is routinely reviewed.

The approach in the United States is a combination of fixed-ratio maintenance and cash flow analysis. Smaller banks are evaluated primarily on the basis of liquid asset levels. Larger banks, considered to have greater access to money and capital markets, are assessed on the basis of projected cash flow or maturity mismatches.

The CAMEL rating system is used in the United States. The specific qualities considered are:

C   Capital adequacy
A   Asset quality
M   Management and administrative ability
E   Earnings level and quality
L   Liquidity level

Each bank is scored between 1 (best) and 5 (worst). Banks with poor results are examined more frequently by federal regulators.

Loan Concentration

Regulators in the United States also examine bank loan portfolios to spot excessive concentration of *long-term loans*. While commercial banks are not precluded from making loans for 15 to 30 years, if a substantial share of the portfolio is devoted to long-term loans, the bank may be effectively taking equity positions with client firms. Such positions are, of course, to be avoided since banks *are prohibited* from holding nonfinancial corporate stock. This is particularly true if the client is not well capitalized.

The basic premise is that an excessive amount of long-term loans that have a *fixed rate of interest* can also expose the bank to risk if interest rates increase. Deposits are short-term liabilities that can quickly reflect a higher level of interest rates. If the bank holds large quantities of long-term fixed-rate loans, interest expense on deposits can increase much faster than interest income on loans and put considerable strain on bank profitability.

While there is no established maximum percentage of long-term, fixed-rate loans that a bank may hold, concentration in terms of a *single borrower* is more explicitly regulated. If a bank devotes too much of its resources to one borrower, the solvency of the bank itself can depend on the financial circumstances of that client. The concept of single borrower is extended to direct and indirect obligations of the borrower. Indirect obligations include those of a partnership in which the client has ownership interest and those for which the client is an endorser or guarantor for another party. In the case of corporate clients, obligations include those of both parent and subsidiaries.

National banks in the United States may not lend more than 15 percent of capital to any single borrower that is not completely collateralized. If the loan is completely collateralized by readily marketable assets, the limit is 25 percent of capital (an additional 10 percent). State banks are also subject to single borrower limits, but these limits vary from one state to another.

There are legal guidelines on loan concentrations to single borrowers outside the United States. In OECD countries, most of the guidelines are set in terms of capital, as is true in the United States.[2] However, the percentages vary from 10 percent of capital plus 1 percent of local currency deposits in Portugal to 50 percent of capital in Austria, Belgium, France, and Norway. The limits fall somewhere in between for Canada, Denmark, Greece, Japan, Luxembourg, the Netherlands, Switzerland, and the United Kingdom. In Austria, France, Germany, and Italy, there are specific limits on "large loans."

The definition of large loans ranges from those which exceed 15 percent of capital (in the case of Germany) to those which exceed 25 percent of capital (in the case of France). In Austria, France, and Germany, all large loans may not exceed 800 percent of capital. In Italy, these loans may not exceed 40 percent of deposits.

No explicit guidelines exist in Finland and Sweden, but concentration levels are monitored by regulators. In Spain undue concentration is discouraged by requiring higher and higher amounts of capital to offset the risk that such concentration adds to the bank.

These regulations underscore a universally recognized principle borrowed from financial theory. Diversification is an essential element for sound loan portfolio management. Significantly, in the United States, this basic goal is frustrated by the lack of a federal provision for nationwide branching.

Capital Standards

In a commercial bank, capital serves much the same functions as capital in a nonfinancial firm. It provides a *buffer for temporary operating losses*. Capital absorbs these losses until profitability is restored so that the firm remains *solvent*, that is, its assets exceed its liabilities.

Theoretically, the solvency of a bank should be determined by *market value* of assets and liabilities rather than *book value*. However, the market value of some bank assets, especially loans, is difficult to specify. Bank regulators are studying ways in which more market value accounting (MVA) can be used. As a step in the direction of full MVA, in 1991, the Financial Accounting Standards Board (FASB) framed the Statement of Financial Accounting Standards 107 (SFAS 107). This statement requires footnote disclosure of the market value of all financial instruments, including loans, for financial statements issued after December 15, 1992.[3] For 1994 financial statements, SFAS 115 requires MVA (not merely footnote disclosure) for all marketable securities that are available for sale. Any associated gains or losses will be absorbed in earnings for the period. This pronouncement stops short of full MVA for marketable securities, however, because it excludes those marketable securities that are to be held to maturity and any related liabilities (the firm's own bonds payable).

These are measured steps toward market value accounting. In the meantime, it is the book value of equity that determines solvency and that absorbs any operating losses.

The ability of bank capital to absorb operating losses is not, of course, unlimited. Sustained losses will eventually erode the capital base and leave creditors' claims exposed. This will occur when cash inflows from operations (income statement activity) are insufficient to cover cash outflows. Conceptually, under these circumstances, the bank must liquidate assets in order to satisfy the shortfall (excess of expenses over revenues). As assets decline while liabilities do not, the capital base shrinks. If the process continues, asset values decline until liabilities are greater than assets. This function of capital as a cushion is common to all business organizations.

Bank capital also serves other functions that are important to regulators. Perceived capital adequacy increases *public confidence* in an institution. If public confidence is maintained, management can avoid unexpectedly high deposit withdrawals (bank runs). On the surface, bank runs may not appear to present a risk of insolvency since, presumably, the value of liquidated assets equals the value of deposits and other liabilities to be satisfied. However, when large quantities of assets must be sold quickly, the bank may realize less than asset carrying values, that is, sustain losses upon sale. These losses deplete capital in the same way as operating losses. Since a relatively small percentage of bank assets is financed with capital, liquidating as little as 5 percent of assets below carrying value can bring the bank close to insolvency.

Even if asset liquidation is not necessary, a loss of public confidence can increase the bank's cost of funds. If the increase is significant enough, profitability will be hurt, once again putting pressure on an already thinly capitalized institution. Thus, capital adequacy can help preserve public confidence and avoid either bank runs or high costs of doing business.

Also from a regulatory perspective, bank capital places *constraints on bank growth*. In this sense, minimum capital requirements prevent unlimited deposit taking and lending (or other investment activities). With a given capital ratio, dividend payout ratio, and rate of return on equity, a bank can expect to grow in the normal course of operating profitably.

$$\Delta \text{ TA} = (\text{ROE}) \ (\text{E}) \ (\text{b}) \ (\text{EM})$$

where Δ TA = change in the asset base for one year

ROE = return on equity (net income as a percentage of equity)

E = equity (dollar amount)

b = retention ratio (percentage of net income not paid as dividends)

EM = equity multiplier (total assets to equity)

(ROE) (E) (b) is the change in retained earnings that can be projected.[4] This addition to retained earnings forms a new equity layer that will support asset growth. When the equity multiplier is high (or the capital ratio is low), the bank's asset base can grow relatively faster. All other things being equal, regulators usually prefer to see a lower equity multiplier (higher capital ratio) because of the greater buffer against loss that it implies. Of course, regulators must seriously consider the impact of minimum capital requirements on bank profitability and competitiveness. High equity ratios also raise the cost of funds for banks and other financial institutions.

TRENDS IN REGULATION

More Formal Regulation

There are two distinctly different forms of bank regulation. The first is a *formal regulatory system*, complete with specific requirements and guidelines for balance sheet ratios. The objective of such legal stipulation is to ensure stability of bank activity and monetary conditions. Examples of formal regulatory systems are those of the United States, Japan, and continental Europe.

The second type of system involves much more informal control. This is not to suggest that orderliness is a lower priority under less formal systems. Instead, the difference appears to be more related to financial system infrastructure. Where a small number of banks has existed or where banks and other financial institutions have been concentrated within a limited geographical area, a *system of nonstatutory supervision* has evolved.

The geographically concentrated financial markets of the United Kingdom, Belgium, and Luxembourg are examples. Frequent interaction between senior bank management and supervisory authorities has made it possible for authorities to adequately assess bank operations and attendant risks. To the extent that such close contact has been effective, there exists little incentive to formalize the relationships.

Nevertheless, deregulation of financial services and the blurring of past lines of distinction between financial institutions has led to a trend toward *increased statutory guidelines* and even more effective oversight. The U.K. Banking Act of 1979 created a legislative framework for authorization of deposit-taking activity and supervision by the Bank of England. Before 1979, supervision was largely informal.

In Canada, there is a combination of informal and formal controls. The Canadian system developed after its U.S. counterpart, with the first commercial bank being chartered in 1817 and the Bank of Canada (central bank) not being created until 1934. This time difference allowed Canadians to observe some of the problems in the United States associated with having a large number of unit banks. Nationwide branching was accepted in Canada from the outset. As a result, five Canadian banks now control the vast majority of all bank assets. This structure makes it easy to coordinate policies with fewer laws and regulations. Formal controls consist mainly of laws that mandate public disclosure and regulate permissible bank activities. Laws have also been passed to allow supervisory authorities to issue formal regulations with respect to cash and secondary reserves, capital adequacy, and liquidity levels.

International Coordination

Another significant worldwide trend is toward greater *international cooperation* among supervisory authorities. Until the 1970s, there was no formalized international coordination. Then the Herstatt Bank, one of Germany's largest privately held banks, failed. This $900 million bank ran up foreign currency exchange losses in June 1974 that sent it to the Bundesbank for emergency funds. The Bundesbank found that the record-keeping was so poor that it could not determine the extent of loss within a short period of time. The bank was closed at 4:00 p.m., German time. New York banks were still open but unable to complete their currency transactions with the closed Herstatt. This, of course, also exposed the U.S. banks to loss. In the final accounting, Herstatt's losses amounted to $500 million. The growing interdependence of systems and the ease with which risk is sometimes spread across borders has led to more structured international communications.

The European Community (EC) has an ultimate goal of uniform bank regulation throughout the region.[5] The 1977 banking directive was the first step in this direction. Guidelines for bank licensing and supervision were to be formulated in as consistent a fashion as possible across EC members. To encourage the flow of information across borders, the second banking directive in 1989 is based on the concept of a single banking license. With one license a bank has the right to operate throughout the EC. (Similar provisions have been made for securities firms and insurance companies.) With this license, banks will be able to engage essentially in universal banking throughout the EC as long as there is "mutual recognition" in the home country of the bank.

The list of permissible activities includes:

- deposit-taking and other forms of borrowing

- financial leasing

- money transmission services

- guarantees and commitments

- trading for the bank's own account in CDs, bonds, government securities, futures and options, foreign currency, and securities

- issuance of securities

- money brokering

- portfolio management

- securities safekeeping services

- credit reference services

Mutual recognition essentially means that the banks from the host country must be permitted the same scope of activities in the home country of the bank being licensed. This provision has raised serious concerns on the part of U.S. banks, given the limited scope of activity they are permitted by U.S. federal regulators vis-à-vis the scope of activity for their European counterparts.

International cooperation extends beyond the EC. The Organisation for Economic Co-operation and Development (OECD) organized the Basel Committee on Banking Regulations and Supervisory Practices to address the relevant issues of international banking. The committee's report, known as the *Basel Concordat*, was completed in 1975 and subsequently revised. It was endorsed by the regulators of the Group of Ten and Luxembourg in 1983 and subsequently endorsed by the regulators of several other countries.[6] The concordat is the basis for international coordination among banking authorities.

The two broad, primary principles of the concordat are that (1) no foreign banking institution in a given host country should be without supervision, and (2) supervision should be adequate. The concordat also outlines basic areas of responsibility for oversight, assigning some functions to host country authorities and others to parent country authorities.

Functional assignments are in the areas of *solvency*, *liquidity*, and *foreign exchange operations*. Supervision to assure solvency of foreign *branches* is the primary responsibility of the parent country. The solvency of foreign *subsidiaries* is assigned to the host country, while that of *joint ventures* falls to the country of incorporation.

The level of liquidity of both branches and subsidiaries falls within the purview of host country supervisory bodies. Again, for joint ventures, the country of incorporation is held accountable. However, the liquidity of foreign offices can affect the liquidity of the group to which it belongs. So, parent countries are held responsible for adequacy of control systems and procedures.

Lastly, foreign exchange operations are the shared responsibility of host and parent countries. The host country monitors the foreign exchange position of those institutions operating within its territory. The parent monitors the position of the entire institution.

Recently, the central bankers of major industrialized countries (the so-called Group of Seven or G7) have broached the issue of whether foreign currency markets should be more closely monitored by regulators. Volatility in currency markets has frustrated steps being taken to achieve a unified European currency. The central bankers with these concerns are led by Hans Tietmeyer, successor to Helmut Schlesinger at the Deutsche Bundesbank. The problem is that highly leveraged, unsupervised hedge funds (involved in speculative currency dealings) are trading currencies and currency futures for short-term profits and complicating the management of currency values by central banks.

Steps that have been suggested to remedy this situation include levying transactions taxes on currncy trades, requiring deposits with central banks as collateral for trades, and placing a capital requirement on currency positons. Implementing any of these strategies would involve a universal and multilateral agreement. While the level of international coordination has increased substantially, there remains real doubt about the feasibility of any of these approaches. Moreover, such measures could considerably restrain the international flow of capital for all parties, not just the targeted hedge funds. As a result, it is unlikely that these measures will be instituted. Instead, central banks will be forced to adapt to market conditions and fulfill their obligations for currency management through skillful trading techniques.

In general, regulators seek to coordinate their financial systems across national borders with the same objectives that operate within—safety and soundness, efficiency, and competitiveness. As these systems evolve, the changing environment will require flexibility for the oversight function to keep pace with, but not constrain, the evolution.

The Federal Reserve worked within the OECD to encourage a harmonization of capital policy among the member countries. The objectives of these coordination efforts were:

- to reduce international differences in capital levels that gave some countries competitive advantages

- to make capital requirements sensitive to the differences in risk profiles of bank balance sheets

- to take into account the level of off-balance sheet risk exposure

- to remove any disincentives for holding safe, liquid assets

As a first step, in January 1987, the Federal Reserve and the Bank of England announced an agreement on common standards of capital. Capital would be defined as:

- equity

- retained earnings

- minority interest in subsidiaries

- perpetual debt

Also, each class of assets would be weighted depending upon riskiness of the category, and contingent liabilities would be included in the calculations.

The Federal Reserve and the Bank of England then attempted to get support for this scheme from other OECD members, especially France, Japan, and Germany. However, Japan and Germany resisted the plan for similar reasons. Japanese banks have significant amounts of land and equity stock recorded on their balance sheets at historical book values that are considerably below market value. Under the U.S.-U.K. plan, these "hidden" reserves could not be used to satisfy capital requirements. Likewise, German banks have large holdings of equity stock that would be considered capital. The Japanese, Germans, and French argued that defining an appropriate capital standard for all banks would be impossible.

In December of the same year, the Cooke Committee (Committee on Banking Regulation and Supervisory Practices of the Bank for International Settlements, also known as the Basel Committee) announced agreement on international convergence of capital standards. This agreement, the *Basel Accord*, addressed concerns of Japan and Germany in two ways. *Capital definitions* included asset revaluation reserves. Within prescribed limits, *risk weights* were left to the discretion of individual countries.

The definition of capital under the Basel Accord is as follows:

Tier I (core) capital:

- shareholders' equity
- perpetual preferred stock, net of goodwill

Tier II (supplemental) capital:

- perpetual and term subordinated debt
- mandatory convertible debt
- asset revaluation reserves
- other supplementary items at the discretion of individual countries

Tier II capital is limited to 100 percent of Tier I capital. According to the Accord, beginning January 1993, international banks must maintain both Tier I and Tier II capital equal to 4 percent of risk-weighted assets for a total capital ratio of 8 percent. Germany and Japan are permitted to use 45 percent of unrealized gains on equities held as investments toward the Tier II capital requirement. In late 1991 and early 1992, the value of Japanese equities fell dramatically because of a collapse in real estate prices and a general recession. As much as half the unrealized gains that had been available were eliminated in the sharp market decline, threatening the ability of Japanese banks to comply with the Basel Accord.

The imposition of stricter capital standards has prompted U.S. banks to respond by raising capital in the stock and bond markets, especially the large money center banks that have consistently operated with lower capital ratios than smaller regional banks. In 1992, total bank issuances amounted to $46 billion, with stock representing $10 billion and debt $36 billion. This topped the 1991 record of $29 billion in total offerings. The $1.2 billion common stock issue of Chemical Banking ranked as the largest bank issue and the fourth largest overall corporate issue for 1992.

The structural differences in the United States and Japan create a different environment for the response of banks in raising capital, however. The major Japanese banks, the *city banks*, are members of Japanese *keiretsu*. As much as 80 percent of stock of these firms is owned by other firms in the group—commercial and industrial firms. Since the mid-1980s, between 60 and 90 percent of all new common stock issued by Japanese banks has been purchased by other *keiretsu* members. In addition, the banks have raised funds through subordinated bonds issued through offshore subsidiaries and subordinated loans borrowed primarily from domestic life insurance companies, generally members of their own *keiretsu*. For example, in the last few months of fiscal year 1992, Bank of Tokyo, Mitsubishi Bank, Fuji Bank, Sanwa Bank, and Tokai raised the equivalent of $1.9 billion in this way.

The recent improvement in the Japanese stock market also has helped the Japanese city banks meet the requirements of the Basel capital standards. As of September 1992, the city banks were comfortably above the minimum 8 percent level of total capital to risk-weighted assets.

Bank	Ratio
Dai-Ichi Kangyo	8.5%
Hokkaido	8.9
Bank of Tokyo	8.8
Sakura	8.4
Mitsubishi	8.7
Fuji	8.7
Sumitomo	8.8
Daiwa	8.9
Sanwa	8.8
Tokai	8.7
Asahi	8.6

Thus, despite periodic reverses in the Japanese stock market and the attendant erosion of Japanese bank capital ratios, the capital levels in the Japanese banking system are less easily compared with U.S. counterparts. In the United States, commercial and other financial firms may not hold significant equity stakes in commercial banks. Nor are there groups of firms that consider it in their best interest to preserve the long-term viability of a specific bank.

ADVOCATE VS. ADVERSARY

This difference in the U.S. and Japanese systems goes well beyond the issue of adequate capital levels. In fact, there are significant differences in the regulatory environment of banks in the United States and those in other countries. These differences help to explain the major influence of foreign banks in the United States. The dynamics of the relationship between the banking industry and its regulators have far-reaching impact.

The United States

For historical reasons, in the United States, the relationship between government and business has been a somewhat arms-length arrangement. This appears to be attributable to two primary factors. First, large concentrations of financial power have never been readily accepted, as evidenced by an extensive body of antitrust law and court cases. Secondly, strong emphasis on public disclosure of government activity has produced "sunshine" and freedom-of-information laws.

These factors have made it difficult for commercial banks and government officials in the United States to develop extremely close working relationships. From the banks' perspective, the loss of confidentiality that would accompany a closer relationship with government could be a disadvantage, particularly if the bank sought greater market share or contemplated a politically unfavorable (albeit completely legal) strategy.

As a result of these factors, the relationship between U.S. banks and government may be accurately characterized as adversarial. The focus of U.S. legislation has been geared more towards protecting consumers and less towards reviewing policies to ensure the international competitiveness of U.S. banks.

Active Consumer Protection. In 1968, the *Consumer Credit Protection Act* was passed. This multi-faceted law was quite explicit in protecting the rights of consumers from any misconduct on the part of banks in their consumer banking activities. The primary legislation was contained in seven different sections of the act:

- *Truth-in-Lending Act* (TILA)—effective July 1969. TILA is designed to ensure that consumers more easily understand the terms of credit and avoid the uninformed use of credit.

- *Fair Credit Billing Act* (FCBA)—effective October 1975. FCBA addresses the resolution of billing errors in connection with credit card accounts.

- *Consumer Leasing Act* (CLA)—effective March 1977. CLA essentially covers the same type of disclosure as for loans (TILA) in the area of consumer leases of personal property for personal, family, or household use.

- *Fair Credit Reporting Act* (FCRA)—effective April 1971. FCRA regulates consumer reporting by placing disclosure obligations on users of credit reports; requiring fair, timely, and accurate reporting of credit information; restricting use of credit reports; and requiring deletion of obsolete information.

- *Fair Credit Opportunity Act* (FCOA)—effective October 1975. FCOA prohibits treating any applicant or group of applicants less favorably than others on the basis of race, color, religion, national origin, sex, marital status, age, or receipt of income from public assistance sources.

- *Fair Debt Collection Practices Act* (FDCPA)—effective March 1978. FDCPA is intended to protect consumers from abusive, deceptive, and unfair debt collection practices.

- *Electronic Fund Transfers Act* (EFTA)—fully effective May 1980. EFTA establishes the rights and responsibilities of participants in electronic funds transfer systems.

Enforcement of most of these acts is effected through Federal Reserve regulations. In addition to these provisions of the Consumer Credit Protection Act, other laws have been enacted that govern consumer banking. The *Fair Housing Act* (a component of the Civil Rights Act of 1968) has been interpreted by the courts to prohibit lending institutions from such practices as redlining (denying mortgage loans in certain areas even though applicants otherwise qualify), making excessively low property appraisal values in the case of minority applicants (forcing higher down payments), or establishing excessively burdensome qualification standards for minority applicants.

The *Community Reinvestment Act* (CRA) of 1977 is another significant consumer protection law. It requires federal regulators (Comptroller, Federal Reserve, and FDIC) to encourage the banks they oversee to provide for the credit needs of the communities they serve.[7] The law mandates that regulators assess an institution's record of providing for the credit needs of the entire community, including low- and moderate-income neighborhoods. This record is to be considered when a bank seeks a new charter, acquires shares of another bank, or merges with another bank.

The objective of the CRA is to discourage the practice of redlining. If banks wish to expand, this legislation requires that they demonstrate that they are not neglecting underserved, disadvantaged areas, although if a bank is not located to serve such an area, the law has virtually no effect on it.

The Financial Institutions Reform, Recovery, and Enforcement Act of 1989 (FIRREA) strengthened the 1977 law by requiring that regulators regularly prepare a written evaluation of each bank's community reinvestment. A portion of this evaluation that must now be made public includes the institution's rating:

- outstanding
- satisfactory

- needs to improve

- substantial noncompliance

The documentation for the rating must also be made public.
Other laws which impact consumer banking practices include:

- The Real Estate Settlement Procedures Act of 1974, requiring relevant and timely disclosures as to the nature and cost of the real estate settlement process.

- The Expedited Funds Availability Act (a component of the Competitive Equality Banking Act of 1987), placing restrictions on the length of time that a bank may deny funds availability after a customer deposits checks.

- The Bank Secrecy Act of 1970 and its 1986 amendment contained in the Money Laundering Control Act of 1986, requiring banks to report deposit, withdrawal, or other exchange of currency in the amount of $10,000 or more.

- The Right to Financial Privacy Act of 1978, prohibiting the disclosure of customer information to federal authorities in the absence of specific documentation.

- The Truth in Savings Act of 1987, requiring full disclosure of interest rates, fees, minimum balances, term, and penalties for all demand or interest-bearing accounts.

As illustrated by this partial list of laws that cover consumer banking, the government has been quite focused on the protection of consumer rights. While such protection is clearly warranted, some have also argued that the burden of compliance has become excessive. It has been estimated that the U.S. banking industry spends $11 billion annually to comply with bank regulations—fully a third of the industry's net income for 1992.

Benign Neglect of the Banks. At the same time, U.S. lawmakers have been less consistent in their attention to necessary legislative remedies to make the banking system more internationally competitive. Federal bank regulation has limited the natural expansion of the banking system almost from the outset. From 1933 to 1978 this regulation was particularly restrictive. Since that time, the remedies that have been afforded only partially address the issue of international competitiveness.

The National Bank Act of 1863 created a banking organization that would be chartered under federal law by the Office of the Comptroller of the Currency. The national bank would not repeat the "mistakes" of the First Bank of the United States (1791–1811) or of the Second Bank of the United States (1816–1836). These earlier federal banks had branched nationwide, had infringed on the perceived territorial rights of state-chartered banks, and (as a direct result) had not been granted renewal of their 20-year charters.

Because the earlier banks had been so unpopular with certain powerful political forces, the geographic scope of national banks was restricted to one location. Thus, national banks were originally unit banks with no branches, rendering them less threatening and more readily accepted. Meanwhile, state banks were granted a much wider geographic scope of operation and given less restrictive guidelines as to capital, lending, and liquidity requirements. State bank charters offered many advantages not shared by national banks. At the same time, national banks were expected to help solidify the banking system and the currency by issuing bank notes (bank liabilities convertible into gold or silver) that were uniform regardless of the state in which they operated.

Such contradictions in policy did not address the need for a strong, unified national banking system. Instead, a *dual-banking* system developed, with banks chartered by both state banking authorities and the Comptroller of the Currency. This is an early example of the lack of a comprehensive, coherent policy to address the banking needs of the country.

After persistent money panics continued to occur, the Federal Reserve Act of 1913 created a central banking mechanism with 12 districts, presumably to address the problems of the fragmented banking system that had evolved. (By 1920, there were over 30,000 banks in the United States—with both state and national charters.) The Federal Reserve Act also began to loosen the restrictions on national banks. Up to this time, only state banks and private, nonincorporated banks were permitted to establish foreign branches. Essentially, there had not been much interest in international operations before World War I because Great Britain was the primary exporter of capital and had assumed the role of world banker.

Around the turn of the century, industry in the United States grew and, along with it, U.S. exports. In 1860 the U.S. trade surplus (exports in excess of imports) was $38 million; by 1920, it had increased to almost $3 billion. In 1913, there were only six state-chartered banking organizations that engaged in overseas banking. The Federal Reserve Act gave national banks permission to establish foreign branches by obtaining permission from the Comptroller of the Currency. To qualify, a bank was required to have $1 million in capital and to agree to full disclosure with respect to foreign branch operations.

Edge Act and Agreement Corporations. A 1916 amendment of the Federal Reserve Act empowered national banks (with $1 million in capital) to invest up to 10 percent of capital in state-chartered banks or corporations that were engaged primarily in international banking. These *Agreement corporations* agreed to be subject to limitations and restrictions imposed by the Federal Reserve Board.

Another amendment of the Federal Reserve Act in 1919 created *Edge Act corporations*, which are federally chartered institutions for foreign transactions. An added advantage of Edge Act corporations is that they may invest in nonbank financial institutions, a privilege not explicitly granted to Agreement corporations.

The McFadden Act. With these laws, federal legislators exhibited an interest in encouraging the international competitiveness of U.S. banks. This intent is further evidenced by enactment of the McFadden Act of 1927 which gave national banks the ability to branch within their home states to the extent allowed by state law. National banks were no longer required to maintain a unit banking structure. The McFadden legislation thus represented a kind of liberation of the national banking system. However, in the context of today's banking environment, the McFadden Act is much more restrictive than the laws that govern branching in other countries. The conditions under which U.S. banks must compete has changed dramatically, but federal law with respect to branching has not.

The Glass-Steagall Act. The Banking Act of 1933, often referred to as the Glass-Steagall Act, represented a significant shift in legislative attitude toward the U.S. banking system. The commercial banking industry was stripped of the ability to meaningfully participate in long-term financing of corporate America. Before the Stock Market Crash of 1929, major U.S. banks frequently engaged in both short-term and long-term financing. However, the banks were accused of conflict of interest—promoting questionable securities and then selling them to their deposit clients and trust accounts. The two types of activities would be separated and commercial banking made safer.

The Federal Deposit Insurance Corporation was created to give depositors confidence in the new, more narrowly focused banking system. Interest paid on demand deposits was prohibited; interest paid on savings and time deposits was regulated. Moreover, no institution that engaged in securities transactions could issue deposits. Thus, commercial banks received a bank-financed insurance program and a steady source of low-cost funds.

Bank failures on the scale that had been experienced would hopefully be averted in the future. From a high of 30,000 banks in 1920, the number of U.S. banks plummeted to 15,000 by 1933. From 1929 to early 1933, the money supply shrank by more than one-third. The crisis had not been contained by the Federal Reserve. In fact, the country's banking problems were exacerbated by Federal Reserve actions. The Fed engaged in open-market operations to purchase securities and increase the money supply in 1932 for only a brief period of time. Beginning in April, the Fed bought as much as $100 million in government securities per week. When the effort abruptly ended in early summer, massive bank failures soon resumed. As a result of the Depression and the accompanying banking crisis, the Federal Reserve was reorganized to give more power to the Federal Reserve Board of Governors in Washington.[8] The Federal Open Market Committee was established to set government monetary policy.

While the Federal Reserve was reorganized in the aftermath of the crisis, the commercial banking system was effectively punished.

Exclusive rights to issue deposit instruments, interest-rate ceilings, and deposit insurance were exchanged for the ability to compete in the long-term financing of corporate clients. This was an inappropriate response to the problems of the 1930s. The Depression and massive bank failures occurred as a result of depressed prices, accompanying business failures, and a contracted money supply—not because commercial banks underwrote corporate stocks and bonds. To make matters worse, foreign banks with U.S. affiliates were not affected by the Glass-Steagall reforms. This was a significant turning point in the relationship between the banking industry and the U.S. legislature. It marked the beginning of a period of neglect of the competitive needs of the banking system.

Growth of International Banking. Ironically, the industrial production associated with World War II (1939–45) helped to revitalize the U.S. economy to a great extent. As a result, the vulnerability of the banking system that had been legislated in 1933 was not immediately apparent. After the war, the United States enjoyed a competitive advantage in that it supplied the capital and the goods to rebuild much of Europe through the $12 billion Marshall Plan. As European economies recovered and U.S. demand for goods (pent-up by wartime restrictions) expanded, international trade expanded. U.S. companies established overseas operations and the Eurodollar market developed.[9]

As U.S. banks sought to participate in the Eurodollar market, foreign banks also entered the United States when foreign companies also established U.S. operations. Because these foreign banks were not subject to Glass-Steagall, they were not limited in scope of activities. Nor were they limited to geographic expansion in one state by provisions of the McFadden Act. Foreign banks frequently operated their U.S. affiliates under the laws of applicable states. Under these laws, they could cross state lines, engage in nonbanking activities, maintain lower capital levels than national banks, avoid federal reserve requirements and interest rate ceilings, and decline federal deposit insurance. The vulnerabilities of federal bank legislation were becoming more apparent.

The Bank Holding Company Act. U.S. banks reacted by forming bank holding companies that obeyed the letter, if not the spirit, of federal regulation. Bank holding companies enabled banks to operate across state lines and to engage in nonbank activities. The 1933 Banking Act had made some provision for the regulation of bank holding companies, but had essentially left them free to compete in other lines of commerce. Moreover, under the 1933 act, if the existing bank holding companies already had interstate activities, these were exempted from federal regulation, that is, they were grandfathered.

Federal legislators again exhibited a restrictive attitude toward U.S. banks by enacting the Bank Holding Company Act of 1956. There were several motivations for this legislation:

- There was a fear of financial concentration that would result from a few multistate bank holding companies controlling a large share of the banking assets of the United States.

- If major nonfinancial corporations were affiliated with commercial banks, these firms could dominate the U.S. economy.

- It was felt that banking should not be exposed to undue risk. If a particular activity was considered unsafe for a commercial bank, it should also be considered unsafe for a bank holding company.

- There was a concern that nonfinancial firms that were affiliated with a bank would have an unfair advantage over those firms that did not with respect to preferential financing arrangements.

The Bank Holding Company Act required that holding companies that owned more than one commercial bank divest of those activities that could not be classified as "closely related" to banking. The 1966 Douglas Amendment to the Bank Holding Company Act restricted the ability of bank holding companies from acquiring institutions in other states by prohibiting such acquisitions unless specifically authorized by the laws of the state of the bank being acquired.

U.S. banks were forced to find the loopholes in federal regulation in order to expand and diversify. One such loophole was the one-bank holding company—not subject to federal regulation. Typically, this form of business organization involved a small commercial bank with one or several other nonbank businesses, frequently including insurance. However, there were a few one-bank holding companies that represented more prominent industrial firms. These latter companies were clear examples of the combination of banking and commerce that Congress had sought to avoid. And their numbers increased dramatically—from 117 in 1955 to 783 in 1968. It was found in a study of 684 of the one-bank holding companies that 578 conducted 20 different *financial* nonbank activities and that 397 were involved in 99 different *nonfinancial* nonbank activities.

Such combinations proliferated because of natural synergies. These synergies had been observed in the United States before Glass-Steagall and can still be observed in Japanese *keiretsus*. However, the U.S. legislature chose to further restrict the banking industry. In a 1970 amendment of the Bank Holding Company Act, Congress extended the regulations to one-bank holding companies. Any impermissible activities begun after June 1968 were to be divested within 10 years. Those begun before this date were grandfathered on the condition that the Federal Reserve review the grandfathered status of nonbanking activities for bank holding companies with assets in excess of $60 million.

Certain activities have been exempted from provisions of the Bank Holding Company Act. Currently, holding companies can own:

- shares in an investment company which is not a bank holding company and which is not engaged in any business other than investing in securities

- shares of any company which is an export trading company[10]

- up to 5 percent of any company, including nonfinancial firms[11]

Notably, foreign banks were also exempted from the 1970 amendment of the Bank Holding Company Act. Foreign banks in the United States continued to enjoy a full range of privileges not available to U.S. banks.

Regulation K. The restrictions on U.S. banks were partially relieved by a 1962 amendment of the Federal Reserve Act which allowed U.S.

national banks to participate in activities on foreign soil that were classified as impermissible if conducted on domestic soil. Regulation K (which governed the international operations of national banks) was amended to include a statement of national purpose with respect to U.S. bank competitiveness overseas.[12]

> The Congress, in enacting section 25(a) of the Act, provided for the establishment of international banking and financial corporations operating under Federal supervision with powers sufficiently broad to enable them to compete effectively with similar foreign-owned institutions and to afford to the United States exporter and importer in particular—and to United States commerce, industry, and agriculture in general—at all times a means of financing international trade.

> In light of the purposes involved, Corporations should be able in their activities abroad to operate, as best meets their corporate policies, through branches, agencies, and correspondents or through direct and indirect ownership in foreign-chartered companies engaged in banking or other international or foreign operations so as their credit and other activities are in the interest of the United States.

This was recognition of the need for U.S. banks to be internationally competitive overseas. The permissible activities for overseas affiliates includes commercial banking and finance; leasing as functional equivalent of an extension of credit; providing investment advisory services; operating a general insurance agency; managing a mutual fund; providing management consulting services; operating a travel agency in connection with financial services offered abroad; and underwriting, distributing, and dealing in debt and equity securities with certain dollar limits. In some cases, banks have also been permitted to underwrite insurance in other countries.

The dollar limits that are imposed on national banks with respect to their securities operations can be quite restrictive, however. No foreign affiliate may underwrite more than $2 million and total underwritings for all subsidiaries may not exceed $15 million. Such low underwriting limits make it exceedingly difficult for U.S. banks to become lead managers, that is, major participants, in large public offerings overseas. In addition, a foreign affiliate of a U.S. bank may underwrite no more than 20 percent of the equity of a commercial firm.

Moreover, until the Fed approval of Section 20 subsidiaries in 1989, no U.S. bank was permitted to participate in *any* corporate securities underwriting domestically. For the years that elapsed between 1933 and 1978, foreign banks had a clear advantage over domestic banks in the United States. Foreign banks were not subject to the provisions of Glass-Steagall or the Bank Holding Company Act.

International Banking Act. It was not until enactment of the International Banking Act in 1978 that the playing field for U.S. banks was at least partially leveled. The act does not directly make foreign banks subject to Glass-Steagall, but instead, takes the approach of making them bank holding companies. As such, foreign banks must adhere to the list of permissible nonbank activities. Since corporate securities underwriting is not on this list, the act effectively precluded their participation in this activity. However, the securities subsidiaries of the 17 foreign banks that already existed were grandfathered. In addition, any foreign affiliate operating as a federal branch was required to be insured by FDIC if it accepted deposits in amounts less than $100,000.

The International Banking Act placed U.S. banks on more equal footing but it did not remove the advantages that foreign banks had accrued in the United States during the period from 1933 to 1978. Nor did it address the restricted activities of U.S. banks overseas vis-à-vis their counterparts from other countries.

The FDIC Improvement Act of 1991. Provisions of the FDICIA, among other things, attempted to lessen the differences in operational freedom among domestic nationally chartered banks, state banks, and foreign banks.[13] Instead of giving greater freedoms to national banks, however, it reduced the scope of activity for the other two categories. The act restricts state banks' ability to:

- own and develop real estate
- underwrite securities
- act as real estate brokers

- sell or underwrite insurance.

FDICIA limits a state bank's insurance underwriting and equity investments to those allowed for national banks. If a state bank wishes to act as principal in nonpermissible activities, it must comply with all capital standards and have a written determination from FDIC that the activity poses no significant threat to the deposit insurance fund. Those banks that underwrite insurance in Delaware are grandfathered with respect to any underwriting engaged in before November 1991. Savings banks in New York and New England also may continue to offer life insurance.

State-licensed branches or agencies of foreign banks are subject to similar provisions. Specifically, the Fed may approve nonpermissible activities *if* it finds that the activity is consistent with sound banking practices. Additionally, if a foreign branch is insured, the FDIC must find that the activity poses no significant risk to the insurance fund.

An Appeal to Government. In this environment of tightening regulations, the banking industry has appealed to the U.S. government for specific relief. Six major bank trade associations—the American Bankers Association, the Association of Reserve City Bankers, the Consumer Bankers Association, the Independent Bankers Association of America, the Association of Bank Holding Companies, and the Savings and Community Bankers of America—formally have asked U.S. President Bill Clinton to eliminate those requirements that restrict lending and impede economic growth and job-creation. Among their recommendations are:

- repeal certain provisions of the Federal Deposit Insurance Corporation Improvement Act that significantly increase the cost of compliance

- eliminate market value accounting

- use incentives instead of penalties to encourage lending in economically depressed communities

- reduce the frequency of regulatory examinations

- reduce maximum financial penalties on bank officers

These requests reflect the frustration felt by the U.S. banking community. The general feeling appears to be that there is too much regulation and that it chokes the ability of commercial banks to adequately serve their clientele.

In the context of the legislative structure of the U.S. banking system, the adversarial nature of the relationship between U.S. banks and their legislators becomes clear. The regulatory process perhaps is viewed as one which imposes restrictions that leave the banks openly vulnerable to competitive forces that they cannot effectively counteract. This natural tension between bankers and regulators is not as readily apparent in other countries.

The United Kingdom

The United States has three federal bank regulators—the Comptroller of the Currency (national banks), the Federal Reserve (bank holding companies and state-chartered members of the Fed), and the Federal Deposit Insurance Corporation (insured banks and state-chartered nonmembers of the Fed). In addition, there are 50 state banking authorities. In contrast, most of the other G-10 have only one chief bank regulator.[14] This makes coordinating and implementing regulatory policies much less complicated. Even when there are regulators along functional lines, for example, a banking regulator and a securities regulator, one is designated as the "lead regulator" to streamline the process. Implementation is also made more efficient by the existence of a few large banks in these countries, as compared to thousands of banks in the United States.

In the case of the United Kingdom, the primary bank regulator is the central bank, the Bank of England. The role of the Bank has evolved over time and is characterized by a tradition of "gentlemen's agreements" between it and other British banks. There is no equivalent of the Glass-Steagall Act in the United Kingdom. Until recently, specialized financial institutions engaged in narrowly focused activities because of tradition, not regulation. The U.K. financial system developed with relatively few regulatory guidelines. Originally, the Bank of England was given special privileges in exchange for its financial services to the government. U.K. clearing (commercial) and merchant banks are expected to obtain the concurrence of the Bank of England before taking any significant action.

Recently, the United Kingdom has moved away from this informal system and toward a more structured one. Reasons for this trend are:

- required harmonization of banking regulations in accordance with European Community directives

- changes in the structure of the City (London's financial district) caused by the Big Bang of 1986 which accelerated the move toward broad-based, diversified financial institutions

- growth in the number of firms operating in the City

- the failures of several financial institutions

In 1974, several smaller institutions failed and the Bank of England organized a "lifeboat" rescue to maintain liquidity in the system. The 1979 Banking Act formalized the role of the Bank of England as supervisor of the banking system and required all deposit-taking institutions to be licensed by the Bank. When Johnson Matthey Bankers failed in 1984, concerns were raised once again as to the adequacy of bank regulation. The Banking Act of 1987 further strengthened the powers of the Bank of England. Nevertheless, the U.K. central bank continues to exhibit a preference for informal approaches to bank supervision and regulation.

There is a higher degree of informality and flexibility in the U.K. system relative to the U.S. system. The Bank of England does not conduct on-site examinations of banks, but instead relies on regularly filed, detailed statistical reports and on meetings with management. The Bank also uses private audit reports. This approach makes it possible to review each institution on a case-by-case basis. There is little need for extensive regulations to govern each aspect of banking.

When financial institutions acquire other firms or engage in new activities in the United Kingdom, they need not make formal application. Instead, it is only necessary to seek the approval of the Bank of England on an informal basis. The Bank has considerable influence in this informal process and a financial firm is unlikely to act against the advice of the Bank.

Clearing banks have always been permitted to engage in securities activities and there are no formal restrictions on the relationship between banks and nonfinancial firms. Although not required to do so, most banks conduct their securities activities through separate subsidiaries. Also, banks may extend credit to their securities subsidiaries as long as such credit is made available in accordance with prudent banking practice and within those guidelines established by the Bank of England.

British banks may engage in almost any type of financial activity. Three exceptions to this general rule are also permitted but must be conducted in separated capitalized subsidiaries:

- government securities dealings

- life assurance (insurance) activities

- management of a unit trust (mutual fund)

In this way, clearing banks have been permitted to develop into diversified financial services groups that engage in universal banking.

The Financial Services Act of 1987 created an elaborate system of authorization, regulation, and supervision. Under this act, the Department of Trade and Industry (DTI) was given the responsibility to regulate U.K. securities industry. DTI delegated responsibilities for securities regulation to the newly formed Securities and Investments Board (SIB), which it oversees. The SIB is functionally similar to the U.S. Securities and Exchange Commission (SEC) except that it is a private organization, financed by fees of its members. Self Regulatory Organizations (SROs) set the standards of conduct and practice for their members.

The Financial Services Act requires that any firm that engages in "investment activities" be authorized by either the SIB or by its SRO. Investment activities include providing investment advice and the sale or management of:

- equity shares

- corporate bonds

- government and local bonds

- depository receipts

- warrants

- units in a unit investment trust

- options and futures

The SROs that cover various investment activities are:

- Securities Association

- Investment Management Regulatory Organization

- Association of Futures Brokers and Dealers

- Financial Intermediaries Managers

- Brokers Regulatory Association

- Life Assurance and Unit Trust Regulatory Organization

Since British banks perform a number of financial services, they must be members of each applicable SRO. This is considered *functional* regulation, that is, regulation by type of activity. To reduce duplication of effort, however, each type of institution has a "lead regulator," which designation depends on the primary function of the financial institution. For a banking group, the Bank of England is lead regulator and sets requirements for the firm as a whole. The various SROs are responsible for the firm's compliance only in their functional areas.

In terms of nonfinancial activities, there are no legal barriers between banking and industry. Traditionally, however, the Bank of England has indicated that proposals for a combination of banking and industrial/commercial firms would be subject to close scrutiny because of the concentrated nature of banking in the United Kingdom. Commercial banks do own merchant banks that, in turn, own equity in nonfinancial, commercial, and industrial firms. The reverse is not observed—merchant banks do not own commercial banks. Moreover, it is not anticipated that commercial banks will become direct owners of large amounts of industrial equities.

Nevertheless, the full range of financial services is open to British banks. The relationship between the banks and their regulators is based on a kind of mutual respect that transcends rules and regulations. Part of this phenomenon is attributable to common background and experience, particularly with respect to the Conservative Party in the government. Beginning in the 1960s, young members of the Tory party often were invited to spend several years working in the City—providing them with insight into the financial community and perhaps instilling a certain amount of loyalty to the firms operating there. In addition, the case-by-case style of regulation in the United Kingdom makes it easier to avoid offensive or defensive positions that can be encouraged by a extensive amount of written rules. Potential problems are more quickly addressed and the financial system is not exposed to decades of overly restrictive regulation.

Germany

The Banking Act of 1961 defines banking business in Germany. The specified activities include:

- deposit taking

- consumer and industrial lending

- trading (for the account of others) government debt instruments and corporate debt and equity securities

- operating a mutual fund that

- custodial securities business

Any firm that is engaged in banking business is considered a bank and must be licensed and supervised by the Federal Banking Supervisory Office and the Bundesbank (central bank). In addition to the activities specified in the Banking Act, banks offer other services, within the bank itself:

- underwriting and dealing in government and corporate debt and equity instruments

- investment advice that

- management consulting

- factoring

- leasing

- real estate brokerage and investment

These functions are performed in departments within the bank, not in separate subsidiaries. The separation between commercial and investment banking that is observed in the United States does not exist in Germany. Moreover, the structure of subsidiaries to separate the functions within a banking group, as in the United Kingdom, is not used. In fact, it is felt that using such "firewalls" only constrains the flow of funds within the bank.

The subsidiary structure is required in Germany for the following lines of business:

- insurance

- investment fund (mutual fund)

- issuance of mortgage-backed bonds and municipal bonds backed by loans to municipalities

- transactions of building and loan associations

German banks can be classified by legal form and ownership: commercial banks (including the Big Three—Deutsche Bank, Dresdner Bank, and Commerzbank—and regional banks), savings banks (with municipal, regional, or state authorities providing capital), cooperative banks (with members providing capital), and specialized banks (including mortgage banks and building and loan associations). Regardless of legal structure, approximately 95 percent of German banks can engage in universal banking. Historically, many have elected to specialize in particular lines of business. More recently, however, competitive pressures have resulted in an expansion of services offered.

In terms of regulation, the Bundesbank acts primarily to collect data from the banks in a network of regional and local offices. The primary regulatory responsibility rests with the Federal Banking Supervisory Office (FBSO). The FBSO regulates the activities of all forms of German banks. In this role, the agency has a broad range of powers including information gathering, investigation, and intervention. It is also within the purview of the FBSO to determine appropriate levels of capital and liquidity, relying less on routine on-site examinations and more on annual external audits, detailed periodic reports, and special investigations.

As is true in the case of U.K. bank regulation, German regulation is less adversarial. Like their U.S. counterparts, professional banking associations have formed to represent the interests of their members. Unlike the U.S. case, however, the German government is required by law to consult with these banking associations when new or amended banking regulations are being considered. This arrangement gives banking associations a semi-official status.

This relationship between banking and government has not gone without challenge and strong debate about the role of universal banks. The issue has been whether these banks, particularly the Big Three which own a large share of German industrial stocks, wield too much power. In 1979, the Gessler Commission, among other things, examined whether banks faced a conflict of interest. Did their close relationships with clients provide them with insider information that gave them an unfair advantage in equity markets? In its findings the commission endorsed the present system and did not conclude that German banks had excessive control over German industry. The commission did recommend, however, that banks limit their equity holdings to 25 percent of the equity capital of a particular firm. Recently, the German Monopolies Commission recommended that equity participations be limited to 5 percent of bank capital.

Over the last decade, German banks have substantially reduced their stock investments in nonfinancial firms. It is notable that this has been accomplished without the force of law and without stripping German banks of their universal banking powers. The relationship between banks and government works well in that the objectives of both sectors appear to be largely accomplished through consultation and negotiation.

Another example of this working relationship involves the German export sector which consistently has been the key to German economic viability. The banks have generally conducted international business in a way that was consistent with the government's foreign policy interests. An effective way to elicit commercial bank support of overseas trade has been the *government guarantee* of loans for international trade. These guarantees signal official desires, without resorting to directives. *Moral suasion* and implied *future government assistance* (as needed) have also been used.

Standard guarantees, for exports and raw materials, available on a fee basis, help to both stimulate the export sector and to assure adequate quantities of raw materials necessary for the industrial sector. Most individual transactions have little or no impact on foreign policy. Thus, the *Hermes guarantee,* as such a guarantee is called, is important to a German bank only if the financial risk of the underlying international loan exceeds the bank's comfort level.

In some cases, however, specific transactions have considerable significance for foreign policy. In those situations, *exceptional guarantees* may be issued. The standard Hermes guarantees cover from 85 percent of the loan (in the case of a German export) to 95 percent (in the case of a German import). In exceptional circumstances, insurance coverage is reduced or increased.

For example, in 1976, the potential sale of nuclear reactors to Brazil had significant consequences for the German nuclear energy sector. At the time, the domestic market was saturated, with only 70 percent utilization of nuclear power plant manufacturing facilities. The government had invested $5 billion in research and development. Up to 13,000 domestic jobs were at stake. Further, if the transaction were completed, the government would be in a much better position to obtain long-term supplies of uranium from deposits in Brazil.

The Hermes guarantee associated with the sale of these reactors covered 95 percent of the loan, rather than the customary 85 percent. The term of the guarantee was 20 years, an unusually long period of time for an export/import transaction. In this case, the government worked with the banking industry to bring about a desirable outcome for the entire German economy.

More recently, the banking system worked in close partnership with the government to ease the monetary transition of the reunification of East and West Germany. In April 1990, the ostmarks of the East Germany were to be converted to Deutsche marks. Without such a conversion, in advance of formal reunification, it would have been extremely difficult for the German government to stem the flow of East Germans to the West. This involved providing 16.5 million East Germans with cash in two days, exchanging Deutsche marks for ostmarks on a one-for-one basis (using bank accounts as well as notes and coin) and converting 28 million savings and checking accounts on July 1 from ostmarks to Deutsche marks.

In 1989, when it became clear that, in the future, West German banks would be permitted to operate once again in East Germany, Deutsche Bank began to give crash courses in banking to the staff of East German banks. Managers were taught the basics of the West German social market economy during weekend seminars. East German bankers learned the modern technology of electronic funds transfer. Other West German banks joined the crusade to update the East German system. In the process, Deutsche Bank, Dresdner Bank, and Commerzbank have collectively opened over 300 new offices. Each of the Big Three has already spent or plans to spend up to DM1 billion in acquisitions and start-up costs in eastern Germany. It is clear that the banking system played a critical role in those early days of German reunification. It is equally clear that the relationship between the German government and banking sectors is typically one of mutual support.

Japan

The Japanese regulatory structure for banks is even more streamlined than the German. The Ministry of Finance is the principal regulator of the entire Japanese financial system. It is made up of seven bureaus: Budget (government expenditures), Tax (government revenue), Finance (government debt), Customs (customs revenue), Banking (banking sector), Securities (securities sector), International Finance (foreign operations of Japanese financial institutions). With the exception of the minister and two vice-ministers, the Ministry of Finance is composed of bureaucrats that typically spend their entire 30-year careers with the Ministry. While there is potential for conflict between the bureaus, most personnel rotate assignments within the Ministry, generally every two years. This enhances the amount of cooperation and coordination between the bureaus.

The Ministry of Finance is thus one unified regulator with duties that parallel a number of U.S. agencies—the Federal Reserve Board, the Office of the Comptroller of the Currency, the Federal Deposit Insurance Corporation, the Office of Thrift Supervision, the Securities and Exchange Commission, the Commodities Future Trading Corporation, and the U.S. Treasury (including the Internal Revenue Service).

The Bank of Japan (central bank) is under the direction of the Ministry of Finance. The Bank also exerts control over commercial banks because it lends funds to Japanese banks to a much greater extent than U.S. banks are permitted to borrow from the Federal Reserve. Also, the Bank monitors bank positions and uses "window guidance" to tell banks what it feels is appropriate with respect to lending policy. While banks are not required to comply with these suggestions, the Bank's control over credit markets ensures compliance.

While this system appears to offer the banks very little input into the process of regulation and operation, the relationship between Japanese banks and regulators is characterized by negotiation. For example, in 1965 the Diet (federal legislature) was faced with an economic recession. Together the Diet and the Ministry of Finance constructed a plan for deficit spending to spur the economy. A Government Bond Syndicate was formed in the fall of 1965 that would function as an alternative to the open market issuance of government bonds. Leaders of the banking community worked with members of the Debt Division of the Finance Bureau. Together, they agreed upon a mutually acceptable bond issue for the entire year. Each month the syndicate purchased the allocation and one year later the bonds were repurchased by the government at par.

The banks agreed not to deal in bonds, as this was the right of securities firms. Over time, bank holdings of government bonds grew—to ¥4.5 trillion in 1975, ¥11 trillion in 1977, and then ¥18.4 trillion in 1978—and the government grew less willing to buy back large quantities for fear of the inflationary effects. Understandably, the banks sought the right to trade these government bonds. The securities firms (perhaps just as understandably) resisted this infringement on their turf, noting that Article 65 expressly prohibited banks from engaging in securities activities.

Together, the Banking Bureau and the Securities Bureau within the Ministry of Finance reached a compromise. In the Banking Act of 1982, banks were given the ability to sell government bonds over the counter to profit from price fluctuations beginning April 1983 and in the secondary market beginning June 1984. In exchange, securities firms were allowed to lend money to customers using government bonds as collateral. By 1984, the bond market in Japan was second only to that of the United States, with most of the activity in government bonds. Other bank reforms have followed—all the result of compromises between the banking system and the Ministry of Finance.

Essentially, major Japanese banks view matters from a long-term perspective in which their own success is tied to the nation's economic viability. This process of compromise is also apparent in the area of international banking. Japanese banks frequently concentrate on lending and deposit-taking in countries that are major trading partners. Since Japan depends so heavily on imported raw materials and other goods, there are numerous overseas bank locations in resource-rich nations. Frequently, the government has used international lending to offset deficits and surpluses in the country's balance of payments.

In the early 1970s, Japan enjoyed trade surpluses and a buildup of official international reserves (foreign currency). From 1970 to 1973, foreign-currency-denominated loans were permitted for the first time and restrictions on capital export (overseas loans and other investments) were relaxed. The government itself deposited substantial amounts of foreign currency in the banking system which enabled commercial banks to develop a Euroloan portfolio.

From 1973 to 1975, Japanese surpluses turned into deficits as steep crude oil price increases took their toll. The government reacted by restricting medium- and long-term loans to nonresidents denominated in foreign currency. At the same time, incentives to encourage capital inflow (borrowing from overseas sources) were instituted. As the balance of payments has changed from surplus to deficit and then back again, the Japanese government has adjusted the restrictions on international banking accordingly. At times, action has gone beyond even these measures.

In 1980, special incentives were put in place to attract OPEC trade surpluses to Japan. The 5.5 percent interest rate ceiling on yen deposits was lifted and normal withholding taxes on interest earned on bank deposits were waived for deposits by foreign governments and by international institutions. The Japanese government supplemented these measures with direct diplomatic consultations with Middle Eastern governments. Predictably, foreign deposits rose dramatically. Although implemented in a different way, Japanese government policy with respect to international banking has been as effective as the German.

Technically, the Japanese government (through the Ministry of Finance and the Bank of Japan) wields considerable influence over that country's banking system. In practice, however, it is clear that the government is only as powerful as the economy that it oversees and that the economy depends to a large measure on the banking system and industrial firms. Thus, in considering Japanese government, banking, and industry, it is not appropriate to view the government as dominant or all-powerful, but instead as "first among equals."

CONCLUSION

The regulation of commercial banks is justified by the same concerns in all industrialized countries. Safety and soundness of the banking system is a critical component of economic viability. From the relatively informal regulatory system of the United Kingdom to the highly regimented system of Japan, there is always a natural tension between the banking industry and its regulators. Nevertheless, the U.S. system presents a sharp contrast to the more negotiated process of compromise that can be observed outside the United States. This a critical difference, whether operating within U.S. boundaries or in a more global setting.

SELECTED REFERENCES

Baker, James C., and M. Gerald Bradford. *American Banks Abroad: Edge Act Companies and Multinational Banking.* Praeger Publishers, New York, 1974.

"Bank Financings Hit a Gusher." *United States Banker*, February 1993, pp. 16–21.

Coulbeck, Neil. *The Multinational Banking Industry.* New York University Press, New York, 1984.

Dale, Richard. *The Regulation of International Banking.* Prentice-Hall, Englewood Cliffs, New Jersey, 1986.

Friedland, Jonathan. "Into the Whirlpool: Japan's Banking Crisis Looks Set to Worsen As Loan Losses Mount." *Far Eastern Economic Review*, April 8, 1993, pp. 70–74.

Greider, William. *Secrets of the Temple: How the Federal Reserve Runs the Country.* Touchstone/Simon & Schuster, New York, 1989.

A Guide to the FDIC Improvement Act. Price Waterhouse, March 1992.

Hales, Michael G. *Handbook of Consumer Banking Law.* Prentice-Hall, Englewood Cliffs, New Jersey, 1989.

Hilton, Anthony. *City within a State: A Portrait of Britain's Financial World.* I. B. Tauris & Co., London, 1987.

International Monetary Fund. *International Capital Markets: Developments and Prospects.* Washington, D.C., 1989.

Johnson, Hazel J. *The Banking Keiretsu.* Probus Publishing, Chicago, 1993.

Johnson, Hazel J. *The Bank Valuation Handbook: A Market-Based Approach to Valuing a Bank.* Probus Publishing, Chicago, 1993.

Khambata, Dara M. *The Practice of Multinational Banking: Macro-Policy Issues and Key International Concepts.* Quorum Books, New York, 1986.

Lee, Peter. "Banks Lean on Clinton." *Euromoney*, February 1993, pp. 34–38.

Pecchioli, R. M. *Prudential Supervision in Banking.* Organisation for Economic Co-operation and Development, Paris, 1987.

Rosenbluth, Frances McCall. *Financial Politics in Contemporary Japan.* Cornell University Press, Ithaca, New York, 1989.

Shirreff, David. "Can Anyone Tame the Currency Market?" *Euromoney*, September 1993, pp. 60–69.

Spong, Kenneth. *Banking Regulation: Its Purpose, Implementation, and Effects*, 3rd edition. Federal Reserve Bank of Kansas, 1990.

Subcommittee on Financial Institutions Supervision, Regulation, and Insurance. *Report of the Task Force on the International Competitiveness of U.S. Financial Institutions*. Committee on Banking Finance and Urban Affairs, Washington, D.C., 1990.

U.S. Department of the Treasury. *Modernizing the Financial System: Recommendations for Safer, More Competitive Banks*. Washington, D.C., 1991.

Wilson, J.S. *Banking Policy and Structure: A Comparative Analysis*. Croom Helm Ltd., London, 1986.

ENDNOTES

1. See also Chapter 3 for a discussion of Euromarkets.

2. OECD is an acronym for Organisation for Economic Co-operation and Development—a group of the major industrialized countries.

3. The December 1992 compliance date applies to all firms with year-end assets in excess of $150 million. Smaller firms have until December 1995 to comply, although they are encouraged to comply sooner.

4. (ROE)(E)(b)
   = $(NI/E)(E)(\Delta retained\ earnings/NI)$
   = $\Delta retained\ earnings$

5. This objective is part of the larger goal of creating *one* economic market that is composed of the 12 member nations. See Chapter 3 for a full description of the EC initiative.

6. The Group of Ten consists of Belgium, Canada, France, Germany, Italy, Japan, the Netherlands, Sweden, the United States, and the United Kingdom. Switzerland is an associate member.

7. Similar provisions apply for savings and loan associations.

8. The reorganization of the Federal Reserve was accomplished through legislation in 1935.

9. See Chapter 3 for a description of the development of the Eurodollar markets.

10. An export trading company (ETC) is a trading organization that supplies support services required for export trade. A business is qualified as an ETC if over 50 percent of revenues are derived from the export of goods or services. The Export Trading Company Act of 1982 gave bank holding companies and Edge Act corporations the right to acquire, partially or wholly, ETCs through equity investment. The objective of the legislation was to support U.S. exports.

11. The Bank Merger Act of 1966 established the ranges of stock ownership that govern the Federal Reserve in determining what is considered control by a bank holding company. Up to 4.9 percent of the voting shares does not constitute control and a bank holding company may own up to this percentage without Fed approval. Between 5 and 24.9 percent, the Federal Reserve has discretion to determine whether control exists. At or above 25 percent, control is assumed to exist.

12. See Baker and Bradford, p. 137.

13. The FDICIA also addresses deposit insurance assessments. See Chapter 3 for a discussion of these provisions.

14. The Group of Ten, also called G-10, is a group of major industrialized countries that coordinate monetary and fiscal policies. The members are Belgium, Canada, France, Germany, Italy, Japan, the Netherlands, Sweden, the United Kingdom, and the United States. Switzerland is an associate member.

5 The Learning Curve

INTRODUCTION

Within the context of their respective regulatory environments and the banking systems, the United States, Germany, the United Kingdom, and Japan present interesting contrasts in terms of their comparative advantages. The United States is clearly dominant in the areas of innovation and technology. Germany has mastered the art of corporate relations. The United Kingdom is perhaps the world's most internationalized banking system. Even in the face of recent financial reverses, Japanese banks present a model for coordination and control. As the global banking community becomes more integrated, these advantages will no doubt be exploited.

INNOVATION IN THE UNITED STATES

U.S. banks have been pioneers in bank innovation, which has been applied in both corporate and retail markets. Loan sales, asset-backed securities, index CDs, swaps, and mezzanine finance are but a few examples.

Loan Sales

Commercial banks are being transformed from deposit-takers and loan-makers into institutions that offer a wide range of financial services. Money market funds and deregulation have made it impossible for banks to fund themselves at below-market rates on deposits and borrowings. The ability of blue-chip corporate clients to obtain lower-cost financing in the commercial paper market has seriously eroded the traditional loan market. The more "bankable" middle market of corporate America now has access to private placement funding and to below-investment-grade bond issuance.[1] Moreover, overcapacity in the U.S. banking system, the formidable presence of foreign banks, and the growth of nonbank financial institutions have increased competition significantly. At the same time, regulatory restrictions on the scope of activity and geographic dispersion have limited the available responses by commercial banks.

The sale of loans represents one of these responses. The process of originating and then selling loans de-emphasizes the traditional role of deposit-taker and loan-maker and enables a bank to better diversify its portfolio. Moving loans "off the books" also reduces the amount of required capital. When a bank performs these functions, it is considered an originator or seller in this market.

Another bank that is less competitive in terms of originating loans can also participate in attractive loans to which it otherwise might not have access. In this role, the bank is considered an investor in the loan sales market. An investor may be an *assignee*, that is, one with the same rights and responsibilities as the original members of the loan syndicate in the primary market. Alternatively, an investor may be a *participant* whose rights, by market convention, are limited to a vote on amendments that would (1) lower the rate of interest or commitment fees or (2) forgive interest on principal.

The originator in the market must consider relationships with *borrowers*, relationships with *investors*, and *portfolio* management and profitability. In structuring a loan, the originator must be sensitive to competitive conditions with respect to price and terms for the *borrower*. For its part, the borrower is likely to be concerned about the size and sophistication of the lending group, with the original syndicate usually drawn from the borrower's traditional banking group. There is often an implicit understanding that the original and assignee lenders will buy back portions of the credit if the borrower requests a loan agreement amendment that the participating lenders are reluctant to grant. While this has historically been the case, this implicit understanding may become less prevalent as this market becomes more standardized.

At the same time, the originator also must be aware of features that are important to the *investor* in terms of structure and pricing. In an investment-banking tradition, originators develop a group of loyal assignees and participants that will consider seriously any deal presented by the originating bank. In some cases, an originator uses its specific information about its investors to "source" loans for assignees and participants that may not fit its own lending interests. An originator may even review its existing loan portfolio to identify credits that would appeal to its investors. Besides the loans themselves, investors should feel confidence that the originator is able to handle the operational aspects of the sale, including timely notification of borrowings, repayments, and repricings.

Volatility in credit markets has resulted in some bank managers seeking only those new loans that can be sold in secondary markets, to ensure needed liquidity of the *asset portfolio*. Of course, profitability is also a consideration. When loans are sold and origination fees are collected, both return on assets and return on equity increase. If market conditions warrant, it may also be possible to earn a "skim," that is, the difference between the contract interest rate earned by the original syndicate and that required by the investors. Also, the originator must be sensitive to diversification in terms of location, industry, and type of loan arrangement.

Foreign banks were the first major investors in the loan sales market. Recently, nonbank financial institutions have become more prominent, including insurance companies, pension funds, savings and loan associations, and mutual funds. There is even a short-term equivalent to commercial paper that has attracted a significant number of nonbank investors.

An area of special interest currently is the sale of real estate loans. NationsBank, Fleet Financial, Mellon Bank, First Chicago, First Interstate, and BankAmerica have negotiated large sales of these loans in 1993. In 1992 Chase Manhattan realized $130 million. During just the last quarter of 1992, Chemical sold $150 million of these loans. During the same period, First Chicago sold $190 million in book value and is contemplating the bulk sale of as much as $1 billion to a single buyer, perhaps GE Capital. In total, banks have sold or contracted to sell $8 to $10 billion of original face value in commercial real estate loans. It has been estimated that the market can absorb as much as $30 billion in face value before the market prices decline.

Those banks that have written down their commercial real estate loans to 45 percent of face can often realize profit by selling in the secondary market at 55 percent of face. The gains are often reflected in other operating income and not broken out separately. Cash proceeds can be reinvested in low-risk Treasuries or even in other real estate-related products. For example, Fleet, during its own bulk disposal of real estate loans, bought into a $105 million private placement by Bankers Trust.

The primary buyers of these loans include the property users, syndicates, individuals, and small institutions. Specialty funds are also often interested buyers, notably those run by Morgan Stanley, Goldman Sachs, and international investment manager George Soros. Foreign money is flowing in from Asia (particularly Taiwan), the Middle East, and Europe.

As the general loan sales market expands, the structure of sales will no doubt become even more standardized. There have been securitized corporate loans such as FRIENDS B.V. (Floating Rate Enhanced Debt Securities—offered by Continental Bank), which consist of diversified senior debt of 25 different borrowers with no more than 8 percent of the pool in any one industry. Investors may choose either Class A or B notes. Class A notes pay LIBOR plus 80 basis points (bp) while Class B notes are subordinated to Class A notes and pay LIBOR plus 350 bp.

BankAmerica is another useful example, recently agreeing to sell $1.7 billion in original face value of real estate assets that it obtained in connection with its acquisition of Security Pacific. The loans were sold to a special purchase vehicle owned by Morgan Stanley Real Estate Fund and are expected to generate $1 billion for BankAmerica.

In addition, the bank will probably invest $100 million in nonvoting participation certificates that entitle the owner to share in residual cash flow from the assets once the more senior debt has been serviced, with the certificates being distributed to shareholders. These and other securitized loan sales have followed and promise to continue the trend toward asset-backed securities.

Asset-Backed Securities

An asset-backed security is a claim against a pool of loans. In this arrangement, the functions of loan originator (discussed above) are split between the original lenders and the issuer of the asset-backed securities. While it is possible for one party to perform both functions, it is not uncommon for an investment banker to act as issuer. This often has been true in the case of bank loan securitization in which legal constraints forced banks, in the absence of a Section 20 subsidiary, to turn over the actual issuance to investment bankers. However, federal regulators have ruled that banks may securitize loans that they have originated or purchased. The investors in asset-backed securities arrangements buy discrete securities rather than a portion of a loan pool.

Government agencies were the first to securitize loans to create a secondary market for mortgages—Federal National Mortgage Association (Fannie Mae), Federal Home Loan Mortgage Corporation (Freddie Mac), and Government National Mortgage Association (Ginnie Mae). In addition to the more traditional residential mortgage loans, Fannie Mae is expected to begin to purchase "reverse mortgages." These loans, sometimes also referred to as "home equity conversion loans," are particularly attractive for banks in areas with a high senior citizen population or with a high real estate appreciation potential. The typical borrower is 76 years of age, lives alone, has an annual income of approximately $8,000, and owns a home worth $100,000. Under the arrangement, the bank pays a stipend to the homeowner (collateralized by the real estate) until the house is sold, at which time all interest and principal are repaid.

In a pilot program to begin in early 1994, the Federal Housing Authority (FHA) is creating a secondary market in these mortgages, which grew at the rate of 350 percent to a total of 12,000 during the three years ended 1992. Under this pilot program, FHA will insure up to 25,000 reverse mortgages in amounts less than $151,725. Original lenders will retain the servicing rights but pass the loans to Fannie Mae. Although a small market at this point, these transactions will add to the already strong secondary markets for mortgage loans in the United States.

Originally, in the secondary markets, instruments were merely "pass-throughs" that paid investors their proportional share of interest and principal each month. Likewise, the risks of default and prepayment were also passed through to the investor. For many investors, this was an undesirable situation. The next generation of mortgage-related securities was the mortgage-backed bond that paid interest and principal as a normal bond, with more customary semiannual or quarterly payments and without any prepayment or (original mortgage) default risk.

The most advanced of these instruments is the collateralized mortgage obligation (CMO), introduced by Federal Home Loan Mortgage Corporation but now primarily offered by private investment banks. The various "tranches" of a CMO reduce prepayment risk by devoting all principal payments to the first tranche until it is completely repaid, then to the next tranche until it is completely repaid, and so on. Meanwhile, all tranches receive interest payments unless there is a "Z-bond," that is, a tranche structured like a zero-coupon bond. Growth of mortgage-backed securities has been dramatic since their inception during the 1970s.

The asset-backed securities market now extends well beyond residential mortgages. Beginning in the mid-1980s, General Motors Acceptance Corporation began issuing securities backed by automobile loans. First Boston contributed $40 million in capital and formed a separate corporation, Asset-Backed Securities Corporation (ABSC), to purchase $4 billion in loans from GMAC and to issue the securities. The notes were issued in fast-pay, medium-pay, and slow-pay tranches. Investors received limited protection against default risk from GMAC (5 percent) and First Boston (1 percent). Credit Suisse provided a standby letter of credit that insured timely payment of interest and principal. Because of these financial enhancements, the issue received a AAA rating from Standard and Poor's. After this inaugural issue, Chrysler Financial Corporation, Marine Midland Bank, Empire of America, and Western Financial Savings thereafter also became significant issuers.

Securities backed by credit card loans were also issued. Some of the most significant early originating lenders were First Chicago National Bank, Maryland Bank, Sears, Bank of America, and Manufacturers Hanover (before its merger with Chemical).

Asset-backed securities are either *pass-through* or *pay-through* arrangements. In a pass-through, the loans are sold to a trust. Investors purchase certificates that represent a proportional share of cash flows from the underlying loans. In order to avoid taxation, the trust must passively transfer all cash flows through to investors. In a pay-through, the loans are transferred to a separate corporation. In this case, there are no restrictions on the management of cash flows, and payments to investors need not be tied to cash flows from the underlying loans.

The pay-through structure can be used to eliminate prepayment risk for the investor, when the issuer guarantees a fixed prepayment rate. Should prepayments exceed this guaranteed fixed rate, the proceeds can be invested in a guaranteed investment contract (GIC, commonly issued by insurance companies). When prepayments are less than this guaranteed rate, the issuer can draw on a borrowing facility, perhaps a standby letter of credit from a commercial bank.

The credit risk of an asset-backed security is not tied to the credit risk of the originating lender. The rating agencies (typically Moody's Investor Service and Standard & Poor's Corporation) examine the historical default rate of the classification of loans, the specific loans in the pool, and the manner in which the loans were selected. These agencies assume the worst general economic conditions in their evaluations.

Credit risk is also affected by both external and internal credit enhancements. External credit enhancements include standby letters of credit, surety bonds, and financial guarantees. When such facilities are used, the credit rating of the asset-backed security is based on that of the party providing the enhancement. Should the credit rating of this party decline, the credit rating of the security will also. Typically, a letter of credit is issued to cover a fixed percentage of the original principal of the underlying loans and is reduced by actual draws. Draws are reimbursed by either the originating lender or a reserve fund. When a commercial bank is the original lender, the reserve fund method is most often used because bank regulators will not permit a bank to treat the transaction as an asset sale unless there is "no recourse" involved in the credit enhancements. A reserve fund satisfies this no-recourse requirement.

A surety bond, or pool insurance, is an insurance contract that protects investors from losses. Most insurers will provide protection only for the entire pool and require that the original structure (without insurance) be eligible for an investment-grade rating. This can be a difficult condition to satisfy. So surety bonds are typically not the primary credit enhancement.

A financial guarantee by the original lender, like a standby letter of credit, usually covers a fixed dollar amount or percentage of the issue. Since the rating of the security depends on the rating of the credit enhancement provider, this form is used primarily by high-rated companies. Also, in the case of commercial banks, the issue of recourse must be addressed in order for the transaction to qualify as a sale of assets.

An asset-backed security also can include an internal credit enhancement. This is accomplished by issuing at least two classes of securities: one senior and one subordinate. The subordinate (junior) class absorbs all default risk while the senior class receives an AA or higher rating. Frequently, the junior class is not rated at all.

All of the features and enhancements associated with asset-backed securities help make them more marketable. Thus, asset-backed securities are an innovation through which U.S. bankers (and other financial institutions) have been able to better manage their lending risk. In the case of those banks that have requested and received permission to operate a Section 20 subsidiary, it is also an area in which they can demonstrate their ability to perform effectively many of the functions of investment banking.

Indexed CDs

Another product innovation of U.S. banks is the indexed certificate of deposit (CD). The Garn-St. Germain Act of 1982 gave all depository institutions the power to offer a money market deposit account (MMDA) with an interest rate tied to money market rates. These deposits help banks compete with money market mutual funds. The Market Index Investment Account, offered by Chase Manhattan Bank, is an extension of the MMDA. This deposit has a fixed term with a rate of return that is partially tied to the performance of the S&P500 stock index. Customers select one of three maturities—three months, six months, or one year. Within these maturities, an investor can select a specific rate of return formula. For example, for one-year certificates the choices may be:

- a zero guaranteed minimum return plus 70 percent of the increase in the S&P500 index for the year

- a 2 percent guaranteed return plus 60 percent of the S&P500 increase for the year

- a 4 percent guaranteed return plus 40 percent of the S&P500 increase for the year

An obvious attraction is that the deposit is federally insured for up to $100,000. Moreover, the depositor has a minimum return built in with the possibility of a much higher return. While an investor could conceivably earn a higher rate of return in a stock mutual fund, the mutual fund investment also exposes an investor to the risk of loss of principal. The indexed CD offers a floor that is not provided in a mutual fund investment.

Other banks now also offer their own version of the Market Index Deposit (MID), with variations that include deposits whose return declines with the stock index or moves with gold prices. These are liabilities whose rate fluctuates with the stock market. On the asset side, issuing banks frequently reduce their portfolio risk by investing in S&P stock index futures contracts. These investments do not violate the Glass-Steagall prohibition against stock investments because contracts are settled in cash rather than in stock.

However, the Internal Revenue Service considers the MID to be two separate instruments: a zero-coupon bond and a call option on a stock index. The option is either exercised at maturity or expires worthless. The issuing institution must stipulate what share of the original purchase price is for the bond and what share represents payment for the option. Each year, the investor pays tax on the imputed bond interest for that period. This information is provided to the investor through a 1099 notice of income earned. If the option component is a nonequity option, gains and losses are deferred until it either expires or is sold. On the other hand, if the option is an equity option, it must be marked to market each year and the appropriate taxes paid.

Because of these complicated tax implications, many banks will sell these instruments only to IRAs or Keogh Accounts.[2] Nevertheless, like the asset-backed security, the indexed CD is an instrument that has enabled commercial banks to cope with the limitations of restrictive regulation.

Swaps

An interest rate swap is the exchange of cash flows between two parties for a specific period of time.[3] The terms of an interest rate swap involve a notational amount, and the interest rate on that notational amount to which each counterparty is obligated. These arrangements help counterparties manage the interest rate risk associated with their asset or liability portfolios. Commercial banks may be either counterparties or intermediaries. An intermediary arranges the transaction, often bringing the two counterparties together. U.S. banks have been instrumental in the development of this market and swaps are a source of fee income to those banks which act as intermediaries.

Banks also can offer swaps to their corporate clients to accommodate their need to manage interest rate risk.

- A floating-rate debt can be transformed into a synthetic fixed-rate debt. The issuer attaches a floating interest rate to the bond. Under the terms of a swap, the issuer agrees to pay a fixed rate and to receive a floating rate on a specified notational principal. The issuer uses the floating-rate receipts to satisfy its own interest obligations.

- Likewise, a fixed-rate debt can be converted into a synthetic floating-rate debt. The issuer attaches a fixed interest rate to the bond. In the swap, the issuer agrees to pay a floating rate and receive a fixed rate. Fixed-rate receipts satisfy the issuer's obligation.

- An issuer can effectively change the basis used for a floating-rate debt instrument. The bond can be issued with a coupon that floats with LIBOR in the Eurobond market.[4] The swap may be structured to exchange the LIBOR basis for a U.S. Treasury rate basis.

- Interest rate protection can be provided for some specific time period that may be a subset of the full term of a bond. The issuer may be concerned about interest rate exposure for the first two years of a 10-year bond. In this case, a two-year swap contract can provide the needed protection.

These are but a few examples of the uses of swap contracts. Such applications are not limited to bank clients, but may be used by banks themselves to offer competitively structured products and, at the same time, protect against undue interest rate risk.

The concept of swaps has been expanded to other areas. In 1993, the first real estate property swap was constructed. Aldrich Eastman & Waltch, a Boston money management firm, sought to change the asset allocation mix of one of the pension funds that it managed. The objective was to reduce the real estate component in order to invest in the equities market. Selling the real estate in a depressed market would have resulted in a loss, however. Instead the company retained the real estate and agreed to pay the return on the Russell-NCREIF Property Index (a benchmark index that reflects the yield on 1800 properties in the United States). In exchange the fund received the return on a range of U.S. broad-based indexes and several European indexes.

The swap was arranged by Morgan Stanley with a notational amount of $20 million for five years. The firm actually engaged in two transactions: a swap of property-index return for LIBOR, followed by a LIBOR-for-equity swap. The company currently is working on other applications of the concept.

Within applicable legal constraints, banks can offer equity-related swaps to give themselves and other investors access to foreign markets. These applications are particularly important for banks in their overseas operations and offer a good alternative for tapping into the fast-growing equity markets.

The use of swaps is part of the practice of *financial engineering*, in which financial structures are designed that would otherwise not be available. Other tools used in financial engineering are interest rate caps (maximum rate), interest rate floors (minimum rate), options (the right but not the obligation to enter into a future transaction), and swaptions (option on a swap). As major participants in the swap market—as both counterparties and intermediaries—U.S. commercial banks have contributed much in terms of the innovations of the 1980s.

Mezzanine Finance

Mezzanine finance is positioned between senior-level debt and common equity, represents another innovative form of financing in which U.S. commercial banks participate, and is frequently used in "friendly" management buyouts. While there are natural comparisons with the junk bond market, there are some important differences:

- Junk (below investment grade) bond transactions often involve financings of $200 million or more. Mezzanine finance is more often used for transactions of between $3 and $40 million.

- The aggregate junk bond market is well over $100 billion while total mezzanine finance is estimated at $30 billion or less.

- Junk bonds are publicly issued; most mezzanine finance is privately placed or directly negotiated by the issuer with a private purchaser.

- The relatively illiquid nature of mezzanine finance often results in more restrictive covenants than are normally associated with junk bonds, including limits on the issuer's rights to sell assets, incur additional debt, or distribute cash to investors.

U.S. banks have the power to engage in private placements. Thus, mezzanine finance is an area of investment banking that capitalizes on the relationships built up through other banking contacts. Continental Bank uses several guidelines to identify potential companies for mezzanine financing, as illustrated in Exhibit 5-1.

A typical arrangement will involve the issuance of several classes of securities—both debt and equity. The classifications are *senior debt*, *common equity*, and *mezzanine finance*, which is somewhere in between the first two in terms of risk and reward. The actual proportions of each may be based on the purchase price, for example:

- 60 percent senior debt
- 30 percent mezzanine finance
- 10 percent common equity

These guidelines could also be based on some multiple of operating income, for example:

- senior debt, 4x
- mezzanine finance, 2x
- common equity, .5x

The *senior debt* portion can include a floating interest rate (perhaps, LIBOR plus 2.5 percent), have a term that does not extend beyond eight years, and be secured by assets of the firm. Restrictive covenants subordinate the claims of other investors to this class of securities. Purchasers of the senior debt probably would be commercial banks.

Mezzanine finance investors could include high-yield investment companies, private equity companies, and perhaps some senior debt holders. The mezzanine finance instruments can be either senior or junior. Senior mezzanine instruments can pay, for example, 400 to

EXHIBIT 5-1

MEZZANINE FINANCE

The following characteristics have been specified by Continental Bank as useful in identifying potentially good candidates for mezzanine finance.

- Strong proven operating management at all levels.

- Products that are not subject to rapid technological change.

- Proprietary products with a strong market position.

- Manufacturing efficiencies that qualify the company as a low-cost producer in its industry.

- Products that are sold to industrial customers.

- Cash flow predictability.

- Balance sheet that can support additional leverage.

- Purchase price for the company that does not exceed eight times operating cash flow.

- Operations not subject to significant import threats.

- Stability of earnings during economic downturns.

- Good asset quality with a substantial share of liquidity assets vis-à-vis fixed assets.

- Quantifiable liabilities.

Source

Donald Chew, Editor, *New Developments in Commercial Banking*, pp. 326–27.

---

500 basis points over Treasury and offer some equity participation. The term would be longer than that of senior debt, perhaps 10 to 12 years, with a provision for exit before then.

Junior mezzanine debt would pay a still higher rate, for example, 600 to 800 basis points above Treasury. While the term would be comparable to that of senior mezzanine debt, this instrument would contain fewer restrictive covenants, have warrants or be convertible into common, and may even pay interest in-kind, that is, add scheduled interest to the principal until some specified future date.

Common equity is sold to management, private investors, pension funds, and investment banks. These investors often seek high annual rates of return (40 percent or more) and anticipate an exit in three to seven years.

Mezzanine finance is a vehicle through which medium-sized companies can access capital. U.S. commercial banks fulfill important roles in both structuring and participating in these arrangements.

U.S. Bank Management

The innovation displayed by U.S. banks in product development is also reflected in bank management. Under assault from nonbank competitors such as mutual funds, U.S. banks have found the need to reconsider their market positions. In some cases, this has meant expanding their scope of operation. In other cases, it has meant dramatic curtailment of services in specific areas. Citicorp and Bankers Trust present two compelling illustrations.

Citicorp. Citicorp and Citibank, its lead bank, have pursued an agenda of expansion and conquest for several decades. During the 1920s, National City Bank followed a strategy to become a financial department store with a strong presence in:

- retail banking

- investment banking, capitalizing on its "placing power," that is, distribution capabilities

- international finance, including operations in Latin America, the Far East, and Europe

However, the McFadden and Glass-Steagall Acts seriously altered the bank's expansion plans. Like other money center banks immediately after passage of these legislative measures, Citibank focused on the now more narrowly defined scope of commercial banking activity—accepting deposits and making loans.

It was not until George Moore began to promote his vision for First National City (so renamed after a merger with First National

Bank in 1955), that the bank started to distinguish itself. Beginning in the 1950s, Moore, who later became president, then chairman, developed the overseas network, expanded the functional scope of the bank's business, upgraded management personnel, and emphasized decentralized decision-making.

The culture of the bank had historically been one in which seniority was the key to advancement. Moore changed this by hiring bright, newly graduated M.B.A.s, and instituting a system of recognition for meritorious performance. His efforts along these lines included personally recruiting students on campus and assuring them that they had a promising and exciting future at First National City Bank. Moore arranged summer internships for students before graduation to stimulate their interest in banking. Once hired, a new crop of management trainees was carefully trained and given full opportunity to compete for promotions.

One of these shining stars was Walter Wriston. Unlike some of his peers, Wriston's academic background did not include business school training. Instead, he had a classical background with a master's degree from the Fletcher School of International Law and Diplomacy. Wriston worked with Moore in the Overseas Division before Moore was named president of the bank in 1959. Wriston shared Moore's vision of the bank as an international presence. The overall plan was to first establish commercial links in other countries, then set up small locations throughout the country, and finally employ the banking expertise shipped in from New York.

Wriston also understood the importance of protecting the bank's deposit base. The large corporate treasurers, who traditionally had invested excess liquidity in large, short-term bank deposits, were being enticed by the issuers of commercial paper. While bank deposits were safer, commercial paper was more liquid because its issuers agreed to buy it back at face value before maturity if an investor required earlier-than-anticipated redemption. Wriston believed a secondary market in bank CDs could neutralize this apparent advantage. In 1960, the "Banker's Certificate" was offered by the Overseas Division and designated as "marketable." The first $1 million certificate was issued to Union Bank of Switzerland, but the initial investor quickly found that there was no market for the certificate.

Wriston then took a more active role in development of a secondary market. He approached Discount Corporation, a government securities dealer, suggesting that the firm make a market in the new certificates. On the condition that First National City provide a $10 million *unsecured* loan to finance the operation (a practice that violated a long-standing rule at the bank), Discount Corporation agreed to do so. In February 1961, the bank announced the new certificates would be sold in $1 million denominations with Discount Corporation making a market in them. Thus, the negotiable CD market was officially launched and would go on to rank second only to the Treasury bill in terms of importance in U.S. money markets.

This head-on approach to banking characterized Wriston's tenure with the bank as he went on to become president in 1967 and CEO in 1970 (retiring in 1984). During his reign, Wriston encouraged the entrepreneurial spirit, established wide-ranging divisions, and championed the cause of deregulation. Wriston was known for pitting his managers against each other, giving an assignment to two different divisions to stimulate in-house competition. As the organization developed into autonomous divisions, this sometimes spilled over to other areas. For instance, product teams sometimes served the same customer without awareness of the others or coordination of their efforts. This type of management created three separate and distinct subcultures within Citicorp: the provision of standardized *consumer* services, the maintenance of long-term relationships with corporate clients in the *institutional bank*, and the expansion of *investment banking* activities.

The *consumer bank* has distinguished the organization in no uncertain terms, with Citicorp being the largest issuer of bank credit cards. The next competitor, Chase Manhattan, has only one-fourth of Citicorp's market share. In addition, Citicorp has a formidable presence in the mortgage market, having established an efficient mortgage-processing facility in St. Louis. The consumer/mortgage network has been strengthened by Citicorp's acquisition of troubled savings and loan associations in California, Florida, Illinois, and Washington, D.C. The bank's goal is to develop centralized support mechanisms for a national system of locations that are decentralized enough to deliver customized products.

The *institutional bank* has not shown as much promise. In this division, long-standing corporate customers are served through a combination of products, including foreign exchange, risk management, real estate finance, transaction processing, highly leveraged transactions, asset securitization, and loan syndications. Results have been mixed in this division, with notable disappointments in real estate loans to Donald Trump for which the bank was either lead manager or a participant, in senior debt associated with leveraged buyouts, and in real estate loans to Olympia & York in Toronto.

The reverses in commercial banking notwithstanding, Citicorp has faced perhaps even greater challenges in the resumption of *investment banking* activities domestically. Into its new investment bank it also has transferred the treasury functions, mergers and acquisitions, and trading activities. The bank has recruited talented business school graduates and built trading facilities in New York. Other facilities have been established in important financial centers such as London, Tokyo, and Hong Kong. However, there was a certain resistance to paying the high salaries that investment bankers typically command. These strains have, at times, led to mass resignations of entire groups of investment bankers. While the issue of compensation for commercial vis-à-vis investment bankers is not unique to Citicorp, it seems to have been exacerbated by the strength of the consumer (that is, lower paid) bank within the same organization.

The increase in staff and resources in Citicorp's climate of in-house competition also led to unproductive conflicts during the pursuit of certain deals. For their part, the commercial bankers did not trust the instincts or tactics of the investment bankers. The commercial bankers felt that the investment bankers had little loyalty for the bank and were interested only in their own transactions and bonuses.

The bankers on the investment side tend to be more entrepreneurial and unorthodox, while those on the commercial side are more sensitive to organizational goals and protocol. As a result, giving investment bankers managerial responsibilities often did not work well.

As a remedy for these problems, Citicorp consolidated the investment and institutional banks in 1987. There is a division of labor in the new unit: institutional bankers originate deals and investment bankers execute them and perform trading functions. The Citicorp approach to investment banking was as aggressive as its approach to consumer banking. Unfortunately, the combination of the stock market crash of 1987, reverses in commercial real estate, a much more subdued junk bond market, and lingering Third World debt problems have combined to confront Citicorp with a serious expense control dilemma.

The bank's response has been to reduce annual costs by $1.3 billion, increase its 1993 loan loss reserve to $.78 per dollar of nonperforming assets (up from $.54 the previous year), and increase its capital ratio from 5.1 to 7.2 percent. While necessary restructuring is not complete at Citicorp, the bank is recovering from the negative effects of its hard-charging approach to banking. At the same time, the positive effects remain in that Citicorp:

- is the leading issuer of bank credit cards

- has the most advanced technology network to support its nationwide consumer banking activities

- understands the importance of customer orientation in product development

- is arguably the leading U.S. bank in the international arena

Bankers Trust. Bankers Trust was founded as a trust company in 1903 to provide New York money center banks with a reputable trust operation to which they could refer their commercial and investment banking clients. It fulfilled this function until the 1913 Federal Reserve Act also gave commercial banks the right to engage in trust activities. From that point on, Bankers Trust developed as a full-service commercial bank with securities underwriting capabilities and international operations. During this developmental phase, Bankers Trust became known primarily as a wholesale bank.

Its involvement in retail banking began primarily after World War II when pent-up consumer demand was unleashed. Financing for homes, automobiles, and appliances was a growth industry for banks and other financial institutions. Bankers Trust opened branch offices throughout the state of New York.

At the same time, the institution expanded its overseas facilities with representation in 30 countries and correspondent relationships with 1,200 banks. In addition, specialized groups were developed in areas such as oil and gas, construction, and public utilities. The bank was one of the first to computerize its support functions.

Profits were healthy during the 1950s and 1960s, but began to deteriorate in the 1970s. The bank analyzed its management approach and took the dramatic step in 1971 of significantly reducing its workforce. This was rare in the banking industry, where lifetime employment had been virtually assured. In further restructuring the following year, Bankers Trust discontinued its stock transfer and related activities.

Then, as the bank continued to review its position in various markets, the real estate market in New York City suffered major reverses in the mid-1970s. Bankers Trust had made loans to real estate developers and to real estate investment trusts (REITs) that supported construction and real estate development. A subsidiary of the bank even advised a REIT named Bankers Trust Mortgage Investors. With an exposure of almost $700 million, Bankers Trust suffered major losses.

At the same time, challenges to the retail area arose. Citibank announced that it would invest $100 million in automated teller machines (ATMs). By the time of this announcement, Bankers Trust had expanded its branch network, but not to the same extent as other money center banks. Retail banking contributed only 10 percent of total revenues. Under the circumstances, competing with Citicorp's investment in ATMs did not appear feasible. In 1978, the difficult decision to exit retail banking was made. Both the retail branches and the credit card operation had been sold by 1982.

Beginning in 1978, Bankers Trust became a *wholesale* institution with major divisions in:

- wholesale banking (traditional corporate loans)

- fiduciary operations (trust and private banking)

- capital markets (government and municipal bond underwriting and trading)

- corporate finance (mergers and acquisitions)

Although substantial investments were made in the capital markets and corporate finance divisions, Bankers Trust continued to emphasize the wholesale business.

Over time, however, the investment banking culture began to emerge. First, the corporate finance group was organized into five areas—mergers and acquisitions, public finance, private placements, leveraged buyout equity financing, and leasing. Members of this group worked apart from the commercial bankers and received performance-related bonuses—bonuses that tended to alienate the commercial bankers, as was the case at Citicorp. In addition, under the leadership of Charles Sanford (who would become president in 1983 and CEO in 1987), the capital markets group positioned itself more like a Wall Street firm than commercial bank. It was physically established in separate facilities in the Wall Street area and paid competitive salaries and bonuses. In the late 1970s and early 1980s, Sanford's power within the bank increased and he persistently argued for more emphasis on investment banking.

Beginning in 1983, Bankers Trust redefined its mission as that of a full-service investment bank. Accountability in the bank has shifted from a common pool of resources that is spread throughout the bank to individual profit centers. The exact configuration is always subject to change based on market conditions, but the major areas of operation are:

- financial services (merchant and investment banking)

- global markets (corporate finance)

- nonbanking activities (investment management and other activities)

Bankers Trust has emerged as an interesting contrast to Citicorp. While Citicorp also has a decentralized organizational structure, there appears to be more coordination between divisions at Bankers Trust. Having eliminated its retail functions, Bankers Trust is a smaller, more agile organization. Because of its trading and investment banking focus, Bankers Trust also has a more volatile earnings stream than Citicorp. Citicorp has made a substantial investment, perhaps more than any other U.S. bank, in consumer banking. Bankers Trust has elected to exit the retail market altogether.

The experiences of these two institutions illustrate the dynamic nature of the banking industry in the United States. It is a market in which regulatory necessity has been the mother of invention and in which customer relationships are very fluid. Market niches are won, then lost, and appropriate strategies are often short-lived. Nevertheless, the U.S. banking industry remains a fertile ground for innovation and entrepreneurship.

UNIVERSAL BANKING IN GERMANY

In contrast to the United States, Germany banking is more stable and predictable. This is primarily because the German economy is bank-centered. In their pivotal role, German banks routinely engage in *universal banking,* that is, the provision of all financial services. The strong bonds that tie German businesses to German banks present a fascinating case study in client relations.

Client Relations

Almost from the beginning, German banks have been major shareholders in German companies and have had representation on boards of directors. This presence is observable in both large and small firms.

Large firms in Germany often developed in regions where there was not even a local handicraft infrastructure. This meant that a firm was forced to build capacity for all necessary components within the firm itself, requiring massive capital infusions. German banks provided these funds. The first products were large machinery such as locomotives and steel-making equipment. Later, the firms diversified into other areas of machinery to maintain employment and operational stability.

Because the European market was composed of dissimilar product standards and preferences, large German companies often manufactured high-quality products in short production runs. Employees were skilled at every phase of their jobs so as to accommodate these rapid changes. In this sense, the large companies became adept at reacting to changing market conditions. If shareholders had not understood these dynamics, dedicated capital would have been much more difficult to secure. As major shareholders, German banks were less concerned with temporary fluctuations and more concerned with long-term viability of their clients.

Deutsche Bank is the largest of the three major universal banks in Germany. (The other two are Dresdner Bank and Commerzbank.) It is also one of Germany's largest shareholders. Its equity stakes include:

- Daimler-Benz (automotives, 28 percent)

- Allianz (Europe's largest insurance company, 10 percent)

- Munich Re (world's largest re-insurance company, 10 percent)

- Karstadt (trading company, 25 percent)

- Philip Holzmann (construction, 35 percent)

- Heidelberger Zement (construction materials, 25 percent)

- Hapag Lloyd (shipping, 12.5 percent)

- Metallgesellschaft (industrial group, 7 percent)

Moreover, Deutsche Bank managers occupy more than 400 seats on the boards of other German firms.

While the three large universal banks have established relationships with major firms, other German banks have fueled growth within the *Mittelstand* group—a group of small- and medium-sized firms. The larger industrial firms developed in regions without a handicraft or supplier infrastructure, but the Mittelstand firms emerged in regions with considerable infrastructure. In these areas, there was little need for each firm to construct facilities to provide all components of production. Firms remained relatively small and usually family-owned. Financing often came in the form of cooperative banks, similar in form and function to credit unions.

Over time, even smaller firms became involved in the export drive of the German economy and more advanced banking services were required. As incomes grew in the late 1950s and 1960s, overall liquidity increased. Savings banks, regional banks, and credit cooperatives offered a full range of loans and other financial services to Mittelstand companies. Today, more than 75 percent of all German banking institutions are engaged in universal banking.

There is also a trend toward "network" financing. Traditionally, the House Bank or main bank provides the full range of services for a particular client. In a network arrangement, several banks provide financing for a network of commercial or industrial firms. Network bank representatives sit on the boards of network industrial firms and vice versa. This is quite similar to the Japanese *keiretsu* arrangement in the sense that there are interlocking relationships between groups of financial and industrial firms. Thus, in both large and small firms, there are close ties between banking and commercial firms.

An interesting byproduct of this system is that the takeover phenomenon of the 1980s in the United States was not witnessed in Germany. Continuity of management in Germany is considered quite important. German banks, as major shareholders, generally adopt the view that industrial management must not be constrained in making appropriate long-term decisions by the prospect of a hostile takeover.

This is in sharp contrast to the situation in the United States, where other institutional investors, including pension funds, mutual funds, and insurance companies, hold well over 40 percent of publicly traded stock. The difference in the United States is that institutional investors are evaluated in terms of the rate of return they generate in the short term. Since this rate of return is measured solely in terms of dividend yield and capital gains yield, investments that pay off in the long term often have negative short-term consequences with respect to earnings (and hence dividends and stock prices). Industrial managers are increasingly coming under fire by these so-called "supershareholders." While the concerns of institutional investors may indeed be warranted in many cases, there is no doubt that U.S. industry has adopted a much more short-term focus than its German counterpart.

In fact, German industrial firms and banks have been known to work together to prevent an unwanted foreign takeover. For example, in 1990 Deutsche Bank worked to block the acquisition of Continental AG, a German tire maker, by Pirelli SpA, the well-known Italian firm. When Leopoldo Pirelli (head of the Italian firm) first approached Ulrich Weiss (the Deutsche Bank representative who sat as head of Continental's board), Weiss was generally receptive to the idea of a merger. The combination would help enhance the presence of Deutsche Bank in the larger European arena and boost the value of the bank's 5 percent stake in Continental. Furthermore, if the two companies combined, the new firm would control 15 percent of the world tire market, only slightly below the 17 percent share held by Bridgestone.

Nevertheless, Horst Urban of Continental believed that the Pirelli overtures were a thinly veiled hostile takeover. After all, Pirelli had begun to buy Continental shares even before the talks began. Furthermore, the terms of the DM2 billion deal were unacceptable. Under Pirelli's plan, Continental would buy Pirelli shares at a premium over their market value. Continental was to raise the cash for this deal by both issuing more stock and borrowing funds. The projected operational savings of DM400 million per year appeared exaggerated in Urban's view. Besides which, Pirelli had not revealed who was actually buying Continental shares. If there were unknown investors involved on Pirelli's side, this would tend to establish the hostility of the offer. This seemed especially true in light of the commonly adopted corporate rule that no single shareholder can exercise more than 5 percent of voting rights, regardless of shareholdings. Multiple parties on Pirelli's side could sidestep this provision and force the merger.

After reviewing Urban's objections, a somewhat embarrassed Weiss reversed his earlier endorsement of the merger and the rest of the Continental board members followed suit. Then Urban enlisted the support of Continental's clients, including Daimler-Benz, BMW, and Volkswagen. Even Allianz, the insurance giant that is partially owned by Deutsche Bank, joined in the defensive front. Together, these German companies formed a pool to buy a 25 percent shareholder interest in Continental. This was enough to block the merger because German corporate law stipulates that no major decision affecting a company may be made with less than 75 percent of the voting shareholders. In addition to this 25-percent block, Deutsche Bank controlled (via proxy) shares that it held in trust.

In response to this obvious show of power, Pirelli attempted to negotiate somewhat more reasonable terms, but Urban refused to discuss the matter. Meanwhile, Continental suffered business reverses that led to the closing of some of its General Tire production facilities in the United States. At this point, Deutsche Bank (again) reversed its position and supported the merger. When Weiss met with Pirelli to discuss the possibility of reopening negotiations, Pirelli agreed on the condition that Urban not act as the negotiator for Continental. Not long thereafter, Horst Urban was replaced by Hubertus Von Grünberg, a previous employee of ITT in the United States.

The talks were aborted, however, when it was revealed that the financial situation of Pirelli was worse than Continental had realized. Urban's earlier suspicions were confirmed, albeit belatedly. Other investors were involved on Pirelli's side and, in fact, Pirelli had guaranteed to cover any losses they sustained. The losses turned out to be substantial—approximately $300 million.

The failed Continental takeover helps illustrate the power of German banks and the close relationships between banks and industrial firms. This environment contributes to a more stable environment in which industrial managers are not as subject to the threat of hostile takeovers as is true in the United States. Also, the short-term-profits pressure is not as intense because pension funds are primarily managed within the companies that sponsor the plans, and large mutual funds are managed by banks. Thus far, German insurance companies have shown no desire to assert their shareholder rights in any way that seriously challenges traditional German methods of cooperation.

German Bank Management

The Deutsche Bank also provides some insight into the management of German banks. Before his death in a terrorist bombing in 1989, Alfred Herrhausen pursued an agenda of making Deutsche Bank a truly global presence. In contrast, his successor, Hilmar Kopper, is inclined to adopt a somewhat less expansionist position.

Herrhausen was a trained economist and an experienced industrialist when he joined Deutsche Bank at the end of the 1960s. At that time, the bank barely ventured beyond national borders. Post-war trauma in German banking had included the break-up of the "Big Three." Even after this initial division was reversed, the mood remained tentative. Having reached maturity after the war, Herrhausen did not share these reservations.

He joined the bank's board in 1970 and set the course. He felt the need to build for the future—not just the Single European Market of 1992, but the global economy of the 21st century. Under Herrhausen's leadership, the bank began to take risks in a more entrepreneurial spirit. His was an independent spirit that would not even entertain the notion of a joint venture. Instead, the bank made wide-ranging international acquisitions, as illustrated in Exhibit 5-2.

Hilmar Kopper assumed leadership after Herrhausen's death. Unlike his predecessor, Kopper has had a lifelong career in banking. In fact, he entered Deutsche Bank as a trainee immediately after completing his education. His strength is considered to be his technical banking background rather than his strategic vision. He believes that the key to success is a healthy home market, in which he includes the Single European Market. Accordingly, the expansion of Deutsche Bank into Eastern Germany is a source of particular pride for him.

Even with Kopper's somewhat less global focus, Deutsche Bank will continue to wield considerable power in German industry, as will Dresdner Bank and Commerzbank. One of the primary challenges for the German banking system will be to compete more effectively in international capital markets. In this bank-dominated economy, certain phases of financial services have not been as well developed as they might otherwise have been. For example, stock of medium-sized firms is often not widely traded. Also, when issues are brought to the public market, there are indications that there may not always be as much free competition as should exist. Even a major industry firm may alternate the underwriting of its common stock issues between two of the major banks. If, for a particular reason, that firm wishes not to award the underwriting to the bank whose turn it is next, its wishes to engage the other bank may be refused precisely because it is not that bank's turn.

EXHIBIT 5-2

DEUTSCHE BANK ACQUISITIONS IN THE LATE 1980s

Location	Firm
London (England)	Morgan Grenfell (merchant bank)
Amsterdam (Netherlands)	H. Albert de Bary (stockbroker)
Vienna (Austria)	Antoni Hacker (private bank)
Milan (Italy)	Banca d'America e d'Italia (commercial bank)
Barcelona (Spain)	Banco Commercial Transatlantico (commercial bank)
Toronto (Canada)	McLean McCarthy (stockbroker)
Buenos Aires (Argentina)	Bank of America branches (commercial bank)
Sydney (Australia)	Bain & Co. (stockbroker)

Source

"The Deutsche Bank Juggernaut Will Keep On Rolling," *Euromoney*, January 1990, p. 43.

Without a doubt, the strong central and dedicated capital of German banks has been one of the critical factors in the development of the German economy. A less desirable side effect of this arrangement, however, has been less innovative banking and capital market developments. As the Single European Market continues to evolve, German banks may find it necessary to look for alliances with institutions that have made greater strides in terms of refining new financial services.

INTERNATIONAL TRADITION IN THE UNITED KINGDOM

While Germany has remained relatively insulated from the impact of aggressive competition, the British banking system has become one of the most internationalized in the world. With this openness to foreign influences, it has been touched by some of the same innovation noted in the United States and has been forced to manage change associated with the "Big Bang" and the Single European Market.

A Diverse Financial Market

The financial system of the United Kingdom shares attributes with both its German and U.S. counterparts. Its banking system is dominated by a few large institutions—Barclays, National Westminster, Midland, and Lloyds—as is the case in Germany. At the same time, a vibrant community of other financial services firms exists, as in the United States. This perhaps paradoxical situation is the result of a highly concentrated financial district referred to as the City that has developed a particular expertise in international trade and investment. The City both operates and "thinks" on a global scale.

The factors contributing to this focus are a tradition of international finance, ties from past colonial relationships, and the Euromarket development. London is one of the three most important cities in foreign exchange markets along with New York and Tokyo. During the 1980s, the volume of foreign exchange trading in London was often twice as great as that in the other two cities combined. Before the U.S. dollar became the most dominant world currency, the British pound held this distinction.

In terms of the international connections of British clearing banks, Barclays and Lloyds have long-standing operations in Africa and Latin America, respectively. Midland and National Westminster have expanded into international markets primarily by building in-house expertise and through overseas acquisitions. Standard Chartered is the result of a merger between Standard Bank (with sizeable interests in Africa) and Chartered Bank (with significant interests in the Far East). Hong Kong and Shanghai Banking Corporation is not actually a British bank. Its head office is in Hong Kong and until recently acted as central bank and note issuer.[5] However, its shares are quoted on the London Stock Exchange and its staff contains a number of British citizens. Thus, British banks, over time, have been completely at ease in international transactions and have freely invested overseas.

With respect to the attractions of the City for foreign banks, one of them is that London is situated in the middle time zone that links New York and Tokyo. It is possible to talk to Tokyo in the early morning and New York in the afternoon. Another critical factor has been that London did not have laws that separated commercial and investment banking or that restricted the rates of interest on deposits. Eurodollar deposits were issued in London without the constraint of interest rate ceilings. Eurobonds, first in dollars, then yen and Deutsche marks, were issued in London.

Ironically, British banks did not participate in early Eurobond issuances as much as other institutions. One reason for this is that the United Kingdom imposed currency exchange controls on nonresident sterling transactions until 1979. The British banks were thus not familiar with the new instruments initially and exhibited a certain amount of hesitancy to become involved. Foreign institutions were not so hesitant. Fully seven years after exchange controls were lifted, the top fifteen Eurobond houses did not include one British firm. Exhibit 5-3 shows the rankings and nationalities of these firms.

Where the British firms feared to tread, foreign firms rushed in. When exchange controls were lifted, British fund managers began to invest overseas vigorously. After two years, it was found that 95 percent of these overseas investments were being handled by non-British firms. It was this foreign presence in the bond and stock markets that convinced the Bank of England and the U.K. government to orchestrate the Big Bang in 1986. Under this initiative, British securities firms became more competitive and banks were encouraged to invest in securities activities. The sweeping changes of the 1986 Big Bang would hopefully remedy the absence of British firms from the ranks of major Eurobond participants noted during the same year. Nevertheless, it is clear that the international nature of the British financial markets is firmly established.

British Bank Management

The Big Bang brought the acquisition of a number of firms. All the British clearing banks acquired or expanded already existing securities operations. For example, Barclays formed Barclays de Zoete Wedd through a merger of its merchant bank subsidiary and two other London financial firms. County NatWest is the merchant banking and stockbroker affiliate of National Westminster. Many other mergers took place such that more than $5 billion was spent by Brit-

EXHIBIT 5-3

EUROBOND HOUSES—1986

Rank	Firm	Amount*	Nationality
1	Credit Suisse First Boston	$20.4	Swiss/U.S.
2	Nomura Securities	14.3	Japanese
3	Deutsche Bank	12.2	German
4	Morgan Guaranty	9.8	U.S.
5	Daiwa Securities	8.8	Japanese
6	Morgan Stanley	8.8	U.S.
7	Salomon Brothers	8.4	U.S.
8	Banque Paribas	6.8	French
9	Merrill Lynch Capital Markets	5.9	U.S.
10	Nikko Securities	5.1	Japanese
11	Union Bank of Switzerland	4.8	Swiss
12	Yamaichi Securities	4.4	Japanese
13	Shearson Lehman Brothers	4.1	U.S.
14	Goldman Sachs	3.7	U.S.
15	Société Générale	3.1	French

*Amounts in millions of dollars.

Source

Anthony Hilton, *City within a State*, 1987, p. 55.

ish and non-British firms to acquire securities affiliates. As it turned out, many of these mergers were hastily structured and have not fared well. The clash of cultures between commercial and investment banking has contributed to some of the problems that these mergers encountered.

The most successful has been Barclays de Zoete Wedd (BZW). The chairman of BZW and deputy chairman of Barclays Bank, Sir Peter Middleton, has adopted the philosophy that a multinational firm needs a global investment bank that can offer a wide and ever-widening range of services. BZW's services include foreign exchange and money market instruments, futures and options, and currency and other swaps on a worldwide basis. The firm's equity trading involves more than two dozen stock exchanges. Mergers and acquisitions, buy-out financing, and privatizations are also among the services rendered by BZW.

This is not to say that British banks have not suffered reverses. In fact, a serious restructuring is currently taking place. The nationwide network of branches has proved too costly to maintain intact in the face of severe recession. Branches are prized as a network because there appears to be a positive connection with market share. But the United Kingdom may be "overbanked." In Britain there is one branch for every 1,400 people. This is considerably less than the 2,200 people per branch in France or the 3,000 in Italy. Recessionary conditions in the United Kingdom placed tremendous pressure on profits in the late 1980s and early 1990s, forcing, for example, Barclays to close 350 British branches, and to sell its U.S. banking operations in California, Delaware, and North Carolina.

Barclays realized its first-ever operating loss in 1992. As recently as 1988, the bank was considered one of the best managed, with profits in excess of $2 billion. However, when National Westminster briefly became Britain's largest bank, Barclays issued a $1.4 billion rights offering and invested much of the proceeds in loans to real estate developers in Britain and the United States. Many of these loans soured, pushing 1992 loan losses in North America alone to over $250 million.

Analysts blame the management at Barclays for these problems. In the 19th century, 20 banks combined to ward off takeovers and became Barclay & Company. The combined organization then began to take over other banks. However, the leadership of Barclays has consistently been drawn from the families associated with the merger of the original 20 banks. In almost 100 years, all but two chairmen have been descendants. Critics charge that such close family links have discouraged the installation of better control mechanisms with respect to operations and credit decisions. In 1992, steps were taken to separate the jobs of chairman and president. The chairmanship remains occupied by Andrew Buxton, who was at least partially responsible for past expansion errors. However, in 1993, the post of chief executive was filled from the outside by Martin Taylor, formerly chairman and chief executive of textiles manufacturer Courtaulds.

The growth pains of Barclays and the other major British clearing banks have been relieved at least temporarily by across-the-board profits during the first half of 1993. Combined pre-tax profits for Barclays (£335 million), National Westminster (£421 million), Midland (£385 million), and Lloyds (£498 million) amount to £1.6 billion. Over the long term, the banks hope to balance their retail banking and commercial loan portfolios with sales of mutual funds, insurance, and private-banking services. Having positioned themselves and survived the Big Bang, British banks have the advantages of a truly internationalized environment and freedom to operate in all the financial services that fit their comfort zone.

THE QUEST FOR INTERNATIONAL COMPETITIVENESS IN JAPAN

There are clear contradictions in the role of Japan in international banking. On one hand, Japanese banks top the list of the world's largest. On the other hand, their entry into international banking has been characterized by a series of progressive steps in terms of their range of financial activities. These contradictions are best explained in the context of the Japanese philosophies of international conquest and domestic cooperation.

Measured Steps toward Internationalization

The philosophy of international conquest by Japanese banks is framed by the objective of supporting the companies within their respective *keiretsu* groups. In the 1960s and 1970s, Japanese banks took extraordinary steps to understand the industries that they served, sending hundreds of executives to the companies for assignments in financial, marketing, technical or planning departments. Within a bank, departments were set up to:

- track macroeconomic trends

- study specific industry segments

- perform detailed industrial market surveys

- retain engineers that evaluated both foreign patents and the technological competence of the bank's clients

Thus, the driving motivation was not so much to advance the bank as to advance the fortunes of bank clients.

When bank customers moved overseas, Japanese banks followed. The Euromarkets were attractive to both Japanese industrial and banking firms. However, the unrestricted market was a challenge to the delicate balance between banks and securities firms. The negotiations surrounding the Euromarket participation of Japanese banks served to temper their quest for market share.

By the time Euromarkets developed, lines of demarcation had been drawn between banks and securities firms in the bond markets. In the 1920s, however, banks were free to underwrite corporate bonds, hold them in their own portfolios, or sell them to securities firms for distribution to the public. Japanese exports to Europe were healthy in light of the consumer and industrial needs of that war-torn region. When the European economy recovered, Japanese exports collapsed. Many bond issuers defaulted, bondholders lost their entire investment, and the Ministry of Finance was forced to support a number of banks. Even with this support, the number of banks shrank from 1,283 in 1927 to 538 in 1932.

In the midst of the financial confusion, the Ministry of Finance drafted legislation in 1927 that gave the ministry broad regulatory oversight in exchange for its protection and the assurance that there would be no further entries into the banking industry. Next, the 30 largest bond-underwriting banks formed the Bond Issue Arrangement Committee. With the approval of the Ministry of Finance, the Bond Committee established rules such that no future bonds were to be issued without sufficient collateral. Furthermore, only "trustee banks" would hold the bond collateral, earning a fee for their services. Eight banks, including the Industrial Bank of Japan, formed the core of the Bond Committee. Securities firms were allowed as underwriting members. But only banks could earn the collateral fee. Moreover, the Ministry of Finance blocked attempts by securities firms to acquire trustee banks.

The whole arrangement was effectively designed to reduce corporate reliance on bond financing and increase reliance on bank financing. Even after the imposition of Article 65 by Occupation Forces following World War II, the Bond Committee remained intact. Article 65 permitted banks to underwrite only private placement bonds, thus establishing similar rules to those in the United States, but did not disband the Bond Committee.

Allied Forces had banned all financial institutions from issuing bonds on the premise that bank bonds would compete excessively with industrial bonds, limiting capital available to commercial firms. This ban was lifted in 1950 and, one year later, the Bank of Tokyo was permitted to issue bonds with three-year maturities. Three long-term credit banks and eight trust banks were given similar privileges but with seven-year maturities. The Bank of Tokyo specialized in international finance, had few domestic offices, and represented little threat in the domestic market. The long-term bonds of the long-term credit and trust banks would not compete with short-term deposits. All other banks were precluded from bond issuance.

In the 1970s, the oil-price shock induced recessionary conditions in Japan which, in turn, led industrial corporations to seek cheaper sources of funds. The Euromarkets offered such alternatives. The Ministry of Finance stipulated asset and capital requirements for any firm issuing Eurobonds. Nevertheless, the instruments were an attractive form of financing for those firms that qualified because there were no collateral requirements, no mandatory prospectuses, and lower interest rates. Moreover, the firms had access to variable rate instruments and swaps that were not available domestically. In the first half of the 1970s, the Euromarket accounted for 1.7 percent of Japanese corporate fundraising. In the second half of the decade, the percent was 19.6 percent.

Japanese commercial banks followed their clients and established wholly-owned investment bank subsidiaries or formed joint ventures with British banks. After all, there were no Article 65 restrictions in the Euromarket.

This activity did not go unchallenged, however. In 1969 when a subsidiary of the Bank of Tokyo participated in an underwriting for Honda Motors that was led by Goldman Sachs and Nikko Securities, the securities industry reacted to this offshore encroachment on their territory. Such activity could easily lead to obvious violations of Article 65. What would prevent the banks from negotiating all terms on Japanese soil and simply booking the transaction in London? The Ministry of Finance reacted with a characteristically Japanese compromise. The banks were not forbidden to underwrite in the Euromarket. Instead, they were told that they should not actively solicit business clients from Japan. All other potential clients were allowed in an unrestricted manner.

When Fuji-Kleinwort Benson, a Fuji Bank joint venture, acted as a managing underwriter for a Eurobond issue by Canon in 1974, the securities industry reacted once again. This was even worse than the Bank of Tokyo participation. It was a lead management role by a bank with a large branch network—a network that could be used to pursue other Japanese firms as potential underwriting clients. Together, three bureaus of the Ministry of Finance (Banking, Securities, and International Finance) issued a statement warning foreign subsidiaries not to violate the spirit of Article 65 and reminding banks in foreign joint ventures to be sensitive to their own portfolio positions and not hold too much of a specific issue in their own asset portfolios.

This pronouncement was not much in the way of a prohibition. Later the same year, the Industrial Bank of Japan applied to the International Finance Bureau for a license to open a wholly-owned subsidiary for the purpose of securities transactions in the Euromarket. This led to what was referred to as the Three Bureaus Agreement in which the Banking, Securities, and International Finance Bureaus stipulated that:

- Banks and securities firms should cooperate in the Euromarkets.

- Banks should not use their domestic branch networks to solicit clients for their European securities operations.

- Banks should not negotiate with their Euromarket clients within Japanese national boundaries.

- Banks should not act against the spirit of Article 65.

- Banks should be mindful of the order of the institutions listed on issuance announcements.

Banks could operate in the Euromarkets as long as they did not take a more prominent position than the securities firms. The development of this compromise illustrates the measured steps toward internationalization that Japanese banks have taken. It also helps to explain why they have used such aggressive pricing tactics in the pursuit of loan business. At least this was an area in which their right to operate would not be challenged.

Japanese Bank Management

In their international expansion, Japanese banks have felt less able to compete with their counterparts from other countries because of regulatory constraints. They at least partially compensated for this by purchasing foreign expertise. A partial list of such acquisitions in the United States includes:

Japanese Bank	Target Firm
Sumitomo	Goldman Sachs (investment bank, $500 million)
Fuji	Walter E. Heller (finance company, $425 million)
Sanwa	Leasing affiliate of Continental ($500 million)
Mitsui[6]	Finance affiliate of Security Pacific ($100 million)
Dai-Ichi Kangyo	CIT Financial ($1.4 billion)

All the while, Japanese banks continued an aggressive program of lending both at home and abroad. Like banks in other countries, overextension in declining real estate markets has hurt profits. The manner in which these losses have been handled in Japan, however, is unusual. Presumably in an attempt to maintain stability in the banking markets, nonperforming loans are not reported until they have failed to pay principal and/or interest for one year. Banks are even more reluctant to actually write-off the loans because there is no tax benefit to doing so. Write-offs are not deductible if the loan is collateralized and the borrower is not yet bankrupt.

Banks are now offering fees to firms like trading companies to purchase real estate with the understanding that they will buy it back at an agreed-upon premium in perhaps five years. Led by the officials in the Ministry of Finance, Japanese banks and industrial firms attempt to share the pain of any necessary restructuring. This process is an indication of the power of the *keiretsu* system in Japan. Just as the banks positioned themselves to be supportive of industrial firms in the 1960s and 1970s, it should not be surprising that the industrial firms be called upon to assist the banks in some measure under current circumstances.

At the same time, Japanese banks are not shrinking from the international scene as are U.S. banks. Instead, there is a selective process that involves expansion in other parts of Asia accompanied by retrenchment in other areas. For example, Sumitomo Bank is reducing its ranks in the United States and Europe, but opened a new branch in Bangkok, Thailand, in 1993 after the government established more receptive conditions for foreign banks. Also, seven of the eleven city (large commercial) banks are expected to establish branches in the People's Republic of China, bringing the number of Japanese branches to 17. Total Asian loans outside Japan amount to more than $70 billion as compared to $53 billion of loans to the United States and Europe combined.

Japanese bank management does not shrink from opportunity abroad. Nor does it appear to be discouraged by the slow pace at which the Ministry of Finance is permitting internationalization of the Japanese banking industry.

CONCLUSION

German and Japanese banks have perhaps the best relations with their commercial clients among the industrialized countries of the world. However, both systems face specific challenges. While legally free to do so, German banks have not tended to develop innovations that could be considered on the cutting edge of financial technology. Japanese banks, on the other hand, face regulatory constraints that inhibit their scope of services. Banks in the United States and the United Kingdom have not developed the same kind of client relations as their counterparts in Germany and Japan, but have developed markets and products that have led the way to financial innovation. The possibility of global strategic alliances suggests that these individual strengths can lead to the formation of powerful institutions that can better serve both consumer and industrial markets in the 21st century.

SELECTED REFERENCES

Bennett, Rosemary. "Rocket Scientists Produce a Fresh Wave of Solutions." *Euromoney*, March 1993, pp. 46–54.

"Branching Out: Japanese in Asia." *The Economist*, August 7, 1993, p. 69.

de Carmoy, Herve. *Global Banking Strategy: Financial Markets and Industrial Decay.* Basil Blackwell, Cambridge, Massachusetts, 1990.

Chai, Alan, Alta Campbell, and Patrick J. Spain. *Hoover's Handbook of World Business.* The Reference Press, Austin, Texas, 1993.

Chew, Donald, Editor. *New Developments in Commercial Banking.* Blackwell Finance, Cambridge, Massachusetts, 1991.

Coulbeck, Neil. *The Multinational Banking Industry.* New York University Press, New York, 1984.

"The Deutsche Bank Juggernaut Will Keep on Rolling." *Euromoney*, January 1990, pp. 33–44.

Dwyer, Paula, and Kelley Holland. "At Barclays, a Stiff Upper Lip No Longer Suffices." *Business Week*, April 12, 1993, p. 80.

Feldman, Amy. "CDs for CPAs." *Forbes*, July 19, 1993, pp. 92–95.

Glouchevitch, Philip. *Juggernaut, The German Way of Business: Why It Is Transforming Europe—and the World.* Simon & Schuster, New York, 1992.

"Hidden Jewels: Bank Branches." *The Economist*, January 9, 1993, pp. 71–72.

Hilton, Anthony. *City within a State.* I.B. Tauris, London, 1987.

Katzenstein, Peter J. *Industry and Politics in West Germany: Toward the Third Republic.* Cornell University Press, Ithaca, New York, 1989.

Kearns, Robert L. *Zaibatsu America: How Japanese Firms Are Colonizing Vital U.S. Industries.* The Free Press, New York, 1992.

Kim, James. "Steffen Takes His Scissors to Citicorp." *USA Today*, May 21, 1993, p. 3B.

Lee, Peter. "Capitalizing on Distressed Real Estate." *Euromoney*, March 1993, pp. 58–62.

"A Loan Sale to the Rescue? (Japanese Banks)." *The Economist*, November 30, 1991, pp. 78–79.

Middleton, Sir Peter. "Rapid Change and the Opportunities It Presents Investment Banking." *The Economist*, May 2, 1992, pp. 1–5.

Miller, Richard B. *Citicorp: The Story of a Bank in Crisis.* McGraw-Hill, New York, 1993.

Muolo, Paul. "Are Reverses Set to Advance?" *United States Banker*, May 1993, pp. 28–30.

"New Dreams at Deutsche Bank." *The Economist*, June 22, 1991, pp. 79–82.

"The New Look: Barclay's Bank." *The Economist*, December 12, 1992, p. 86.

"On the Mend: British Bank." *The Economist*, August 7, 1993, pp. 67–68.

"Overburdened: Japanese Banks." *The Economist*, July 25, 1992, pp. 77–78.

Robinson, Danielle. "Tailored for All Tastes." *Euromoney*, February 1993, pp. 63–64.

Rodgers, David. *The Future of American Banking: Managing for Change.* McGraw-Hill, New York, 1993.

Rosenbluth, Frances McCall. *Financial Politics in Contemporary Japan.* Cornell University Press, Ithaca, New York, 1989.

Simon, Hermann. "Lessons from Germany's Midsize Giants." *Harvard Business Review*, March-April 1992, pp. 115–123.

Smith, Eric Owen. "Equity Stakes: Are U.K. Banks Following the German Pattern?" *Banking World*, June 1991, pp. 28–30.

ENDNOTES

1. It should be noted that legislative restrictions such as the Glass-Steagall Act still prevent small and medium-sized businesses from obtaining adequate long-term financing. Also, the new risk-based capital standards require higher capital for corporate loans than for Treasury securities or residential mortgage loans. Such laws, regulations, and capital requirements discourage financing in this critical area.

2. IRAs are Individual Retirement Accounts for employees. Keogh Accounts are retirement accounts for self-employed persons.

3. Foreign currency swaps involve the exchange of currencies at one date and the reversal of the transaction at a specified future date. Currency swaps are derived from parallel loans. In the 1970s, companies in different countries made loans in different currencies to facilitate their multinational operations. In the 1980s, these transactions evolved into currency swaps.

4. LIBOR is an acronym for London Interbank Offering Rate.

5. The People's Republic of China has begun to establish a more official presence in Hong Kong in preparation for its resumption of power in 1997.

6. Mitsui is now part of Sakura Bank, the product of a merger between Mitsui and Taiyo Kobe.

6 Strategic Alliances

INTRODUCTION

Deregulation, European market integration, privatization of state-owned enterprises, and the emergence of Asian markets are factors that collectively are leading to strategic alliances. Some of these new working relationships take the form of ownership stakes, but others take the form of contractual relationships for specific services. Together, these changes help to make the banking industry a dynamic, changing field with growing opportunities across industry lines and national boundaries.

WITHIN THE UNITED STATES

With permission by federal regulators to offer securities services, U.S. commercial banks have formed alliances with securities firms and increased the general level of activity in securities trading. This trend is evident in regional banking circles as well as in the money center institutions.

Mutual Funds

A joint venture between a bank and a securities firm helps move the bank in the direction of a full-service provider of financial products. The greatest asset a commercial bank possesses is its relationship with customers, a characteristic that enables it to cross-sell products. As a group, however, commercial banks were precluded from engaging in securities transactions for many years and, thus, many have not developed the full set of skills appropriate in the securities industry.

In forming such an alliance, a bank must carefully guard its reputation for being a safe haven for investing. In this connection, guidelines were developed in 1993 to protect the bank customer. After federal regulators issued advisory guidelines in July, six banking associations formulated similar guidelines in September.[1] It is suggested that banks locate the areas designated for mutual fund sales away from teller windows so that customers do not confuse FDIC-insured products with mutual funds, which do not protect investors from loss of principal. Also, customers should be informed clearly that mutual funds are not traditional deposit instruments and should be asked to sign a statement to acknowledge their awareness of this difference. Such guidelines are particularly important in view of the popularity of mutual funds, with sales through banks amounting to over $40 billion in 1992 (or 14 percent of the total sales of $300 billion).

Clearly, if a joint venture between a bank and a securities firm goes well, the bank has gained a potentially lucrative fee-income generating operation. If it does not go well, for instance, if the mutual fund partner becomes invasive and uses client lists in ways that create internal friction, the benefits may not justify the costs. If the partnership falls apart, then the bank has wasted valuable time and resources in an arena with little future prospects and has also damaged its image in the financial community. Thus, selecting the right partner is critical.

Early in 1993, IDS and First Bank System (FBS) announced a pilot program to provide financial planning and products through two First Bank offices in Albert Lea and Owatonna, Minnesota. IDS is owned by American Express Company and concentrates primarily on financial planning, with more than 7,300 financial planners in 50 states. The arrangement promises an attractive sales channel for IDS. FBS hopes that the arrangement will help it develop a sharper sales focus and lead to greater revenues. In the Albert Lea office, an IDS licensed representative will offer IDS products while, in the Owatonna office, a sales representative from FBS will offer the same set of products. The results of the pilot program will help determine the direction of future efforts.

Chemical Investment Services is a joint venture between Chemical Banking Corporation and Liberty Financial Services, a subsidiary of Liberty Mutual Insurance, that is expected to be operational by the end of 1993. Products offered to customers will be The Hanover Funds (a family of nine funds managed by Chemical affiliates), five Liberty Financial funds, third-party mutual funds, annuities, stocks, and bonds. Liberty Financial Bank Group will act as broker-dealer, with Chemical focusing on customer delivery. Over time, Chemical Investment Services is expected to grow from its current sales force level of 60 seasoned securities representatives to more than 300, with 190 in Chemical branches in the New York area.

NationsBank has teamed up with Dean Witter in what may be one of the most ambitious combinations to date. There are hundreds of "investment officers" in specific NationsBank offices, with half from each organization. It is projected that by the end of 1993, there will be 620 officers working in 400 NationsBank branches. The bank will concentrate on Dean Witter's mutual funds but will also sell other funds, depending on customer demand. The characteristics that attracted the bank to the brokerage firm are Dean Witter's operational systems, software support, and sales experience. NationsBank hopes that the venture breaks even in 1993 and projects annual profits of up to $60 million by the fifth year of the arrangement. There is even discussion of syndicating their arrangement with other banks.

Securities Trading and NationsBank

NationsBank has been no less aggressive in its approach to securities trading. With the goal of expanding this activity, NationsBank has purchased Chicago Research and Trading (CRT). The $225 million acquisition brought to NationsBank a primary government securities dealer and an experienced trader in options and futures contracts.

NationsBank will now be able to offer its clients a wider array of products through which financial risk can be managed. CRT is one of Chicago's biggest and most respected futures and options traders and is also experienced in currency swaps, forward-rate agreements, and interest-rate options—derivative products that many bank clients find particularly useful.

NationsBank can also use CRT's expertise to manage the risk within its own balance sheet, which grew from $7 billion to roughly $120 billion in the 10 years ended 1993. Its securities investment portfolio is in excess of $25 billion, composed largely of government bonds and mortgage-backed securities.

CRT employs approximately 800 people and has 150 memberships in 19 exchanges worldwide. It trades between 100,000 and 200,000 contracts daily with an average aggregate face value of $10 billion. Its overall strategy is to lock in small, but low-risk profits by capturing arbitrage profits in different markets. It trading expertise should add to NationsBank bottom line in the trading division.

Regional Expansion

NationsBank. The alliances of NationsBank have not been limited to improved product offerings but have also revealed the objective of wide regional expansion, with a ranking of fourth largest U.S. commercial bank. With 1,900 offices, NationsBank has the largest branch network in the country and dominates the Southeast.

The predecessor institutions of NationsBank include NCNB (North Carolina National Bank), Sovran Bank of Virginia, and Citizens & Southern of Georgia. Before NationsBank was formed, NCNB had been the largest bank in North Carolina since 1979. In 1982, NCNB became the first non-Florida bank to expand its retail banking into Florida when it purchased First National Bank of Lake City. During the next two years, it bought banks in Boca Raton, Tampa, Miami, and Bradenton. The acquisition of Pan American Bank in

Miami in 1985 added another 51 offices. By 1988, NCNB was the fourth largest bank in Florida.

The bank's interstate presence was expanded by purchases of Southern National Bankshares, Inc. (Atlanta), Bankers Trust of South Carolina (122 branches statewide), and Prince William Bank of Dumfries (Virginia). By 1986, it was the first bank to operate in five southern states. The following year, it bought CentraBank (Baltimore) to bring the number of southern states to six.

The asset base of NCNB doubled in 1988 when FDIC selected the bank to manage the banks that had been part of failed First RepublicBank Corporation, formerly the largest commercial bank in Texas. NCNB had been permitted to buy 20 percent of the institutions in 1987; by 1989 the remaining share belonged to NCNB. National Bancshares of San Antonio became part of the organization in 1990.

Also in 1990, Citizens and Southern (Georgia) and Sovran (Virginia) merged into C&S/Sovran. The following year, NCNB took over C&S/Sovran to become NationsBank. With a presence in North Carolina, South Carolina, Georgia, Florida, Texas, Maryland, and Virginia and $7 billion in Tier I capital, the selection of the name NationsBank is certainly appropriate. Through regional agreements as to interstate acquisitions and through purchases of troubled financial institutions in other parts of the country, NationsBank has formed alliances to position it for the eventual relaxation of federal branching restrictions. At the same time, the bank is expanding into those activities that will help it remain competitive in both corporate finance and retail banking.

Banc One. With its $61 billion in assets and $4.7 billion in Tier I capital, there are few U.S. banking institutions that have a higher ranking (in terms of capital) than Banc One Corporation— BankAmerica, Citicorp, Chemical Banking Corporation, NationsBank, J.P. Morgan & Company, and Chase Manhattan.

In 1929, the two Columbus banks, Commercial National and City National Bank of Commerce, merged to form City National Bank and Trust. John H. McCoy was the bank's first president. His son John G. McCoy took over in 1958 and shortly thereafter started to break with tradition. In 1966, the bank introduced the first Visa credit card outside of California (then BankAmericard). McCoy formed First Banc Group in 1967, a holding company of which City National was a subsidiary. Then in 1968, the company bought Farmers Savings and Trust of Mansfield, Ohio. By 1985, the holding company owned a total of 44 Ohio banks.

In a 1977 alliance, First Banc Group was designated as the bank to manage the Cash Management Account (CMA) for Merrill Lynch. This innovation brought together a retail brokerage account, a checking account, and a debit card, representing an aggressive post-Glass-Steagall combination of services.

In 1979, First Banc Group changed its name to Banc One and all bank subsidiaries included Banc One in their names.[2] When the third generation McCoy, John B., took over the reins in 1984, the emergence of multistate regional agreements with respect to bank acquisitions had begun. Banc One expanded into Indiana, Kentucky, Michigan, and Wisconsin. With FDIC guarantees against loss, Banc One purchased the loans of 20 of the branches of MCorp (Texas), paying $34 million for $11 billion in assets ($2.5 billion of which were troubled). In 1991, Illinois was added to the list of states in which Banc One operates.

Early on, Banc One grew by acquiring smaller banks, consolidating back-office operations, and mixing local control with regional marketing power. The company continues to stress retail banking, quickly taking advantage of technological advances such as ATMs and home banking systems. With its technology, Banc One maintains a master file that records which products each customer is likely to buy. Its corporate clientele is the middle market. The bank's overall strategy involves conservative lending, innovative technology, dedicated customer service, and mergers with other banks.

In identifying potential candidates for merger, Banc One follows certain guidelines:

- Never merge with a peer.

- Do not buy a bank more than one-third the size of the existing Banc One organization.

- Leave the existing management in place.

- Allow each bank to make its own decisions in a decentralized fashion.

These decentralized operations are coordinated through a system of common products, technology, and monthly reporting requirements.

As the result of these strategic alliances, Banc One's 1993 asset base of $61 billion is twice its 1990 level. With locations in Ohio, Kentucky, Indiana, Illinois, Michigan, Wisconsin, and Texas, the Banc One presence now reaches from the Great Lakes to the Gulf of Mexico.

PNC Financial Corporation. One notch below Banc One in the capital rankings is PNC, with Tier I capital of $3.7 billion and assets of $51 billion. The First National Bank of Pittsburgh was one of the first banks chartered in 1863 under the National Bank Act passed in the same year. The bank merged with Second National Bank of Pittsburgh in 1913. By 1921, the institution had also merged with Peoples National Bank (Pittsburgh).

In the 1940s, the bank made strategic acquisitions to establish a strong trust business, acquiring Pittsburgh Trust, Sewickley Valley Trust, and Monongahela Trust. The name of the bank was then changed to Pittsburgh National. In 1965 the bank entered the credit card business and joined the Bankamericard program in 1969. The holding company Pittsburgh National Corporation was formed in 1968 and a series of holding company acquisitions followed: Pittsburgh National Discount (commercial paper), PINACO (insurance on commercial loans), Pittsburgh National Leasing (lease financing), and Pittsburgh National Life (credit life, health, and accident reinsurance). These acquisitions enabled the bank to enter nonbank financial activities that were permitted within the scope of bank holding companies.

In 1983 another strategic merger strengthened the institution's position in money management and trust operations. Pittsburgh National combined with Provident National of Philadelphia to become PNC Corporation. Acquisitions followed in other parts of Pennsylvania, Kentucky, Ohio, New Jersey, and Delaware.

It should be noted that PNC has had to absorb significant loan losses in recent years, due primarily to real estate exposure in eastern

Pennsylvania. Write-offs in 1990 drove return on assets to an uncharacteristically low 0.2 percent. The bank has also undergone a restructuring of back-office operations to achieve greater efficiencies.

Nevertheless, the strategic alliances that bolstered the fee-generating activities, such as trust operations, have paid handsome dividends. In 1988 fee income was not quite $550 million. By 1992, it was $900 million and the bank was earning 1.17 percent on assets. PNC Securities, which offers mutual funds and related products, is projected to employ 500 to 600 brokers by the end of 1995. The bank also has significant operations in the area of private placement investment banking. In 1992, the 70 private placements in which the bank participated generated $4 billion. PNC appears to have found its niche, a strong and diverse regional banking presence with a diversified scope of services.

BankAmerica. In terms of capital, BankAmerica is the top-ranking U.S. bank with $6 billion in Tier I capital. Its $179 billion in assets earn it a rank second only to Citicorp. The San Francisco-based holding company is similar to Citicorp in other ways as well. BankAmerica has always aggressively sought to become a truly national bank.

Amadeo Giannini founded the Bank of Italy in 1904. His philosophy of banking leaned toward providing financing for small merchants and farmers as well as reasonably priced mortgage loans, with attention to the personal aspects of banking. For example, after the earthquake of 1906, Giannini retrieved the gold, cash, and notes from the bank before the resulting fire destroyed them and promptly opened a makeshift branch on a pier from which he made loans for reconstruction.

Accomplishing the objective of serving the whole state of California (and ultimately the entire United States) meant that the bank had to operate outside San Francisco. To circumvent the prohibition against intrastate branching, Giannini purchased the Bank of America of Los Angeles with 21 branches. In 1928, Giannini formed a holding company, Transamerica Corporation, to manage the banks and other enterprises. By 1930, both the Bank of Italy and Bank of America were operating as Bank of America.

Through strategic alliances via the holding company format, Transamerica reached outside California, eventually controlling 41 percent of commercial bank office locations, 39 percent of commercial bank deposits, and 50 percent of commercial bank loans in Arizona, California, Nevada, Oregon, and Washington. This much control of commercial banking interests in one company led the Federal Reserve to bring an antitrust action against Transamerica in 1948. Essentially, the court ruled in favor of Transamerica, requiring it to divest of Bank of America, but allowing it to retain the remaining 46 banks and to expand into other states if it elected to do so. It was this case and the apparently sympathetic ruling of the courts that led to the Bank Holding Company Act of 1956. The act was intended to prevent the spread of bank holding companies and the broad-based financial services that they offered.

Neither the court decision nor the Bank Holding Company Act dissuaded the Bank of America from its goal of nationwide banking. Transamerica divested its Bank of America in 1958. In the same year, Bank of America introduced Bankamericard, which would later become Visa in 1977. The bank also dramatically increased its international presence, becoming one of the most active international lenders in the 1950s and 1960s in the United States. In 1968, Bank of America became a subsidiary of BankAmerica Corporation.

When A. W. Clausen became CEO in 1970, the bank embarked on an aggressive plan for international and real estate lending. During his tenure, earnings and assets quadrupled. When Clausen left in 1981 to become head of the World Bank, he was replaced by Samuel Armacost, who inherited a number of problems, the most serious of which was large loan losses. The aggressive international lending was done with little strategic focus, poor communication between headquarters and overseas locations, and few credit controls. Overhead costs soared out of control and domestic loans to energy, agriculture, and real estate sectors soured. Earnings slumped, as Bank of America lost its ranking as largest U.S. bank to Citicorp. By 1985, Armacost was forced to lay off employees for the first time in the bank's history. The following year, Armacost himself resigned under fire.

Clausen returned as CEO until 1990, during which time the bank reduced both costs and the troubled domestic loan portfolio. In 1990 under the new CEO, Richard M. Rosenberg, BankAmerica acquired eight troubled thrifts and expanded its presence from three states to seven. The back-office operations were modernized in 20 regional centers. At the same time, the bank retrenched from international markets, closing down or consolidating many of its branches.

Clearly, the focus of Bank of America shifted to consumer banking in California. Branches adopted aggressive merchandising initiatives, including calling on customers to ask what they needed and giving branch managers and employees performance-related bonuses. Under Rosenberg, the vision of BankAmerica is not unlike that of Giannini, that is, nationwide banking. With the acquisition of Security Pacific in 1991, BankAmerica tops the ranks of U.S. banks in terms of capital. The strategic alliances with thrifts and Security Pacific have provided BankAmerica with a solid platform from which it may eventually orchestrate a nationwide expansion.

EUROPEAN ALLIANCES

As many U.S. banks retrench from their overseas activities because of international and domestic loan losses and because of more stringent capital requirements, there remain a number of opportunities that have not been completely exploited. In order to realize some of these opportunities, it will be necessary to form alliances—not necessarily mergers, but instead other working relationships that capitalize on the competitive advantages of each of the partners.

Capitalizing on U.S. Strengths

Despite the reverses in international lending, U.S. banks have been successful in making a niche for themselves in overseas markets. Foreign currency and investment banking are two of these areas.

Foreign Exchange. In 1993, *Euromoney* surveyed 1,000 industrial corporations, banks, insurance companies, institutional investors, and state agencies whose foreign exchange turnover rate was $500 million or more annually.[3] The respondents were asked to name specific financial houses that received the highest proportion of their foreign exchange business and the total amount of foreign exchange business that they conducted. The surveys themselves were sent to institutions that represented North America (31 percent), the United Kingdom (25 percent), the rest of Europe (29 percent), the Far East (10 percent), and the Middle East (5 percent).

Among the 15 favorite houses in an overall ranking, seven were American—Citibank (1), Chemical (2), J.P. Morgan (4), Chase Manhattan (8), BankAmerica (12), Goldman Sachs (14), and Bankers Trust (15). *Euromoney* had asked respondents to rank houses with respect to their proficiency in currency-specific transactions. Among the top five houses, U.S. names again appeared frequently:

Currency	*U.S. House (Rank)*
German DM	Citibank (1), Chemical (3), Chase Manhattan (4)
Japanese yen	Citibank (1), BankAmerica (2), Chemical (3), Chase Manhattan (5)
British pound	Citibank (2), Chemical (3), Chase Manhattan (#5)
Swiss franc	Chase Manhattan (3), Chemical (5)

U.S. institutions had similar favorable showings among the top five houses in the categories of currency derivatives and forward contracts:

Contract	*U.S. House (Rank)*
Swaps	Citibank (1), Bankers Trust (2), Chemical (3), J.P. Morgan (4)
Options	Chase Manhattan (2), J.P. Morgan (3), Bankers Trust (4)
Forwards	Up to one year: Citibank (1), BankAmerica (2), J.P. Morgan (3), Bankers Trust (5) From one to three years: Citibank (1), Chemical (3), Chase Manhattan (5)

Over three years:
Citibank (1), J.P. Morgan (2), Chemical (3)

The expertise of U.S. banks is clearly recognized in actual transactions. Yet it is even more pronounced in the area of economic research for currency transactions, where U.S. firms completely dominate the top ranks.

Type of research	U.S. House (rank)
Short-term	Chase Manhattan (1), Citibank (2), Goldman Sachs (3), J.P. Morgan (4), BankAmerica and Chemical (tied for 5)
Long-term	Citibank (1), Goldman Sachs (2), Chase Manhattan (3), J.P. Morgan (4), Chemical (5)

Investment Banking. While the results of this poll point to the competitive advantage that U.S. institutions have in foreign exchange markets, it should also be noted that there are certain elements that will be critical in terms of the ability of a financial institution to adequately serve institutional clients, which are an increasingly important segment of investors. Because of the extent of new issues on a global basis, one of these elements is an *investment banking* capacity.

Bilateral lending, that is, a borrower receiving funding through one institution only and eliminating the need for a syndicate, can be risky business. Attempting to compete in bilateral lending, a bank usually must go head-to-head with a borrower's relationship bank. Such attempts generally will be successful only if the bank offers some form of concession—either on price or on the covenant contained in the loan agreement. Those banks that make such concessions are actually placing lower credit into their investment portfolios, which can affect the market as a whole. From the borrower's perspective, these concessions may be misleading and the borrower may be disappointed in subsequent financings. In later attempts to access mainstream funding, the borrower may discover that the terms it has come to anticipate (because of bilateral concessions) are unrealistic.

Furthermore, market analysts believe that the demand for syndicated loans is likely to increase as corporate and sovereign borrowers come forward. This anticipation is in stark contrast to recent experience. In 1992, primary market loan syndications fell nearly 25 percent from 1991 levels to $134 billion. However, the first half of 1993 was only marginally lower than the corresponding period in 1992—$62 billion vs. $63 billion. Belief in the return of corporate and sovereign borrowers is supported by large issues by British Aerospace (£1.4 billion refinancing jointly arranged by four U.K. clearing banks) and by the Kingdom of Spain (Ecu5 billion standby revolving credit arranged by NatWest Capital Markets). In addition, there may be demand on the part of U.K. insurance companies that are seeking to increase their capital. There are no guidelines (such as the Basel Accord capital arrangements for banks) for appropriate capital levels for insurance companies, but there are competitive benefits associated with strong capital bases, including the ability to acquire other insurance companies. A likely structure for these loans is a nonrecourse arrangement that is backed by the insurer's underlying policy cash flows, with the nonrecourse feature qualifying the issue as capital. Chase is already assembling a group of banks that may be interested in participating in these loan syndications. Thus, investment-banking style underwriting skills will be important in global banking markets. The strong research capabilities of U.S. banks are extremely valuable in this regard.

The top 10 loan arrangers in the Euro syndicated loan market in 1992 (and the amount of loans syndicated) include eight U.S. institutions: Chemical Bank ($75 billion), J.P. Morgan ($46 billion), Citicorp ($41 billion), Bankers Trust ($30 billion), Chase Manhattan ($29 billion), First National Bank of Chicago ($24 billion), BankAmerica ($24 billion), and NationsBank ($14 billion).

The demand for research skill is not limited to foreign exchange markets and loan syndications, however. Sovereign borrowers are major bond issuers. Here, the combination of relationship banking and strong research is critical. Specific steps can be taken to improve an institution's likelihood of being given a mandate, that is, being selected as lead manager of a sovereign bond issue:

- *Understand the borrower's program.* This requires that a bank understand the sovereign's financing goals and legal constraints. There is a general trend for sovereign issuers to provide more information so that institutions can submit more informed bids.

- *Determine whether the sovereign is attempting to actively manage its liabilities.* Some issuers have become sensitive to the currency mix and timing of their liabilities. The successful bids will require an understanding of such strategic decisions as well as the more customary funding-level requirements.

- *Be prepared to offer liability management advice.* Not all sovereigns rely on their underwriters for liability management advice, but most will take note of the availability of this service.

- *Be prepared to assist with any credit-rating difficulties.* When borrowers have less than an AAA credit rating, the presentation of the deal to rating agencies can be a critical phase of the offering. The time and energy spent in research and documentation can be instrumental in obtaining the highest possible credit rating for the sovereign issuer.

- *Be attentive to the aftermarket.* When bonds are issued, the performance of the bonds in the secondary market will affect later issuances by the borrower. In addition, a sovereign may expect the firm to which it awards the mandate to make a market in the bonds.

- *Remember that relationships count.* Unless a firm has established some sort of relationship with a soveriegn, it will be difficult to obtain the mandate, or, in some cases, to even be invited to bid.

- *Don't neglect the competitive issues.* While relationships are important for initial consideration, ultimately the bid with the most attractive terms and services will be most competitive.

- *Have the ability to offer a truly global issue.* The bonds that can be promoted in several markets will be the most successful. This means that the underwiting firm must have established allowances (through its own offices or syndication relationships) to offer an international presence.

If these steps are taken, a financial institution can significantly increase its chances of being selected to lead a sovereign bond flotation.

In addition to the opportunities in foreign currencies, loan syndications, and bond issues, there is a growing trend toward direct equity investments, including depository receipt transactions—ADRs, IDRs, or GDRs. *American depository receipts* (ADRs) are negotiable certificates issued by a U.S. bank for shares of stock issued by a foreign corporation. The securities are held in a custodial account, either at the issuing bank or an agent. ADRs are registered with the Securities and Exchange Commission, give the holder the same rights as shareholders, are priced in dollars, and trade in either over-the-counter or organized exchanges. Among the 10 most actively traded ADRs are eight from European countries:

Company	Country	Exchange
Glaxo Holdings	U.K.	NYSE
Hanson	U.K.	NYSE
British Petroleum	U.K.	NYSE
Saatchi & Saatchi	U.K.	NYSE
Telefonica Nacional de España	Spain	NYSE
Wellcome	U.K.	NYSE
Memorex	Netherlands	NASDAQ
SmithKline Beecham	U.K.	NYSE

The remaining two are issues of Telefonos de Mexico (Telmex), one traded on the NYSE (New York Stock Exchange) and the other on NASDAQ (National Association of Securities Dealers Automated Quotations).

An *International Depository Receipt* (IDR) is the non-U.S.-dollar equivalent of an ADR that is sold in Europe. *Global Depository Receipts* (GDRs) are sold in both the United States and Europe. In the case of a GDR, the shares are easily exchanged between different markets.

An increasing volume in these securities is expected. ADRs valued at a record $123 billion were traded on the NYSE, AMEX (American Stock Exchange), and NASDAQ during 1992, with Glaxo leading at $570 million in trading volume. U.S. banks can benefit from these high volumes.

In addition to depository receipts, institutional investors will be attracted by the ability of a bank to provide detailed research on stocks after issuance. As new regions open up for investment, there may a temptation on the part of underwriting units to simply push the latest "hot" investment idea. But institutional investors highly value strong, detailed local research on the market. In addition, the quality of execution of trades is important. Thus, strategic alliances that bring together solid research and demonstrated expertise in trading and execution (in both primary and secondary markets) will lead to a highly competitive operation.

Privatizations

The wave of privatizations that is sweeping the world represents an opportunity to construct alliances that serve investor needs as these markets open up. The privatizations are sell-offs of state-owned assets. For the most part, they involve telecommunications, utilities, and banking and insurance. Salomon Brothers estimates that $120 billion in equity will be raised in privatizations between 1993 and 1995—$55 billion in Europe, $30 billion in Latin America, $20 billion in Asia and the Pacific Rim, $5 billion in the United States, and $10 billion elsewhere.[4] Thus, Europe is the single most promising arena for new, primary market financing.

The United Kingdom led the push to privatization beginning in the 1980s with sales of British Aerospace, British Airways, British Telecom, Cable & Wireless (overseas telephone company), Britoil, Enterprise Oil, British Petroleum, British Gas, and Jaguar Cars. To date these sales of stock have raised £40 billion (approximately $60 billion). More sales are planned as shown in Exhibit 6-1.

France is expecting to raise Ffr40 billion (approximately $7 billion) by the end of 1993, with the total projected at Ffr300 billion ($52.5 billion). The planned sell-offs are listed in Exhibit 6-2. The timing of the sales has not been determined, but Banque Nationale de Paris is expected to be the first enterprise offered for public sale.

EXHIBIT 6-1

U.K. PRIVATIZATIONS

Enterprise	Industry
British Telecom	Telecommunications (third tranche)
British Coal	Mining
British Rail passenger services	Rail
British Rail freight services	Rail
Red Star	British Rail parcel division
36 local bus companies and buses in London	Transport
Belfast International Airport	Airport
East Midlands International Airport	Airport
Parcelforce	Post Office parcel division
Trust Ports	Port
Vehicle Inspectorate and Transport Research Laboratory	Miscellaneous
Property Services Agency's five building management businesses	Miscellaneous
Dairy Crest	Milk products
PowerGen	Utilities
National Power	Utilities

Source

"Who's Selling What: The Global Picture," *Euromoney*, July 1993, pp. 114–25.

Crédit Lyonnais, a lesser credit, may not be offered for two to three years, allowing time for its balance sheet to be strengthened. It should be noted that five banks will be sold in total, as well as five insurance companies.

Italy hopes to raise as much as L27,000 (approximately $19 billion) in its sales of state-owned enterprises over a three-year period. As noted in Exhibit 6-3, these sales include seven banks and two insurance companies.

Among the German privatizations, shown in Exhibit 6-4, is Deutsche Telekom. The sale of this telecommunications enterprise may eventually represent one of the largest public issuances ever offered.

EXHIBIT 6-2

FRENCH PRIVATIZATIONS

Enterprise	Industry
Aérospatiale	Aerospace engineering
Air France	Transport
Banque Hervet	Bank
Banque Nationale de Paris	Bank
Caisse Centrale de Réassurance	Insurance
Caisse Nationale de Prévoyance-Assurance	Insurance
Compagnie des Machines Bull	Information technology
Compagnie Génerale Maritime	Transport
Crédit Local de France	Banking
Crédit Lyonnais	Banking
Péchiney	Metals
Renault	Motors
Rhone-Poulenc	Chemicals/pharmaceuticals
AGF-Assurances Générales de France	Insurance
GAN-Groups des Assurances Nationale	Insurance
UAP-Union des Assurances de Paris	Insurance
SEITA-Société Nationale d'Exploitation Industrielle des Tabacs et Allumettes	Tobacco
Société Marseillaise de Crédit	Bank
SNECMA-Société Nationale d'Etude et de Construction de Morteurs d'Aviation	Technology
Elf Aquitaine	Energy/oil
Thomson	Electronics
Usinor-Sacilor	Steel

Source

"Who's Selling What: The Global Picture," *Euromoney*, July 1993, pp. 114–25.

Half of the stock could raise as much as DM30 billion (approximately $18 billion). The Treuhand (short for Treuhandanstalt) sale is interesting because this holding company has been responsible for restructuring and selling the East German enterprises absorbed by the

EXHIBIT 6-3

ITALIAN PRIVATIZATIONS

Enterprise	Industry
Crediop	Banking
Credito Italiano	Banking
Banca Commerciale Italiana	Banking
Banca di Roma	Banking
Banco di Napoli	Banking
BNL's Efibanca subsidiary	Banking
Istituto Mobiliare Italiano	Banking
ENEL	Utilities
AGIP	Energy/oil
AgipCoal foreign coal mining	Mining
SNAM	Energy/oil
ENI Group	Energy/oil
SME	Food
INA	Insurance
STET	Telecommunications
Finnmeccanica	Engineering
Nuovo Pignone	Engineering
Assitalia	Insurance
Iritecna	Construction
Saipem	Energy equipment
EFIM subsidiaries	Industrial holding company
SIV	Glassmaker
Railways	Transport

Source

"Who's Selling What: The Global Picture," *Euromoney*, July 1993, pp. 114–25.

country after reunification in 1990. By the end of 1992, the Treuhand had sold 7,092 companies and operating units (366 to foreign investors). Virtually all the small- and medium-sized retailers, restaurants, and pharmacies are in private hands. The Treuhand still holds many of the farms and forestries that it originally acquired.

EXHIBIT 6-4

GERMAN PRIVATIZATIONS

Enterprise	Industry
Deutsche Telekom	Telecommunications
Lufthansa	Airlines
Treuhand	Holding company
Bonn-Cologne Airport	Airport
Bundesbahn tourism office	Miscellaneous
Bundesanzeiger Verlagsgesellschaft	Printing
Transportgummi in Bad Blankenburg	Manufacturing
Transport businesses in Berlin	Transport

Source

"Who's Selling What: The Global Picture," *Euromoney*, July 1993, pp. 114–25.

Turkey is also an interesting arena, with a broad range of future privatizations in petrochemicals, construction materials, the food industry, airlines, and hotels as listed in Exhibit 6-5.

These and other privatizations represent opportunities for U.S. banks to become involved in new markets in a number of roles. One of these roles is clearly participation in equity issue flotations. Here the same set of principles that apply to a successful sovereign bond issue apply (see previous section). Another possible role is offering trade finance within the national boundaries of the privatizing countries. A third is servicing U.S. industrial clients that are directly involved in the industries themselves. A fourth way of participating is providing investment research services to those institutions that are actively involved in underwriting, lending, or otherwise investing in the newly privatized ventures. It is now apparent that the successful firm may offer research in one of two ways:

- A London-based, pan-European research team will provide insights on entire industries across Europe.

- A local research team can provide invaluable information about specific countries or firms.

EXHIBIT 6-5

TURKISH PRIVATIZATIONS

Enterprise	Industry
Petkim Petrokimya	Petrochemicals
Petrol Ofisi	Petroleum distributor
Tupras	Refinery
Teletas	Telecommunications
Netas	Telecommunications
Eleven equity participations by TKB Development Bank	Various
Citosan	Cement
Trakmak	Engineering
Layne Bowler	Electrical equipment
Konya Seker	Food manufacturer
Ankara Halk Ekmek	Food
USAS	Airline caterer
THY	Airline
Minerals Exploration General Directorate	Mining
Sek Sut Endustris	Dairy producer
Yem Sanayii ve Ticaret	Animal feeds
Five hotels operated by Turban	Hotels

Source

"Who's Selling What: The Global Picture," *Euromoney*, July 1993, pp. 114–25.

The reason for this division is that there are essentially two equity markets in Europe. The first is the set of highly liquid, blue-chip, multinational firms with access to world capital markets. Daimler-Benz is an example of such a firm—one that may be primarily interested in diversifying its shareholder base. Interested investors will want considerable information on the European, if not worldwide, automobile industry. The second set of firms is composed of much less liquid firms about which the investing public may have little, if any, information. Without detailed local information, institutional investors will have difficulty evaluating such firms. Nevertheless, these small and medium-sized firms represent potentially some of the best investment opportunities in terms of rate of return. Thus, a regional bank in the United States could initiate a strategic alliance with a local European firm to fill a niche for research information about a particular country or set of firms within that country.

The European Securities Markets

European markets offer banks a number of vehicles for participation, including the commercial paper, bond, and equity markets. The cost of Eurocommercial paper is competitive with domestic commercial paper and increasingly competitive with bank loan rates. Highly rated borrowers that can generally achieve a cost of LIBOR plus 1/8 percent on loans can issue Eurocommercial paper for a cost below LIBOR.[5]

At the same time, the volume of Eurocommercial paper remains small in comparison to domestic commercial paper in the United States. While outstanding Eurocommercial paper totals approximately $80 billion, U.S. commercial paper is closer to $540 billion.[6] One of the reasons for the difference in activity in the two markets is the growth of domestic commercial paper markets in Europe. Eurocommercial paper investors are interested primarily in credit ratings, while domestic investors are more concerned with name recognition. This means that domestic markets can offer some lesser credits with name recognition a lower cost of funds in their domestic markets than in the Euromarket equivalent.

Another factor that helps determine the degree of interest in issuing Eurocommercial paper is the availability of swaps. Three-quarters of Eurocommercial paper is issued in U.S. dollars but swapped into other currencies. But swaps also are part of the off-balance-sheet activity that has been included in Basel Accord requirements for capital coverage. As a result, the cost of swap opportunities has increased, pushing up the cost of issuing Eurocommercial paper. There are clearly opportunities for banks in the Eurocommercial paper market that can offer lower cost swaps and credit enhancements for client firms to qualify their issue for a high credit rating.

Also, investor demand will have an impact on the aggregate issuance of Eurocommercial paper. Low short-term interest rates have a tendency to push investors into more medium-term securities, such as floating-rate, medium-term Euronotes. This is especially true in the one- to two-year maturity range when the yield curve is fairly steep, as is the dollar yield curve currently, with its low short-term rates.

On the other hand, there continues to be strong growth in the Eurobond market. Projected issuances could go as high as $350 billion in 1993, up from $293 billion in 1992, which was itself a record year. The strong growth is attributed to increased sovereign borrowing to finance budget deficits, greater participation by local governments, and fundraising by corporations that have become interested in financing in anticipation of increases in interest rates.

Although not as large as the Eurocommercial paper and Eurobond markets, the Euroequities markets continue to grow. From new issues of $23.8 billion in 1991 to $24.4 billion in 1992, 1993 volume is expected to show significant increases. This heightened activity will be attributable primarily to the acceleration of cross-border portfolio investment. In the period from 1975 to 1979, private portfolio investment represented 15 percent of total cross-border investment. Currently, private investment is as much as 75 percent of the total. Within these private flows, equity comprised 5 percent during the 1970s and now constitutes 36 percent. The growth in equity markets is expected to continue in light of liberalization of European financial markets, EC harmonization, and widespread privatization campaigns.

Thus, the opportunities of European markets clearly involve securities activities as well as foreign exchange transactions and loan syndications. An examination of specific strategic alliances that have or will capitalize on these opportunities is useful.

European Bank Mergers and Alliances

From 1987 through 1993, more than 240 mergers of European banks occurred, with particularly intense activity during the period 1989 to 1991 when 140 acquisitions occurred. French banks alone represented 74 of the alliances, while Germany (35), the United Kingdom (36), Spain (33), and Italy (27) make up roughly comparable shares of the total. The target countries were fairly uniformly distributed. Spain was the most sought-after country—49 acquired institutions were Spanish. France (44) was next, followed by the United Kingdom (39), Italy (28), and Germany (22).

The predominant form of alliance was outright acquisition (43 percent), but purchases of minority interests (32 percent) were also common. Joint ventures represented only 8 percent of the total alliances. Spanish institutions showed a particular preference for joint ventures and formal cooperation agreements, e.g., the arrangement between Banco Santander and Royal Bank of Scotland.

In France, the acquisitive nature of the banking sector is best illustrated by Crédit Lyonnais. While contracting its own employment from 42,051 in 1986 to 40,411 in 1990, employment outside France expanded from 9,755 to 19,427. Non-French banking offices expanded from 684 to 1,200. The scope of these acquisitions has been wide, including Banco Comercial Español (BCE) in Spain, Crédit Lyonnais PK Leasing in Germany, and Leasing Ethniki Lyonnais in Greece, to name a few. The bank has sought to acquire credit card processing facilities in the United Kingdom and to boost its share of the retail market in Belgium. In the largest bank takeover in Germany since the end of World War II, Crédit Lyonnais became the major shareholder of BfG Bank. Apparently, the level of these expansionary activities created some of the tension in Europartners—the joint venture that it previously shared with Commerzbank (of Germany)—that led to the dissolution of the arrangement. Nevertheless, Crédit Lyonnais has formed important strategic alliances in retail and wholesale banking.

For their part, German banks are now focusing more on developing markets in eastern Germany. The objective is to capitalize on the potentially lucrative retail market where 50 commercial banks represent over 800 branches in the eastern region of the country. In addition to the retail market possibilities, Frankfurt is becoming one of the most desirable locations for European operations, after London. One reason is the strength of the Deutsche mark, which has become an increasing popular currency for Eurobond issues in light of recent instability in the Exchange Rate Mechanism (ERM). Another factor that adds to Frankfurt's attraction is the new Deutsche Börse A.G., a holding company formed early in 1993 to manage Germany's eight stock exchanges. The international appeal of the London market continues to be a challenge for Frankfurt, but the Börse promises to give the German financial capital market a technological edge.

In the United Kingdom, Lloyds Bank has approached its strategic alliances by recognizing that its future strength will lie *not* in deposit-taking and lending, but in providing an array of financial services. Especially important in this evolution are private banking services and the sale of insurance and investment products. At the same time, this has meant exiting its less profitable merchant banking business. And the stock market has apparently endorsed this approach; Lloyds' stock recently has outperformed that of any other large U.K. bank.

In general, the U.K. clearing banks have found it less advantageous to enter cross-border markets through establishing offices under their own names. Along these lines, Lloyds has sold many of its retail operations in continental Europe and has established special correspondent relationships. National Westminster (NatWest) has a somewhat similar approach. In 1993, NatWest, Société Générale (France), and Commerzbank (Germany) entered into an agreement to facilitate cross-border payments in the retail market. The system is slated to become operational in 1994.

These are but a few examples of the types of alliances that are being formed in European banking. There are several ways to form these relationships:

- outright purchase of same-industry firms, that is, commercial banks

- acquisitions of companies in related industries, for example, insurance, investment-related products, or leasing

- special correspondent relationships

- technology-sharing arrangements

There are opportunities for U.S. banks because innovative and technology-driven products can now be offered in Europe with more ease than has been possible in the past. The U.S. institutions that participate in the early formation of strategic alliances can best expect to benefit in the long run.

THE DYNAMIC ASIAN MARKET

While the European banking arena is in a fluid state of evolution, the Asian market is currently the world's most dynamic. To a significant extent, this phenomenon is attributable to the People's Republic of China.

Greater China

In 1993, Chinese investment in real terms increased by 50 percent over 1992 levels. The result has been a booming economy and a double-digit inflation rate.

According to Deng Xiaoping, who has significant moral suasion, growth in the economy should not be constrained from the "healthy" levels that have been evident in recent years. Many banks have over-extended themselves to meet the demands of capital formation and, in some cases, property speculation. There is a major construction boom in the country's coastal regions and this construction is being financed largely by the banks.

Zhu Rongji, the new governor of the People's Bank of China (the central bank), has been charged with containing inflation and with reforming the financial system. The People's Bank of China has enjoyed its current status as a western-style central bank only since 1984. However, with personnel of less than 100 people, the Bank is still seen as essentially rubber-stamping the wishes of the State Council and the State Planning Commission. Over 70 percent of state banks' allocations are directed by the central planning mechanism. Moreover, control of the remaining 30 percent is not much more effective. Allocations by specialized banks, including the Bank of China, People's Construction Bank, and Agricultural Bank of China, have exceeded planned loan allocations for 1993 by more than 50 percent. Because of these lax controls, it has been estimated that actual nonperforming loans of specific banks may range anywhere from 3 to 45 percent of total loan portfolios. Furthermore, many banks operate nonbanking financial institutions, such as leasing and consumer credit companies, to escape the scrutiny of the People's Bank of China altogether.

In order to reform the system, Zhu advocates a new central banking law with clauses to direct the People's Bank of China to act merely as a supervisory and regulatory agency rather than, as is now the case, a hybrid between a commercial and a central bank. Then the specialized banks will be freed from politically motivated, but unprofitable, loans. This will encourage more fundamentally sound investments by these institutions.

In the meantime, Zhu has set down rules to rein in the excesses of the system. He announced several measures at a conference in Beijing shortly after his appointment in July 1993:

- no new loans to nonbanking financial institutions
- recall of Rmb100 billion in such loans[7]
- increased savings deposits by all banks
- visits and inspections of regional banking offices by enforcement teams of the People's Bank of China

Zhu has set the tone for the reformed banking system of China. Of course, it will be a delicate balancing act to perform, given Deng Xiaoping's stated endorsement of an expansionary economy. Nevertheless, these are steps in the right direction for the development of a modern financial system.[8]

The attraction for commercial banks is considerable. Greater China is composed of South China, Hong Kong, and Taiwan. The recent investment wave has been spurred by the synergies created in this region. China contributes a low-cost labor pool and abundant land resources. Hong Kong is a source of marketing and financial skills. Taiwan is a base for technology transfer. Taiwanese companies have set up roughly 4,000 factories in South China to manufacture bicycles, handbags, and sporting goods. Hong Kong companies have approximately 25,000 factories in China that employ three million workers.

The intent of the Chinese government is clearly to encourage development of this economic arrangement. For example, in 1993, the Beijing government remained silent when Japanese banks took significant steps to increase their presence in Taiwan. Previously, Beijing had attempted to block the expansion of Japanese banks in Taiwan because the People's Republic claims sovereignty over the country. Only Dai-Ichi Kangyo Bank had maintained a Taiwanese branch. More recently, the Tokai Bank requested a license for a representative office and Bank of Tokyo requested that its representative office license be upgraded to a full-service branch. Beijing's muted reaction to these applications has signaled other banks from Japan and elsewhere that such alliances would not jeopardize their existing relationships with the People's Republic of China. By overcoming many of the previous political barriers to trade and finance, Beijing is clearing the way to sustained growth in Greater China. Such economic vitality and pragmatic approaches to business are attracting the attention of international banks, which hope to capitalize on the need for a more modern Chinese banking system.

International Banks in China

Also sparking the interest of international banks in China is the privatization of nine state-owned enterprises, the so-called "China Nine":

- Shanghai Petrochemical (petroleum products)
- Qingdao Brewery (food)
- Guangzhou Shipyard (shipping)
- Beijing Renmin Machinery (electronics)
- Yizheng Chemical Fibre (manufacturing)
- Ma-anshan Iron and Steel (metals)
- Dongfang Electric (electronics)
- Kunming Machine Tools (electronics)
- Bohai (miscellaneous)

Over 100 foreign banks are licensed to have representative offices in Beijing and another 31 in Shanghai. More than $2.5 billion has been invested in over 30 funds that specialize in Chinese securities.

Many international banks have elected to open representative offices since foreign banks in China are prohibited from establishing branch networks. With multibranch operations off limits, these institutions effectively do not have access to the retail market in China. Furthermore, they may not conduct transactions in Renminbi, the local currency. Nevertheless, there has been feverish activity on the part of financial institutions to become involved in the market for newly privatized Chinese enterprises with almost 50 financial institutions in Hong Kong vying for the privilege of participation. Not all of the enthusiasm surrounding these privatizations has been justified, however. The July 1993 offering for Qingdao Brewery had been projected to be oversubscribed by 250 to 350 times. The actual response was a more moderated (although still vigorous) oversubscription of 110 times, generating HK$763 million or US$98 million.[9] The issue by Shanghai Petrochemical Company in the same month for HK$2.9 billion (approximately US$372 million) was oversubscribed by only 1.77 times.

Part of the challenge of the Chinese market for foreign institutions is its structure. Most foreign institutions that have an interest in China have used Hong Kong as their base of operation. In the future, however, it is possible that Shanghai will challenge the dominance of Hong Kong. The number of seats on the Shanghai Stock Exchange should reach 1,600 by the end of 1993 and could mushroom to 3,000 by the end of 1995. Stock offerings on the Chinese stock market are either "A" shares that are available only for domestic investors or "B" shares which foreigners may purchase. Approximately 50 "A" share issuances are available to domestic investors and quoted in Renminbi. The "B" shares are quoted in dollars. Foreign firms must trade "B" shares through Chinese members of the stock exchange. Only six foreign securities firms have representative offices in Shanghai: the Big Four Japanese securities firms (Nomura, Daiwa, Nikko, and Yamaichi), Crosby Securities, and Merrill Lynch. Eventually, foreign firms will also be permitted to occupy seats on the Shanghai Stock Exchange.

In the meantime, there are 18 full branch offices of foreign banks in Shanghai (along with the 31 representative offices), including the recently approved Mitsubishi branch. At this time, these banks are restricted to foreign currency business only. There is slow progress, however, toward convertibility of Renminbi along with the reforms aimed at the domestic banking sector. At such time as the People's Republic of China joins GATT (General Agreement on Tariffs on Trade), the Chinese currency will be convertible. When this occurs, the banks will likely lend to joint ventures between Chinese and foreign companies, to government entities, and to private Chinese-majority-owned companies.

Already, Crédit Lyonnais of France, whose Shanghai branch opened in December 1991, is actively engaged in syndicated loans, short-term lending, and trade finance. The bank has also become heavily involved in asset-management for "B"-share companies, joint ventures, and municipalities. The Shanghai branch of Citicorp also manages money for "B"-share companies that frequently have large cash balances on hand. Not surprisingly, Citicorp is also capitalizing on its technological expertise by acting as technical adviser and cash-settlement bank for the Shanghai Stock Exchange "B" market. Other banks such as Hong Kong and Shanghai Banking Corporation, Standard Chartered, Bank of East Asia, and Oversea-Chinese Banking Corporation have operated in Shanghai for a relatively longer period of time because they were permitted to remain after the 1949 change in government. The government planners in China continue to constrain the activities of these and other foreign banks until the indigenous banking system is more competitive.

Nevertheless, it appears quite clear that foreign institutions will play an important role in the future development of China. In 1993, Deng Xiaoping spent 21 days in Shanghai emphasizing the need for development of the Chinese interior regions. The central planners are now focusing on the six provinces and major cities along the Yangtze River. Since Shanghai sits at the mouth of this river, the city will play a critical role in this development.

Thus, the most promising strategic alliances in the People's Republic of China that can be established at this time are in the areas of the payments system, cash management, syndicated loans, and securities underwriting. As the banking and securities markets are further strengthened and liberalized, these opportunities will continue to grow, as well as access to the 1.2 billion potential customers in the Chinese retail market.

CONCLUSION

The world of commercial banking is changing dramatically. Traditional deposit-taking and lending are losing their dominance as the mainstay of the profession. Traditional, blue-chip corporate clients now have increased access to money and capital markets and often can fund their short- and medium-term financial needs more efficiently through domestic and international markets. As a result of these dynamics, the share of U.S. financial assets held by commercial banks has declined significantly while the proportions held by investment companies (mutual funds) and pension funds have increased sharply.

At the same time, legislative constraints have limited the entry of U.S. banks into many of the most important areas of finance, such as securities transactions. To overcome this limitation, U.S. banks have formed strategic alliances that, for example, combine banks that have strong client relationships with mutual fund distributors. Other alliances have overcome the legislative restrictions with respect to geographical expansion, as strong regional banks expand their scope of operation.

No less important are the strong competitive advantages of U.S. banks vis-à-vis banks in other countries. For example, U.S. institutions have a decided edge in terms of innovation and technology and they are the world leaders in foreign exchange transactions. The economic research capabilities of U.S. banks are unparalleled. These international skills will be increasingly important as cross-border alliances form in Europe and Asia. Many of the definitions of commercial banking are, indeed, changing. Nevertheless, U.S. commercial banks have both the skills and the ingenuity to successfully compete in the evolving markets of global finance.

SELECTED REFERENCES

The Banker 1000. Special edition of *The Banker*, July 1993.

Barnathan, Joyce, and Matt Forney. "Between Reform and a Hard Line: China's Economic Czar Is Battling the Old Guard and Local Capitalists." *Business Week*, September 6, 1993.

Bennett, Robert. "Forging a New Bank at PNC." *United States Banker*, July 1993, pp. 22–28.

Bennett, Rosemary. "Universal Banks Play the Investor Card." *Euromoney*, May 1993 supplement, pp. 71–80.

Chai, Alan, Alta Campbell, and Patrick J. Spain, Editors. *Hoover's Handbook of World Business 1993.* The Reference Press, Austin, Texas, 1993.

"Crédit Lyonnais—Europe's Most Expansionist Bank." *Financial Revolution in Europe II.* Lafferty Publications, Dublin, 1992, pp. 258–63.

Dyer, Geoff. "The Going Gets Easier As Spreads Narrow." *Euromoney.* March 1993 supplement, pp. 2–28.

Fitch, Thomas P. *Dictionary of Banking Terms.* Barron's, Hauppauge, New York, 1990.

"French Top Acquisitions League in EC." *European Banker*, August 23, 1993, p. 5.

"The Great Divide in European Research." *Euromoney,* September 1993, pp. 372–90.

Hagger, Euan. "Why the Market's Dinosaurs Are Back in Fashion." *Euromoney*, August 1993, pp. 65–70.

"Here Comes Hugh (Again)." *United States Banker*, July 1993, p. 6.

"How to Sell to Sovereigns." *Euromoney,* September 1993, pp. 46–58.

Jackson, Ted. "NationsBank Buys Big-League Status." *Euromoney*, April 1993, pp. 71–72.

Leung, Julia. "Beijing Remains Silent As Japanese Banks Move into Taiwan." *Asian Wall Street Journal*, February 15, 1993.

Loong, Pauline. "Can the Economy Achieve a Soft Landing?" *Euromoney*, August 1993, pp. 41–42.

Marray, Michael. "Public Issuance Overtakes Private Placements." *Euromoney*, April 1993, pp. 117–19.

Marshall, Jeffrey. "Banks and Brokers Take a Leap." *United States Banker*, August 1993, pp. 13–14,63.

McGill, Peter. "Shanghai Bids to Become a Top Financial Centre." *Euromoney*, April 1993, pp. 57–62.

Miller, Richard B. *Citicorp: The Story of a Bank in Crisis.* McGraw-Hill, Inc., New York, 1993.

"Retail Market Beckons (Country Survey: Germany)." *European Banker*, August 10, 1993, p. 10.

Robinson, David. "Putting the Shareholder First." *European Banker*, May 21, 1993, pp. 9–10.

Robinson, David. "To Stay or Go (UK Banks in Europe)." *European Banker*, August 23, 1993, pp. 8–10.

Schmerken, Ivy. "Germany's Equity Markets Recharge Their Batteries." *Wall Street and Technology*, vol. 11, no. 2 (1993), pp. 32–35.

Shale, Tony. "Foreign Banks Scramble to Win Chinese Business." *Euromoney*, August 1993, pp. 38–40.

Shale, Tony. "Scramble Starts to Win Share of State Sell-offs." *Euromoney*, February 1993, pp. 80–81.

Shale, Tony. "Zhu Rongji's Big Gamble." *Euromoney*, August 1993, pp. 32–36.

Shepperd, Rosie. "The Investor Side of New Issues." *Euromoney*, July 1993, pp. 75–77.

Shirreff, David. "Assault on Frankfurt—Part Two." *Euromoney*, August 1993, pp. 54–60.

"Who's Selling What: The Global Picture." *Euromoney*, July 1993, pp. 114–25.

ENDNOTES

1. The six banking associations that drafted the guidelines are Consumer Bankers Association, Independent Bankers Association of America,

American Bankers Association, Association of Reserve City Bankers, National Bankers Association, and Savings and Community Bankers of America.

2. The holding company assumed the name Banc One, with the "c" because Ohio law restricts the use of the word bank.

3. See Bennett, "Universal Banks Play the Investor Card."

4. See "Who's Selling What: The Global Picture."

5. LIBOR is an acronym for London Interbank Offering Rate.

6. Some analysts believe that the outstandings in the Eurocommercial paper market amount to $120 billion. The $80 billion estimate is by Euroclear, the European clearinghouse. In any event, the difference in volume is significant.

7. Renminbi (Rmb) is Chinese currency.

8. Zhu's reforms also include a new system of taxes to clearly separate national and provincial revenues; privatizations of state-owned enterprises; and new laws on consumer protection, securities regulation, and accounting procedures.

9. The exchange rate is roughly 7.80 Hong Kong dollars to one U.S. dollar.

BIBLIOGRAPHY

Abrams, Richard K., Peter K. Cornelius, Per L. Hedfors, and Gunnar Tersman. *The Impact of the European Community's Internal Market on the EFTA.* International Monetary Fund, Washington, D.C., December 1990.

Bacon, Richard. "EC Finance Rules Face Fresh Obstacles." *Euromoney,* May 1993, pp. 50–55.

Baker, James C., and M. Gerald Bradford. *American Banks Abroad: Edge Act Companies and Multinational Banking.* Praeger Publishers, New York, 1974.

"Bank Financings Hit a Gusher." *United States Banker,* February 1993, pp. 16–21.

The Banker 1000. Special issue of *The Banker,* July 1993.

Bank Profitability, Statistical Supplement, Financial Statements of Banks 1981– 1989. Organisation for Economic Co–operation and Development, Paris, 1991.

Barnathan, Joyce, and Matt Forney. "Between Reform and a Hard Line: China's Economic Czar Is Battling the Old Guard and Local Capitalists." *Business Week,* September 6, 1993.

Barth, James R., R. Dan Brumbaugh, Jr., and Robert E. Litan. *Banking Industry in Turmoil: A Report on the Condition of the U.S. Banking Industry and the Bank Insurance Fund.* U.S. Government Printing Office, Washington, D.C., December 1990.

Bayliss, B. T., and A. A. S. Butt Philip. *Capital Markets and Industrial Invest-*

ment in Germany and France: Lessons for the U.K. Saxon House, Westmead, England, 1980.

Bean, Randall. "Banks' Big Opportunities in Small Business." *Bankers Monthly,* January 1993, pp. 35–36.

Beckwith, Burnham P. "Eight Forecasts for U.S. Banking." *The Futurist,* vol. 23, no. 2 (March–April 1989), pp. 27–33.

Bennett, Robert. "Forging a New Bank at PNC." *United States Banker,* July 1993, pp. 22–28.

Bennett, Rosemary. "Rocket Scientists Produce a Fresh Wave of Solutions." *Euromoney,* March 1993, pp. 46–54.

Bennett, Rosemary. "Universal Banks Play the Investor Card." *Euromoney,* May 1993 supplement, pp. 71–80.

Benston, George J., and George G. Kaufman. *Risk and Solvency Regulation of Depository Institutions: Past Policies and Current Options.* Salomon Brothers Center for the Study of Financial Institutions at the Graduate School of Business Administration of New York University, New York, 1988.

Binhammer, H. H. *Money, Banking, and the Canadian Financial System.* Nelson Canada, Scarborough, Ontario, 1988.

Board of Governors of the Federal Reserve System. *Flow of Funds Accounts: Financial Assets and Liabilities.* Washington, D.C.

Boreham, Gordon F. "Canadian and U.S. Banking Systems: Some Comparisons." *Canadian Banker,* vol. 94, no. 3 (1987), pp. 6–14.

Borowsky, Mark. "Banks Are Betting on Electronic Presentment." *Bank Management,* April 1993, pp. 26–28.

"Branching Out: Japanese in Asia." *The Economist,* August 7, 1993, p. 69.

Bronte, Stephen. *Japanese France: Markets and Institutions.* Germany Publications, London, 1982.

Casey, Robert W. "Foreign Lenders Piling Up Gains in U.S." *United States Banker,* April 1993, pp. 30–32, 71.

Chai, Alan, Alta Campbell, and Patrick J. Spain, Editors. *Hoover's Handbook of World Business 1993.* The Reference Press, Austin, Texas, 1993.

Chandler, Clay. "Japanese Bid to Bail Out Banks Weighed Down by Conflicts, Concern about Using Public Funds." *Asian Wall Street Journal*, October 19, 1992.

Chew, Donald, Editor. *New Developments in Commercial Banking*. Blackwell Finance, Cambridge, Massachusetts, 1991.

Coler, Mark and Ellis Ratner. *Financial Services: Insiders' Views of the Future*. New York Institute of Finance, New York, 1988.

Comparative Economic and Financial Statistics: Japan and Other Major Countries 1988. Bank of Japan, Tokyo, 1988.

Compton, Eric N. *The New World of Commercial Banking*. Lexington Books, Lexington, Massachusetts, 1987.

Cooper, S. Kerry, and Donald R. Fraser. *Banking Deregulation and the New Competition in Financial Services*. Ballinger Publishing Company, Cambridge, Massachusetts, 1984.

Coulbeck, Neil. *The Multinational Banking Industry*. New York University Press, New York, 1984.

"Crédit Lyonnais—Europe's Most Expansionist Bank." *Financial Revolution in Europe II*. Lafferty Publications, Dublin, 1992, pp. 258–63.

Dale, Richard. *The Regulation of International Banking*. Prentice–Hall, Englewood Cliffs, New Jersey, 1986.

Davies, Michael S. "Exploiting Opportunities in Small–Business Lending." *Journal of Retail Banking*, vol 15, no. 1 (Spring 1993), pp. 33–37.

de Carmoy, Herve. *Global Banking Strategy: Financial Markets and Industrial Decay*. Basil Blackwell, Cambridge, Massachusetts, 1990.

"Deposit Insurance, Redux." *United States Banker*, May 1993, p. 13.

"The Deutsche Bank Juggernaut Will Keep on Rolling." *Euromoney*, January 1990, pp. 33–44.

Dwyer, Paula, and Kelley Holland. "At Barclays, a Stiff Upper Lip No Longer Suffices." *Business Week*, April 12, 1993, p. 80.

Dyer, Geoff. "The Going Gets Easier as Spreads Narrow." *Euromoney*, March 1993 supplement, pp. 2–28.

Dyer, Geoff. "Global Bonds Aim to Broaden Their Scope." *Euromoney*, June 1993, pp. 84–88.

Economic and Monetary Union. Commission of the European Communities, Luxembourg, 1990.

Einzig, Paul, and Brian Scott Quinn. *The Eurodollar System: Practice and Theory of International Interest Rates,* 6th edition. St. Martin's Press, New York, 1977.

Europe 1992: The Facts. Department of Trade and Industry and the Central Office of Information, London, 1989.

European Economy: One Market, One Money: An Evaluation of the Potential Benefits and Costs of Forming an Economic and Monetary Union. Commission of the European Communities, Directorate–General for Economic and Financial Affairs, Brussels, October 1990.

Federal Deposit Insurance Corporation. *FDIC Quarterly Banking Profile.* Washington, D.C.

Federal Deposit Insurance Corporation. "Quarterly Banking Profile." First Quarter 1993.

Federal Deposit Insurance Corporation. *FDIC Statistics on Banking 1992.* Washington, D.C., 1993.

Feldman, Amy. "CDs for CPAs." *Forbes,* July 19, 1993, pp. 92–95.

Fitch, Thomas P. *Dictionary of Banking Terms.* Barron's, Hauppauge, New York, 1990.

Folkerts-Landau, David and Donald J. Mathieson. *The European Monetary System in the Context of the Integration of European Financial Markets.* International Monetary Fund, Washington, D.C., October 1989.

Fraser, Donald R. and Peter S. Rose, Editors. *Financial Institutions and Markets in a Changing World,* 3rd edition. Business Publications, Inc., Plano, Texas, 1987.

"French Top Acquisitions League in EC." *European Banker,* August 23, 1993, p. 5.

Friedland, Jonathan. "Into the Whirlpool: Japan's Banking Crisis Looks Set to Worsen as Loan Losses Mount." *Far Eastern Economic Review,* April 8, 1993, pp. 70–74.

Gart, Alan. *Banks, Thrifts, and Insurance Companies: Surviving the 1980s.* Lexington Books, Lexington, Massachusetts, 1985.

Giesen, Lauri. "Debit Cards Get Some Respect—Finally." *Bank Management,* January 1993, pp. 47–51.

Gillis, M. Arthur. "Unscrambling the Jargon: A Glossary of Terms in the Technology Arena." *Independent Banker,* vol. 43, no.4 (April 1993), pp. 26–27.

Glouchevitch, Philip. *Juggernaut: The German Way of Business: Why It Is Transforming Europe—and the World.* Simon & Schuster, New York, 1992.

Grady, John, and Martin Weale. *British Banking, 1960–85.* Macmillan Press, London, 1986.

"The Great Divide in European Research." *Euromoney,* September 1993, pp. 372–90.

Greider, William. *Secrets of the Temple: How the Federal Reserve Runs the Country.* Touchstone/Simon & Schuster, New York, 1989.

A Guide to the FDIC Improvement Act. Price Waterhouse, March 1992.

Haggar, Euan. "How the EEC Can Save the ECU Market." *Euromoney,* February 1993.

Haggar, Euan. "Why the Market's Dinosaurs Are Back in Fashion." *Euromoney,* August 1993, pp. 65–70.

Hales, Michael G. *Handbook of Consumer Banking Law.* Prentice Hall, Englewood Cliffs, New Jersey, 1989.

Hardy, Quentin. "Bank of Tokyo Unit to Buy 28 Branches of Bank America." *Asian Wall Street Journal,* March 9, 1992.

Havrilesky, Thomas M. and Robert Schweitzer, Editors. *Contemporary Developments in Financial Institutions and Markets.* Harlan Davidson, Inc., Arlington Heights, Illinois, 1987.

Hay, Tony. *A Guide to European Financial Centres.* St James Press, Chicago, 1990.

"Here Comes Hugh (Again)." *United States Banker,* July 1993, p. 6.

"Hidden Jewels: Bank Branches." *The Economist,* January 9, 1993, pp. 71–72.

Hilton, Anthony. *City within a State: A Portrait of Britain's Financial World.* I.B. Tauris & Co., London, 1987.

Holstein, William J., James Treece, Stan Crock, and Larry Armstrong.

"Hands across America: The Rise of Mitsubishi." *Business Week,* September 24, 1990, pp. 102–7.

Horne, James. *Japan's Financial Markets.* George Allen and Unwin North Sydney, Australia, 1985.

"How to Sell to Sovereigns." *Euromoney,* September 1993, pp. 46-58.

Huat, Tan Chwee. *Financial Institutions in Singapore.* Singapore University Press, Singapore, 1981.

International Monetary Fund. *International Capital Markets: Developments and Prospects.* Washington, D.C., April 1989.

International Monetary Fund. *International Capital Markets: Developments and Prospects.* Washington, D.C., April 1990.

International Monetary Fund. *International Financial Statistics.* Washington, D.C., Yearbook 1990.

International Monetary Fund. *International Financial Statistics.* Washington, D.C., May 1991.

Jackson, Ted. "NationsBank Buys Big–League Status." *Euromoney,* April 1993, pp. 71–72.

Johnson, Hazel J. *The Banking Keiretsu.* Probus Publishing, Chicago, 1993.

Johnson, Hazel J. *The Bank Valuation Handbook: A Market–Based Approach to Valuing a Bank.* Probus Publishing, Chicago, 1993.

Katzenstein, Peter J. *Industry and Politics in West Germany: Toward the Third Republic.* Cornell University Press, Ithaca, New York, 1989.

Kearns, Robert L. *Zaibatsu America: How Japanese Firms Are Colonizing Vital U.S. Industries.* The Free Press, New York, 1992.

Khambata, Dara M. *The Practice of Multinational Banking: Macro–Policy Issues and Key International Concepts.* Quorum Books, New York, 1986.

Kim, James. "Steffen Takes His Scissors to Citicorp." *USA Today,* May 21, 1993, p. 3B.

King, Mary L. *The Great American Snafu.* Lexington Books, Lexington, Massachusetts, 1985.

Krarr, Louis. "How Americans Win in Asia." *Fortune,* vol. 124, no. 8 (October 7, 1991), p. 140.

Kurtzman, Joel. *The Death of Money: How the Electronic Economy Has Destabilized the World's Markets and Created Financial Chaos.* Simon & Schuster, New York, 1993.

Lawrence, Colin and Robert P. Shay. *Technological Innovation, Regulations, and the Monetary Economy.* Ballinger Publishing Company, Cambridge, Massachusetts, 1986.

Lee, Peter. "Banks Lean on Clinton." *Euromoney,* February, 1993, pp. 34–38.

Lee, Peter. "Capitalizing on Distressed Real Estate." *Euromoney,* March 1993, pp. 58–62.

Lees, Francis A. and Maximo Eng. *International Financial Markets: Development of the Present System and Future Prospects.* Praeger Publishers, New York, 1975.

Leung, Julia. "Bank of America Unveils Asia Plan in Wake of Merger." *Asian Wall Street Journal,* April 27, 1992.

Leung, Julia. "Beijing Remains Silent as Japanese Banks Move into Taiwan." *Asian Wall Street Journal,* February 15, 1993.

Leung, Julia. "U.S. Banks Are Poised for Further Expansion in Asia This Year As Demand for Services Grows." *Asian Wall Street Journal,* February 24, 1992.

Liner, Doug. "Some Trends in Export Financing." *Export Today,* May 1993, pp. 39–41.

"A Loan Sale to the Rescue? (Japanese Banks)." *The Economist,* November 30, 1991, pp. 78–79.

Loong, Pauline. "Can the Economy Achieve a Soft Landing?" *Euromoney,* August 1993, pp. 41–42.

Lorch, Donatella, "Banks Follow Immigrants to Flushing." *New York Times,* August 7, 1991, pp. B1–B2.

"The Maastricht Agreement on Economic and Monetary Union." *Bank of England Quarterly Bulletin,* February 1992, pp. 64–68.

Marray, Michael. "Public Issuance Overtakes Private Placements." *Euromoney,* April 1993, pp. 117–19.

Marshall, Jeffrey. "Banks and Brokers Take a Leap." *United States Banker,* August 1993, pp. 13–14, 63.

Marshall, Jeffrey. "Variable Annuities: Hope or Hype?" *United States Banker,* June 1993, pp. 25–26.

McGill, Peter. "Shanghai Bids to Become a Top Financial Centre." *Euromoney,* April 1993, pp. 57–62.

McRae, Hamish, and Frances Cairncross. *Capital City: London As a Financial Centre.* Methuen, London, 1984.

Middleton, Sir Peter. "Rapid Change and the Opportunities It Presents Investment Banking." *The Economist,* May 2, 1992, pp. 1–5.

Miller, Richard B. *Citicorp: The Story of a Bank in Crisis.* McGraw–Hill, New York, 1993.

Milligan, John W. "Who's Afraid of Proprietary Trading?" *United States Banker,* July 1993, pp. 12–14.

Mitchell, Richard, and Robert Kazel. "Finding New Uses for Debit Cards." *Bank Management,* January 1993, pp. 52–55.

Modernizing the Financial System: Recommendations for Safer, More Competitive Banks. U.S. Department of the Treasury, Washington, D.C.

Mullineux, Andrew. *International Banking and Financial Systems: A Comparison.* Graham and Trotman, London, 1987.

Mullineux, A. W. *U.K. Banking after Deregulation.* Croom Helm, London, 1987.

Muolo, Paul. "Are Reverses Set to Advance?" *United States Banker,* May 1993, pp. 28–30.

Neufeld, E. P. *The Financial System of Canada.* Macmillan Company of Canada, Toronto, Canada, 1972.

"New Dreams at Deutsche Bank." *The Economist,* June 22, 1991, pp. 79–82.

"The New Look: Barclay's Bank." *The Economist,* December 12, 1992, p. 86.

"On the Mend: British Bank." *The Economist,* August 7, 1993, pp. 67–68.

"Overburdened: Japanese Banks." *The Economist,* July 25, 1992, pp. 77–78.

Pecchioli, R. M. *Prudential Supervision in Banking.* Organisation for Economic Co-operation and Development, Paris, 1987.

Pressnell, L. S. *Money and Banking in Japan.* St. Martin's Press, New York, 1973.

Radigan, Joseph. "Can Branch Automation Deliver the Goods?" *United States Banker,* May 1993, pp. 65–67.

"Recent Developments in Overseas Commercial Paper Markets." *Bank of England Quarterly Bulletin,* November 1992, p. 405.

Rehberg, Virginia J. "Letters of Credit: Cracking the Code." *Export Today,* September 1991, pp. 21–23.

"Retail Market Beckons (Country Survey: Germany)." *European Banker,* August 10, 1993, p. 10.

Revell, J. R. S. *Banking and Electronic Fund Transfers.* Organisation for Economic Co-operation and Development, Paris, 1983.

Revell, Jack. *The British Financial System.* Macmillan Press, Ltd., London, 1973.

Robinson, Danielle. "Tailored for All Tastes." *Euromoney,* February 1993, pp. 63–64.

Robinson, David. "Putting the Shareholder First." *European Banker,* May 21, 1993, pp. 9–10.

Robinson, David. "To Stay or Go (UK Banks in Europe)." *European Banker,* August 23, 1993, pp. 8–10.

Rodgers, David. *The Future of American Banking: Managing for Change.* McGraw–Hill, New York, 1993.

Roman, Monica. "The New Currency Gunslingers." *Global Finance,* vol. 6, no. 6 (June 1992), pp. 32–36.

Rosenbluth, Frances McCall. *Financial Politics in Contemporary Japan.* Cornell University Press, Ithaca, New York, 1989.

Schmerken, Ivy. "Germany's Equity Markets Recharge Their Batteries." *Wall Street and Technology,* vol. 11, no. 2 (1993), pp. 32–35.

Scott, Robert Haney, K.A. Wong, and Yan Ki Ho, Editors. *Hong Kong's Financial Institutions and Markets.* Oxford University Press, Hong Kong, 1986.

Shale, Tony. "Foreign Banks Scramble to Win Chinese Business." *Euromoney,* August 1993, pp. 38–40.

Shale, Tony. "Scramble Starts to Win Share of State Sell–offs." *Euromoney,* February 1993, pp. 80–81.

Shale, Tony. "Zhu Rongji's Big Gamble." *Euromoney,* August 1993, pp. 32–36.

Shepperd, Rosie. "The Investor Side of New Issues." *Euromoney,* July 1993, pp. 75–77.

Shirreff, David. "Assault on Frankfurt—Part Two." *Euromoney,* August 1993, pp. 54–60.

Shirreff, David. "Can Anyone Tame the Currency Market?" *Euromoney,* September 1993, pp. 60–69.

Simon, Hermann. "Lessons from Germany's Midsize Giants." *Harvard Business Review,* March–April 1992, pp. 115–123.

Skully, Michael T. *Financial Institutions and Markets in the Far East: A Study of China, Hong Kong, Japan, South Korea, and Taiwan.* St. Martin's Press, New York, 1982.

Smith, Eric Owen. "Equity Stakes: Are U.K. Banks Following the German Pattern?" *Banking World,* June 1991, pp. 28–30.

Smith, Geoffrey. "Fleet's Ship Comes In: Its Bank of New England Unit Has Earned Fat Profits Fast." *Business Week,* November 9, 1992, p. 104.

Spong, Kenneth. *Banking Regulation: Its Purpose, Implementation, and Effects,* 3rd edition. Federal Reserve Bank of Kansas City, 1990.

Subcommittee on Financial Institutions Supervision, Regulation, and Insurance. *Report of the Task Force on the International Competitiveness of U.S. Financial Institutions.* U.S. House of Representatives, Committee on Banking, Finance and Urban Affairs, Washington, D.C., 1991.

Suzuki, Yoshio. *The Japanese Financial System.* Oxford University Press, New York, 1987.

Suzuki, Yoshio. *Money and Banking in Contemporary Japan.* Yale University Press, London, 1980.

Tew, Brian. *The Evolution of the International Monetary System, 1945–81.* Hutchinson & Co., Ltd., London, 1982.

Ungerer, Horst, Juko J. Hauvonen, Augusto Lopez–Claros, and Thomas Mayer. *The European Monetary System: Developments and Prospectives.* International Monetary Fund, Washington, D.C., November 1990.

U.S. Department of Commerce, Bureau of Economic Analysis. *Business Statistics 1961–1988.* Washington, D.C.

U.S. Department of Commerce, Bureau of Economic Analysis. *Survey of Current Business, April 1991.* Washington, D.C.

U.S. Department of the Treasury. *Modernizing the Financial System: Recommendations for Safer, More Competitive Banks.* Washington, D.C., 1991.

U.S. Securities and Exchange Commission. *Internationalization of Securities Markets: Report to the Senate Committee on Banking, Housing, and Urban Affairs and the House Committee on Energy and Commerce.* Washington, D.C., 1987.

Viner, Aron. *Inside Japanese Financial Markets.* Dow Jones–Irwin, Homewood, Illinois, 1988.

"Visa's Corporate Card Push." *United States Banker,* August 1993, pp. 46–47.

"Wall Street Cache." *United States Banker,* August 1993, p. 47.

Weiner, Jerry. "Your Technology: It May Be Better Than You Think." *Independent Banker,* vol. 43, no. 4 (April 1993), pp. 24–25.

"Who's Selling What: The Global Picture." *Euromoney,* July 1993, pp. 114–25.

Wilson, J. S. *Banking Policy and Structure: A Comparative Analysis.* Croom Helm Ltd., London, 1986.

Index